Irish Apartheid

Irish Apartheid

Healthcare Inequality in Ireland

Sara Burke

IRISH APARTHEID
First published 2009
by New Island
2 Brookside
Dundrum Road
Dublin 14

www.newisland.ie

ISBN 978-1-84840-036-8

British Library Cataloguing Data. A CIP catalogue record for this book is available from the British Library.

Book design by Type IT, Dublin

Printed in Ireland by ColourBooks

10 9 8 7 6 5 4 3 2 1

For my inspirational parents,
Helen and Kevin Burke, with big love
and thanks.

Contents

Acknowledgments

Many people have assisted me in writing this book and it is to them that I owe any credit due.

Maev-Ann Wren has written most extensively in this area and I am extremely grateful for her mentoring and for her generosity to me.

Susie Long put a public face and heart on the core inequality in the Irish health system and I thank her for her courage and motivation.

The projects involved in Combat Poverty's Building Healthy Communities Programme kept me in touch with the harsh realities facing communities left behind and further excluded during the boom years. I am privileged to have worked with them. Thanks to Elaine Houlihan for leading me to their door, and for her sustained support, encouragement and wisdom.

Too many people have assisted me in getting the book this far to name individually, but I am extremely grateful to you all for your continued sustenance and back-up. You know who you are.

Unwisely, I will single out a few: to the young people and staff I worked with in Focus Point who first taught me about the structural causes of poverty and inequality in an Ireland of plenty; Owen Metcalfe and Jane Wilde who gave me my first opportunities to work in public health policy – you taught me a lot; Eithne McLoughlin who showed me that knowledge was good and injustices were worth fighting; Vincent Browne who persuaded me to enter the journalism world – the career diversion you provided has given me the courage, freedom and voice to try to hold those in power to account; for this I am very grateful; *Village* magazine, the *Sunday Tribune*, *The Irish*

Times and RTÉ, which gave me the opportunity to contribute to daily and weekly news coverage and analysis over the past few years – some of these stories are in this book; Maureen Browne of *Health Manager* gets me to cover stories I did not know existed and keeps me busy when business is bare; Ursula Barry who persuaded me to write a chapter for a tasc book which sent me down the slippery slope of book writing; my PhD classmates and teachers who have been a great sounding board over the last year – you have allowed me (unbeknownst to yourselves) to tease out the issues I am not quite sure about; those who gave me interviews and information for the book, many of whom do not want to be named specifically – I am eternally grateful to you for your time, guidance and information; to those who read and gave very helpful comments on early drafts of this book; any mistakes and inaccuracies that remain are mine; Deirdre O'Neill and her colleagues in New Island who gave me the opportunity to get this book published.

Finally, I must thank my family and friends who put up with me banging on about the health system and inequalities over the years. Happily for me (and you), you are too many to name.

But I must mention my mum, Helen Burke, who diligently was the first reader of each chapter I wrote in summer 2008 and went through every one of them with her wise and experienced red pen. It is no coincidence that I have ended up in the work that I do. And also my special father, Kevin Burke, who is living proof that quality health services work, and has gently tried to teach me patience and that less *can* be more.

Finally, I have to thank Eoin Ó Broin, whose idea it was that I write this book. As I became increasingly frustrated with the absence of health analysis in the public domain in late 2007, he persuaded me that this book needed to be written and encouraged me throughout.

This book was written with the hope that if people know how unequal and unfair our health system is, they may be motivated to change it. I really hope in some small way this book contributes to a quality Irish public health service that is universal and accessible to all, solely on the basis of need.

Sara Burke
April 2009

Introduction

The world has changed utterly in the months between starting to write this book in summer 2008 and completing it in spring 2009. What had seemed like a soft ending to the Celtic Tiger years changed to the bottoming-out of free-market economies. Each month throughout the summer 2008, then each week in autumn/winter, and each day in early 2009, there was another unfolding, unforeseen economic 'worst' for Ireland and the world. As this book is completed in spring 2009, the economic future is bleak. Ireland is facing the most challenging economic conditions ever in the history of the state. What is apparent is that there will have to be a different way of working to the past thirty years of economic liberalism.

The intention of this book was to bring an explanation to a wider audience of why we have the health system we have in Ireland today; to clarify why the Irish health system seems to cost so much, yet to make the case that we still do not spend enough on it. To tell the story about why we have never adopted a universal system of healthcare, to describe the politics of health in Ireland in the first ten years of the twenty-first century and to unashamedly make the case against our two-tier system of healthcare; to demonstrate unreservedly why inequality in society and in health service provision is bad for the health of individuals and the health of the nation.

Up to the middle of 2008, we had never had it so good. More than a decade of a booming economy, Ireland was the tenth richest country in the world, Irish citizens had more disposable income, lived longer lives and took more holidays than ever before. Yet, there were many facts that did not sit right with the Ireland of plenty. Why did Irish people live shorter lives than those in other, poorer countries in Europe? Within Ireland, why were poorer sections of the population allowed to become sicker and die younger than their wealthier neighbours during the boom times? Why does the poorer half of the population have to wait longer to access what can be life-saving healthcare than the wealthier half?

How come this was allowed to ensue and persist in an Ireland of abundance? Did it just happen by accident or was it the result of the politics of the majority who are well, healthy and happy? Why did governments not use our wealth to change public policies so that our prosperity was more evenly distributed and our health services accessible to all?

Of course, I do not manage to answer all these questions in this book, but I hope I answer some of them and get people thinking about the others.

There is a lot of hype and headlines about a health system in 'crisis' in Ireland in 2009. And for individuals and families who experience poor care, such outcry is warranted and required. There are many sick and vulnerable people who wait hours or days in emergency departments; public patients left waiting up to eighteen months for a cancer diagnosis, so late it can result in premature death; people who die without dignity in crowded, dirty, public wards, frequently from infections acquired in the hospital they went to for care; mothers and fathers who do not qualify for a medical card, but whose wallets are stretched to pay the €60 required to bring their sick child to their GP; communities, often the most disadvantaged, who live without a GP, pharmacy or any health facilities in their neighbourhoods; older people who are left in hospital wards or in nursing homes without the quality and kind of care required for their last precious years and months in life; families of people with disabilities who have to wait endlessly for assessment and care they are entitled to; people with cystic fibrosis, MS, epilepsy, mental health conditions, who are often the hidden, forgotten, unwanted patients of the Irish healthcare system – each of these and more, everyone of us, has a story to tell, and every one of them is valid.

There are many, many wrongs in the Irish health system, but there are also good parts. Each day, hundreds of thousands of patients receive care from ten of thousands of public health staff. All of us who could tell a 'bad' story, could also tell about the kind, caring public health or district nurse who visits week in week out; about the doctors and nurses who provide really good, quality care, under huge pressure, when you get in to the hospital system; about the porters or cleaners who stop to talk and bring kindness to a system that often seems heartless; of hospice care that enables people to die with dignity in their own homes or in the shelter of a hospice; of the therapists, care staff and volunteers who enable sick or dying people to have a good quality of life. There are great components to the health system, there are outstanding staff and some pools of excellence that should not be forgotten or discarded in the legitimate litany of complaints about Irish health services.

Yet, all of the above diverts attention and action away from the four main deficiencies in Irish healthcare.

Firstly, there is a virtual absence of a public health policy in Ireland, it is purely focused on health (or indeed sickness) services. When future generations and historians look back at what will probably be regarded as Ireland's richest ever decade, it will seem unfathomable that inequalities in health and access to healthcare were allowed to develop and persist during the last years of the twentieth century and the first decade of the twenty-first. We know that our recently acquired wealth has raised many boats, but it has not lifted them all. And those people who are left behind are left further behind and more excluded than before.

Secondly, Irish health and social services have been, and still are, underfunded. We have never paid enough – and we still don't – for the really good quality, universal health system that is required. In times of less, the need for good quality, accessible public health services is more than ever. Cutting public health services now is more costly in the long term. To do so is wrong. It is bad for all of society who are entitled to a good quality public health system. But fundamentally it is an attack on those who depend on it most – the old, the very young, the sick, the poor, people living with disabilities, with mental illness, the homeless, the marginalised. It is not acceptable in any modern democracy in 2009, no matter what the economic circumstances, to take away basic services from these particular groups.

Thirdly, and most fundamentally, we have an apartheid system of healthcare, where those who can afford to have access to what can be life-saving diagnosis and treatment, quicker than those who can't afford private care. This has always been the case, but, in the past decade, the two-tier system of healthcare has been accentuated, with increasing numbers of people incentivised to take out private insurance, privileging them over those who cannot afford to skip the queue. But nobody cared enough for half the population who do not have private health insurance to do anything about it. Everyone knew about it, but it was not spoken about. When it was, it was and is denied or shouted down by our political and policy leaders.

Fourthly (and this was the story I stumbled upon rather than sought out while writing this book), while politicians, policymakers and managers have been busy developing, consulting, writing and rewriting policy and the structures of the public health system and the (Health Service Executive) HSE in the first ten years of the twenty-first century, a relatively silent but revolutionary change was happening in the health system, which would change the landscape of Irish healthcare for the foreseeable future. The private healthcare sector boomed, encouraged and supported by government, yet it operated in an unplanned, unregulated and unmonitored way. These developments did not occur by accident or take place in a vacuum; they were largely led from the top, from the highest ministerial office.

This book will tell some of these tales of the Irish health system. Most fundamentally, this book wants to expose the causes and the consequences of our apartheid system of care so that when people look back on Ireland's decade of greatest prosperity, there is no excuse. No excuse that we did not know, because we knew and we allowed the discrimination to prosper.

On a more positive note, circumstances are changing. Certain events have occurred that are raising awareness and tipping public opinion in favour of public health. Susie Long's legacy to the Irish people was to put a brave, human, dignified face on the apartheid system of care. Rebecca O'Malley's gift to the country was, and continues to be, to highlight the absence of quality and regulation of cancer care. *Primetime Investigates*, through their Leas Cross exposé, awakened the nation to the poor quality of care for some of our older people and the state's neglect to monitor it or do anything about it. Janette Byrne's ongoing support, activism and advocacy for patients and the public health system draws attention to the inadequacies that persist and the poor treatment of patients.

Ironically, Charlie McCreevy's 'gift' to older people over 70 years of age of universal healthcare and its withdrawal in the early 'emergency' budget in October 2008 by the Fianna Fáil-led government raised more awareness of the benefits of universal healthcare than any other grass-roots movements or previous efforts had beforehand. Incongruously, it might be the global downturn and the fall of free market economics that will ensure the halting and perhaps the collapse of private for-profit healthcare in Ireland.

In tough economic times, the need for a good quality, universal public health system is greater than ever. Increasingly, people believe that such a system should be in place and are willing to pay higher taxes for that system.

What is amazing to me is that we have not taken to the streets sooner, in solidarity, demanding the good quality, universal health system to which we are entitled.

Sara Burke

Chapter 1

Ireland's unequal system of healthcare – 'I am going to die because of hospital waiting lists'

Susie Long's Story

> Dear Joe,
> Today I had my twelfth session of chemo. I got to talking to the partner of a man who was also getting chemo. She told me that when her partner's GP requested a colonoscopy for him he was put on the waiting list. She then phoned the hospital and told them he had private health insurance and he was seen three days later. He had bowel cancer that was advanced, but it had not broken through the bowel wall and spread to other organs. She said the tumour was the size of a fist and what made him go to the doctor (apart from her nagging) was he started to lose weight rapidly. Thank goodness they got it in time and he's going to recover.
>
> I then came home, flicked on the TV and got into bed. The first ad on the TV was from the government telling people that bowel cancer can kill, but not if caught in time. If Bertie Ahern or Mary Harney or Michael McDowell were within reach I would have killed them. Literally. I'm not joking.
>
> I don't have private health insurance. It's a long story, so I'll start at the beginning …

So began Susie Long's brave, honest testimony to the nation.

At first she was 'Rosie'; she did not want to be identified because her children did not know she was dying. But, within days of emailing *Liveline*, Joe Duffy's radio show, because of the overwhelming response from listeners, she came out as Susie Long, a 39-year-old woman with terminal cancer, living in Kilkenny, with her husband and two teenage children.

Susie Long had suffered from stomach complaints for years. At first, she took Rennies to ease her discomfort, then it got worse. She often had diarrhoea and when blood appeared in her faeces, she got worried. She went to her GP in the summer of 2005, and was immediately referred to the hospital for two tests – an ultrasound and colonoscopy. She had the ultrasound soon after the referral and was diagnosed with gallstones. That explained the nausea. However, months passed and there was still no word from the hospital about either the colonoscopy or the operation to remove her gallstones.

In November, when Susie called the consultant about the colonoscopy, she was told she was on the waiting list. Between November and February 2006, Susie's health continued to deteriorate. She was constantly tired, often staying in bed until just before she went to her job in the late afternoon to save the little energy that she had for her badly paid, part-time social care work. She did not eat until she came home, as she felt too unwell after food.

She called the hospital again after Christmas, and, once more, was told she was on the waiting list.

Finally, on 28 February 2006, four days after she turned 40, Susie was called for a colonoscopy. She was diagnosed with bowel cancer and had surgery to remove the tumour. She spent over fifty days in St Luke's Hospital in Kilkenny and had to undergo a second round of surgery because of complications. She was hopeful she could fight the disease; after all most people recover from cancer, she was relatively young, strong and healthy. Susie did not want to die.

In March 2006, Susie went to the Mater Hospital in Dublin for tests. The cancer had spread to her lungs. Her diagnosis was terminal.

In that same email to Joe Duffy, Susie said:

> I know in my heart and soul that when I started to feel really, really bad, especially from December to February 2006, is when the cancer broke through the wall of my bowel. Of course I can't prove it. But I know. Because it broke through the bowel, I have been given two to four years from diagnosis to live. The chemo is to prolong life, not to save it. I have three years, tops, to go. Despite that, I'm going to try my best to make it for five more till my youngest turns eighteen. He needs me too much now. My husband has suffered right alongside of me in his own way knowing that the woman he loves will be dead soon. My 18-year-old daughter has been told and has gone quiet and doesn't want to talk about it. But I know she's scared. I haven't told my 13-year-old son yet. He's too young to handle it.

Susie Long began her chemotherapy to extend her life. Ten months later, while getting her treatment, she sat beside a man who had a similar or worse bowel cancer than her, yet he started his treatment within three days because he was a private patient. It took seven months for Susie Long to be diagnosed and begin her treatment simply because she was a public patient.

It was the unfairness of the system, combined with the ad on TV encouraging people to go to their doctor if they had the early symptoms of bowel cancer, that motivated Susie Long to go public with her story.

She explained in her email to Joe Duffy that despite one and a half incomes, they could not afford private health insurance. 'But even if we could have we wouldn't have gotten it because we believed (and still do) that all people should get good care despite their incomes. We thought jumping queues was wrong.'

The three years Susie Long was given to live did not materialise. Within eighteen months of her diagnosis, she had died. The email she sent Joe Duffy was entitled: 'I am going to die because of hospital waiting lists'. Unfortunately, Susie Long's prediction was true. She was another victim of Ireland's apartheid system of healthcare.

Susie Long was not an exception; her experience is the norm for what many public patients experience in Ireland. But Susie Long was definitely an exceptional person. Somehow, she found the energy and the courage to speak out, despite her terminal diagnosis and deteriorating health. She and her family took a principled position not to buy private health insurance, 'not to skip the queue'.

As a result, they suffered dearly. But they suffered in the knowledge that Susie Long provided the Irish people with perhaps the greatest public service she could – she exposed in a humane, more personal way than before, the unequal system of Irish healthcare.

Between the time she emailed Joe Duffy in January 2007 and her death in October 2007, Susie Long took opportunities to speak out publicly about the inequality in the public health system. She encouraged people not to re-elect the Fianna Fáil–PD government that oversaw and accentuated the two-tiered system of healthcare.

She highlighted the poor hygiene, innutritious food and overburdened nursing staff in the public hospital system.

She brought attention to the plans to centralise hospital services, the increased privatisation of healthcare and the absence of hospice care in most communities.

She criticised the trade unions (even though she was a

member of one) for not taking a more proactive role in defence of the public health system, against the two-tier system and the privileging of private patients over public patients.

Susie Long's early and untimely death provided a public face to the inequality that is at the core of the Irish health service.

Political response to Susie Long's death

Susie Long's death was a major news story – and the politicians responded in their usual cavalier manner.

'Very regrettably, the system did not live up to its standard in that [Susie Long] case,' the then Taoiseach Bertie Ahern told the Dáil the day after Susie Long's funeral.

Mary Harney, the Minister for Health, in response to media questions about the untimely death of Susie Long said the new consultants' contract, would 'support equity of access for public patients' through ensuring a common waiting list for diagnostics and objectively enforcing a 80/20 ratio of public–private mix in hospitals.

In plain English, what Mary Harney alluded to was that the new consultants' contract (then being negotiated) would end the privileging of private patients over public patients and that the required mix in hospitals of 80 per cent public patients in public beds and 20 per cent private patients in beds in public hospitals would be enforced.

What both the Taoiseach and Minister for Health failed to admit is that in Susie Long's case, the system did live up to its standard, because inequality is inherent to the model of the Irish health system.

Susie Long was not a unique case. The Irish health services are structured on the basis of an unequal, complicated mix of public and private healthcare that produces cases like Susie Long, day in, day out. In the days that followed Susie Long's death, doctors and health union officials spoke out against

Ahern's and Harney's comments in relation to the health system.

'It's disingenuous of politicians to say that Susie Long was a unique case,' said Donal Duffy of the Irish Hospital Consultants Association. 'If Mary Harney wanted to, she could introduce one waiting list for everything, eliminating overnight with the stroke of a pen the two-tier health system, but she hasn't done that,' he continued.

Liam Doran of the Irish Nurses Organisation (INO) also vehemently disagreed with the politicians. 'The system we have perpetuates a two-tier approach, those with the ability to pay have access to diagnostics, consultants and beds quicker than those who can't afford to. Susie Long's experience happens everyday, in every specialty.'

Dr Orla Hardiman, consultant neurologist at Beaumont Hospital and spokesperson for Doctors Alliance, a lobby group of doctors set up in 2007 to defend the public health system, said, 'It's not a figment of imagination, there are hundreds and thousands of Susie Longs who can't go public. We are very grateful to her [Susie Long] for jettisoning her anonymity, for articulating the inequality in access to essential services for those who do not have private health insurance. What Mary Harney is saying just does not wash, it is just more nonsense. There is a general access issue because 80 per cent of admissions to hospitals are through A&E, and 50 per cent of the population have private health insurance so there will always be more than 20 per cent of private patients in public hospitals. The consultant contract is a smoke shield, it simply does not matter.'

The Irish hospital system and access to specialist care is structured so that private patients are privileged over public patients. The statements by Ahern and Harney show that this unequal system is denied right up to the highest political office in the land.

No government in the history of the state has successfully introduced access to health services on the basis of need. In Ireland in 2009, access for the majority of the population to both hospital care and GP services depend on their ability to pay. Efforts in the past to control the public–private mix in order to guarantee equitable access have failed. What history has proved is that it is not possible to have an equitable public–private mix. It has also proved that Ireland's unique blend of public–private care guarantees inequality.

Consistent government measures over the past decade have institutionalised inequality in our health system. The public system and its public patients are the victims of increased state support and subsidy for private healthcare and the failure of consecutive governments to build up a quality, equitable public health system.

What successive ministers have chosen, or not chosen, to do has led to the fundamentally unequal health system we have today. In particular, Mary Harney's tenure as health minister has fuelled the predominance of a Progressive Democrat, free-market ideology in health policy, perpetuating the belief that competition is inherently good and private for-profit healthcare can solve all ills, including the ills of the Irish health service.

During the first decade of the twenty-first century, report after report was being published on the public health system with little effect. Despite a quadrupling of the health budget, no effort was made to change the way the Irish health system was financed, no attempt to dismantle the inequitable access and treatment of patients who are not well-off enough to be able to buy health insurance. Meanwhile, there was a virtually silent but effective privatisation of many aspects of the public health service. Privatisation was not official government policy but it was busily happening despite a growing body of evidence, nationally and internationally, that the market may not be the most appropriate cure for health systems under pressure.

Ireland's unequal system of care

Unlike most European countries, Ireland does not have a unified health service, instead there is a fragmented system of healthcare made up of public, private and voluntary providers who supply different types of healthcare in different settings, often uncoordinated, and usually difficult for the patient to understand and navigate.

Healthcare services are staffed by a variety of different types of employee: full-time salaried employees, such as HSE staff in hospitals and the community; independent self-employed workers such as GPs and many allied health professionals; voluntary sector workers, such as staff in voluntary hospitals and other care providers in the disability and social care area; and private staff, such as employees in private health clinics, hospitals and nursing homes.

A direct result of this disjointed system of care is that differences arise in how a patient accesses care and how that care is paid for, for example how a patient gets in to hospital and specialist care is different from how a patient accesses GP care. And access to these vital health services is sometimes determined by income status and ability to pay, not medical need.

The most public manifestation of inequality in the Irish health system is the discrimination experienced by public patients when accessing the public hospital system.

Routes into hospital and specialist care

By law, all residents in Ireland are entitled to be public patients in the public hospital system, where minimal fees are charged. The public hospital system is made up of voluntary hospitals, traditionally set up and run by religious orders, and publicly run HSE hospitals. All are publicly funded but most receive some additional income through private care.

If a person presents at an emergency department[1] in a

hospital without a letter from a GP and not in an ambulance, there is a fee of €100.[2] For care in the hospital system, patients are charged €75 a day for a maximum of ten days. This entitles you to a bed in a hospital ward, 'consultant-led' care and hospital services as required. If you need to be in hospital for months, there is a maximum charge of €750 no matter how long the stay or how expensive the treatment.

While, technically, everyone is entitled to this, in reality it is patients without a medical card or private health insurance who pay these fees. Having a medical card means you are exempt from any fees, while having private health insurance means that the health insurer covers all charges for inpatient hospital care. People take out medical insurance as it ensures faster access to hospital care and is highly subsidised with public money. By the end of 2008, under 30 per cent of the population had a medical card while 52 per cent of the population had private health insurance.

In 2005 – the most recent year for which analysis of income and insurance are available – the average income of the population with private medical insurance was €25,549, while the average income for those without private medical insurance cover was €14,523.[3] Not surprisingly, wealthier people can afford to take out private health insurance.

This research also found that 25 per cent of the population had neither medical insurance nor a medical card, indicating that some people with medical cards also have taken out private health insurance.

Organisations working with people living in poverty, such as the St Vincent de Paul, reiterate this findings, that some people on very low income take out private health insurance and often have to borrow to do so.

People who have neither a medical card nor private health insurance are usually younger and on a low income but do not qualify for a medical card and cannot afford health insurance.

It is these people who fare worst in the Irish health system benefiting from neither the privileges of a medical card nor private health insurance.

In Ireland, private health insurance is subsidised by the state. People can claim tax exemptions on money spent on health insurance. Also just under two-thirds of all private inpatient hospital beds in 2007 were in public hospitals, where the vast majority of the cost of private care is absorbed by the public health system.[5] For these reasons, private health insurance is significantly cheaper in Ireland than in other European or North American countries where people contribute more to the full cost of their private care. Some, but not all, outpatient fees are not covered by insurance but can be claimed back against tax, for those without medical cards, on an annual basis if the total is over a certain threshold.

There are two ways in to the hospital system in Ireland. The first is through the emergency department. Anyone who presents at an emergency department is treated the same and gains access to a bed in a hospital ward on the basis of medical need.

It is not a coincidence that one of the most vociferous manifestations of the Irish public's dissatisfaction with the health service is the waiting times and conditions in emergency departments, where everyone is treated the same. Money or who you know does not usually enable queue jumping in emergency departments. That said, if you are a member of a hospital board of management or the minister, it is unlikely you will be left to wait for days on a trolley.

When people are in a hospital ward, they are designated as a public or private patient depending on their health insurance status. If they are a private patient in a public hospital, they may be accommodated in a public ward, a semi-private ward (usually rooms with fewer beds) or a single private room, depending on availability. There are very few single rooms in Irish public hospitals. There is a growing body of international evidence showing that single bedded hospitals are more cost effective, are less prone to infection and patients recover quicker in them.

The second access route to hospital care is referral by a specialist doctor through an outpatient clinic. Specialist doctors in Ireland are all consultants.

Generally to access a consultant in Ireland, you need to be referred by your GP. How long it takes to get a hospital bed without going through the emergency department depends on a person's status as a public or a private patient.

If you are a private patient, you can generally get to see a consultant quicker, within days or weeks, often in their private consulting rooms. The consultant will then refer you to hospital, if required. Again, if someone is a private patient, they can access that hospital bed or care within days or weeks. So, being a private patient means getting to see a specialist more quickly and then getting a hospital bed or care more quickly, so both diagnosis and treatment in hospitals can be speedier for private patients.

However, if someone is a public patient, they can wait months, or even years, to see a consultant or get a diagnosis in the first place. And then the public patient may have wait further months or years to access a bed for treatment. While there has been some progress in recent years in reducing waiting times for treatment, accessing that first essential outpatient appointment can still take months or longer.

Also if someone is a private patient, the consultant usually provides any care needed, however, if someone is a public patient, while a consultant may be involved in providing care, much of the time, patients will be seen by a junior hospital doctor who is training under the consultant.

The new consultants' contract in place from spring 2009 introduces a common waiting list for the diagnosis of public and private patients in the public health system. This is a start towards achieving equity, but it is not an end in itself. There are simple ways around it if one can afford to buy private care outside of the public hospital system. Incentives are still in place whereby consultants are paid differently and more attractively for private patients. A common waiting list has been long promised and recommended many times over two decades, yet it still remains unimplemented. There is no plan to remove the incentives in place for how consultants and hospitals are paid for private and public patients. It is still possible for private patients to access care quicker and there is no clause in the consultants' contract about a common waiting list for treatment.

Medical card holders and access to GP care

Thirty per cent of the population, who are medical card holders, have 'free' access to GPs.[6] The remaining 70 per cent, who are not medical card holders, pay €45–60 per visit out of their pockets to see their GP. Some private health-insurance schemes (which are subsidised by the state) now cover GP visits, but most do not.

In 2008, there were three types of medical card holders in Ireland: those who qualify for a full medical card because of their limited income; those who qualify for a full medical card because of their age; and those who qualify for a doctor only medical card on the basis of their income.

Alongside entitlement to free hospital care and GP services, full medical card holders get free prescribed drugs and medicines, with some exceptions; outpatient services; dental, optical and aural services; medical appliances; maternity and infant care services; and a maternity cash grant of €10.16 on the birth of each child. The spouse and children of medical card holders are also entitled to these services.

Medical card holders choose their GP from a panel of participating doctors. GPs have to accept patients and, usually, are located within a ten-kilometre distance of the patient's home.

In some areas, where there are disproportionately high numbers of medical card holders GPs close their lists and people may have to travel some distance to get on a GP's medical card list.

Medical card holders are exempt from paying the health levy portion of social insurance. Having a medical card can act as a gateway to other supplementary welfare allowances, such as the waiver of school transport charges.

Up to 2001, eligibility for a full medical card based on income was assessed through a means test. People could also seek a medical card on the basis of 'hardship'. Community welfare officers in local health offices assess 'hardship' cases and have discretion over issuing medical cards. This 'hardship' clause in eligibility is a direct hang-over from the dispensary system set up to care for the poorest under the Poor Law in nineteenth century Ireland.

In 2001, the Fianna Fáil–PD government changed the eligibility guidelines for a medical card, introducing medical cards for everyone aged 70 and over. This move was a seen as a pre-election stroke by Minister for Finance Charlie McCreevy who was looking for the 'grey' vote in the 2002 election.

Older voters in Ireland always turn out in high numbers and are less likely to switch their party preference. It was a move that was not part of any health strategy or plan and one which benefited the better off, as medical cards were given to older, richer people rather than poorer, probably younger, people. In 2001, when medical cards were introduced for people over 70, fewer people had medical cards on the basis of income than the traditional 35–38 per cent of the population, as had been the case up to the mid-1990s.[7] For the first decade of the Fianna Fáil–PD government, between 1997 and 2007, less than 30 per cent of the population qualified for medical cards. The figure increased during 2008 as numbers of unemployed grew so that the level reached over 30 per cent of the population for the first time in over a decade. At least three per cent of these are over 70-years-olds who qualified on the basis of age not income, so the figure was still about 27 per cent of the population who held medical cards on income or hardship grounds.[8]

Universal entitlement on the basis of age was withdrawn in Budget 2009. As a result of new thresholds, 90–95 per cent of over 70-year-olds are expected to hold on to their medical card. This issue is dealt with in chapter eight and nine.

In 2004, in response to criticisms that many people on a low income did not qualify for medical cards, the government announced a plan to introduce 200,000 'GP Visit' medical cards. People are entitled to GP visit medical cards on the basis of income, but at a higher threshold than full medical cards. There has been slow uptake on doctor-only medical cards, with 85,546 GP visit cards allocated five years after 200,000 were promised.[9]

GP visit medical cards entitle the holder to free GP visits, but the cost of drugs and treatment from allied professionals is not included. Like all other non-medical card holders, the state reimburses the cost of drugs if over €100 per month or €1,200 per annum. Often, the cost of medicines for someone with a chronic illness is substantially more expensive than the cost of the visit to the GP.

Medical card holders get most medicines for 'free', while non-medical card holders pay out of pocket for their prescribed drugs. The increasing cost of the medical card holders' drug costs and the drugs repayment scheme were two main reasons given by HSE management in autumn 2007 for the introduction of cutbacks in the public health service and the withdrawal of medical cards for better off over 70-years-olds in October 2008.

There are also inequalities in access for people on low incomes who do not qualify for a medical card. Research carried out by Combat Poverty in 2007 found that 16 per cent of the population in consistent poverty, approximately 47,000 people, and 30 per cent of people at risk of poverty, 229,000 people did not have medical cards.[10] These figures show that in 2007, there were over a quarter of a million people living on low incomes, in or at risk of poverty, who do not qualify for a medical card.

Unlike hospital care, but similar to emergency departments, public (medical card holders) and private patients (non-medical card holders who may or may not have private health insurance) are treated equally in GP care. They wait the same amount of time to get treated by the same doctor, usually in the same location.

It is hard to estimate the exact numbers of people who do not access GP services because of cost. Research carried out on women living on a low income showed that mothers delayed bringing sick children to the GP – because the cost put further pressure on an already tight budget – to see if the child recovered without seeing a doctor. It also found that women on low income without a medical card were reluctant themselves to go to the doctor because of the cost.[11]

Comparative North–South research on visits to the family doctor found that, in Ireland, 18.9 per cent of patients with medical problems had not consulted a doctor because of cost, compared to 1.8 per cent in Northern Ireland, where there is free universal access.[12]

Geographic inequalities also exist as some communities, often the more deprived urban communities and isolated rural communities, are not serviced by any GP.

Community services, including preventive medicine, public health measures, social services, continuing and long-term care

Some public health, community, continuing and social care services are provided on a universal basis, that is, they are available to everyone. For example, everyone is entitled to free maternity services, free healthcare for babies up to six weeks old and public health nursing. Referral from a doctor is necessary to access public health and community nursing services.

Some specialist services are also provided for everyone (technically). For example, in 2008, Breastcheck, a free breast-screening service, was meant to be available to all women aged 50 to 64, across the country. Yet it was not universal as it was still not available to women in the southwest and northwest of the country as the services were not yet in place in these areas.

Social work services are also provided for free on the basis of need, yet, again in 2008, there is growing evidence that only the children most at risk are receiving a service. Social workers are under increasing pressure to deal with the most 'high risk' cases and to close other cases, resulting in many children at risk falling through the net, often with detrimental results.[13]

Allied health professions, such as physiotherapy, chiropody, speech and language therapy, occupational therapy and counselling, are provided free of charge to medical card holders, while non-medical card holders must pay for them.

Increasingly, there is a blurring of the lines between those who are entitled to free allied professional care, for example between 2001 and 2008 all people over 70 years of age were entitled to this care without charge as they were medical card holders. However, often, such services were so over-stretched that the necessary care was not available, so the entitlement was meaningless because many older people paid out of pocket to receive care within a reasonable time. This is true for the rest of the population as well. Increasingly, schools and organisations such as the St Vincent de Paul pay for people to see professionals such as psychologists, speech and language therapists privately, as the wait for an appointment in the public system could be detrimental in the long term.

The 2001 Primary Care Strategy, envisaged Primary Care Teams around the country, of which allied care professionals were a key part. Yet, the strategy did not state explicitly whether these services were to be provided free to everyone.

In two of the pilot areas, Lifford/Clonleigh, County Donegal, and Virginia, County Cavan, where the teams are successfully up and running, allied care services are available to everyone. In 2008, the Department of Health was reviewing eligibility for all health and social care services. Given that, in some parts of the country, some services are free to all citizens and in others they are free just to medical card holders, no doubt eligibility will be tightened as a result of the review with the introduction of more user charges.

In many instances, such services are restricted because of waiting times and staff shortages. For example, many parents, who are entitled to a 'free' public psychological assessment for their children or occupational therapy, end up paying for private care, as the wait for the public services is too long. For example, delay in getting a psychological assessment can have long-term mental health consequences, while unavailability of speech and language therapy can prevent recovery from a stroke.

Some public health services, such as immunisation, are also totally free. But, again in July 2008, it emerged that sixth class students who are all meant to get the BCG vaccination to inoculate against TB, had not been immunised by the end of the school term.

Conclusion

One of the most distinctive traits of the Irish health system is the complex way people access public health services. Because of the myriad providers, the status of patients, the varied methods of payment, there is no consistent or clear route into or through the Irish health service. Instead, it is a convoluted web of pathways, that depend on income and the type of service that a patient is trying to access.

Ireland's health and social services are unique. They are inimitable to health and social care provision in other European countries, where access is generally universal and paid out of insurance or tax, but fundamentally available to all on the basis of need.

Susie Long put a public face on the most unjust inequality of all in the Irish public health system – inequality in access to the public hospital system. Quite simply, she had to wait seven months for an essential test in order to be diagnosed with colon cancer. If she had been a private patient, she most probably would have taken the test within days and could have begun treatment that could have saved her life.

This inequality in access to hospital care has been the status quo for decades, although denied, or at least avoided, by health-service management, health ministers and governments. While the two-tier hospital access and care is not officially acknowledged, it has been reinforced by legislation and government-agreed contracts, accepted in health strategies and official reports on the health service.

So how is it that we have the health system that we have? How has this system of care been allowed to develop and how does our political elite propagate it? Why are so many people discontented with the Irish public health system despite a €15 billion health budget? How and where does the inequality prevail?

Chapter 2

Why we have never adopted a universal healthcare model

A potted history of health services and policy in Ireland

The history of health policy and services in Ireland is a complicated journey from a minimal, fragmented medical service inherited from the days of the British Empire to a Health Service Executive providing care for over four million people with an overall health budget of €15 billion. It is a social as well as a political voyage, held up by economic constraints and conservative forces, interrupted by changes in government, interfered with by powerful vested interests, most markedly the medical profession and the Catholic Church.

It is a story of a century of politics and policies, well documented by Ruth Barrington[1] and Maev-Ann Wren[2,3], whose work should be read for a detailed analysis of the history of health policy in Ireland.

What follows is a synopsis of the recent history of health services and policy so that the reader can understand how Ireland got to the position that pertains in 2009 – a complex, unequal system of care, which evolved over time in an unplanned, unorthodox way. This brief narrative is told through a public health and inequality lens so as to provide the reader with an understanding of why we have never adopted a universal system of healthcare in Ireland.

The 1970 Health Act

Although many of the foundations of the system we have today were put down in the 1800s and the early parts of the twentieth century, the 1970 Health Act legislated for the health system still in place in Ireland in 2009, particularly in relation to who is eligible for what services.

The 1970 Health Act came into law in February 1970 under the leadership of the Fianna Fáil Minister for Health, Erskine Childers. Eight regional health boards were established, with the majority of the boards made up of local officials.

New eligibility criteria for accessing health services were included in the act. Those with full eligibility were entitled to free GP, hospital and specialist care and prescribed drugs. Those with limited eligibility had to pay for GP care, pay a nominal fee for hospital and specialist care but were entitled to a reimbursement for money spent on drugs over a certain threshold. People with limited eligibility no longer had to pay outpatient fees. The state paid the cost of treatment for people with certain illnesses, no matter what their income. Notably, the act allowed the definition of eligibility to be changed by ministerial regulation, an issue that had caused great controversy decades earlier in the 1940s and 1950s.

The dispensary system which had provided care for the poorest people for over a hundred years was finally abolished and replaced by the General Medical Service (GMS). Critically, GPs providing care for the poor were no longer state employees but were self-employed and provided care for all patients in the same setting. A choice of doctor was introduced to those eligible for the GMS and although not specified in the bill, within two years, doctors were paid by capitation. Children from high-income families were no longer entitled to free hospital and specialist care, but free care was extended to all children with disabilities irrespective of their parents' income.

In the late 1960s, government established a Consultative Committee on General Hospital Services to make recommendations on how best to organise hospitals and where to locate specialties. Professor Patrick FitzGerald, a UCD professor and consultant in St Vincent's Hospital, chaired this committee. Their report, known as the FitzGerald Report, recommended the radical reconfiguration of Irish hospitals, centralising specialities in four regional hospitals, which would be supported by twelve 300-bed general hospitals around the country. The remaining hospitals were to become community hospitals and health centres. The Health Act did not adopt the FitzGerald Report recommendations to separate hospital administration from other health services and the proposed reconfiguration of hospitals never happened.

From 1971, health boards had responsibility for public hospitals in their area. A central body known as Comhairle na nOspidéal was set up and had responsibility for the location of specialties and for where consultants were appointed.

Crucially, in terms of laying the foundations for the two-tier health system that exists today, Minister Childers agreed to allow public hospitals to provide private and semi-private accommodation for those with limited or no eligibility who wanted to be treated as a private patient. This concession was given as 'an attempt to standardise conditions for consultants in public and private hospitals'.[4]

In 1971, a health levy was imposed on middle and high income groups.[5]

According to Barrington, the abolition of the local rate contribution to the health services had two consequences. Firstly, to 'stimulate a dramatic increase in expenditure on health services' and, secondly, to 'jeopardise plans for regionalisation of hospital services. With no financial pain falling locally, every community had an incentive to fight for the development of its hospital to the standard envisaged for a few [hospitals] by Fitzgerald and Comhairle na nOspidéal'.[6]

The central issue of how to finance increasingly expensive health services was not addressed in the 1970 Health Act and remained a controversial issue that raised its ugly head in the run-up to the 1973 general election. Fine Gael and Labour promised to do away with the costly local rate contribution to the health budget.

Fianna Fáil lost power in 1973 and a Fine Gael–Labour coalition took over. The coalition met their election promise and phased out local rate contributions so that, from 1977, almost the entire health budget was publicly financed and came from central government budget. Brendan Corish, leader of the Labour Party and Tánaiste became Minister for Health in 1973, indicating the importance that Labour put on the health remit. Labour's policy was for free medical care for all paid for out of general taxation. Only months in the post, Corish announced the introduction of free hospital services for the whole population by April 1974, which would be funded by a flat rate contribution from all employees.[7]

Previous efforts by Fianna Fáil to introduce 'free and extended medical services to the whole population' in 1945 and Noel Browne's attempt to provide free and comprehensive care for all mothers and children in 1950 were opposed by the medical profession, the Catholic Church, the Department of Finance and opposition parties. Corish's proposals were supported by the Post Vatican II, Catholic Church's Council for Social Welfare.

But the consultants did not like the intention of the Minister for Health to introduce free hospital services for all as it would curtail their private practice particularly in public hospitals. Consultants' private practice was their cash cow and they threatened industrial action immediately.

In particular, the consultants objected to the proposed payment by salary, rather than a fee-for-service which they got for their private practice. Worried about the impact of a strike on hospital patients, Corish postponed the introduction of free hospital services for all and set up a committee to agree the terms and conditions of consultants' pay. The committee failed to make any progress as the consultants refused to participate.

Despite Fianna Fáil's earlier commitments to introduce free medical services for all twenty five years previously, they were now firmly against it, opposing Corish's attempts to have universal access to hospital care. Charlie Haughey, the Fianna Fáil opposition spokesperson on health advocated an extension of the medical card to those who needed it as the best use of limited resources. Haughey, also opportunistically, opposed Corish's attempts to implement the recommendations of the FitzGerald Report to reduce the numbers of general hospitals, and made it a prominent issue in the forthcoming 1977 general election.

The 'sweetheart' deal

Failing to open up free hospital care to all citizens and to rationalise the plethora of rural hospitals in the tight fiscal situation of the mid-1970s, Corish's energy towards the end of his ministerial office went in to reducing expenditure and 'like other incumbents, before and after him, he became preoccupied with value for money'.[8]

An ambitious Haughey became Minister for Health, when Fianna Fáil regained power with a resounding majority in the 1977 election. Having campaigned against Corish's attempts to reduce the numbers of rural hospitals, he regularly gave way to local interests looking for developments in hospitals without any cognisance of a national plan or rising costs. Despite campaigning for increased eligibility for medical cards while in opposition, Haughey failed to increase eligibility while in office despite the fact that health expenditure doubled between 1977 and 1980 under his stewardship.[9]

In 1979, contrary to his previous position, Haughey extended free hospital care to all but the richest 17 per cent, who had to pay for their consultants' fees. People contributed to this cost by paying one per cent of their income towards healthcare. This time, the consultants did not oppose it because private practice was a well-established and growing phenomenon, and consultants already had one-fifth of the population paying private fees directly to them for the care they received. In addition, a new consultants' contract was being negotiated. When Haughey became Taoiseach in 1979, Michael Woods took over the health ministry and completed the consultant contract 'sweetheart deal',[10] which would remain in place until 2008.

It is this overly generous contract perhaps more than any other health policy development which copper-fastened the two-tier health system. Consultants, who had always resisted attempts to introduce a state medical service, salaried pay, and an equal playing field for treatment of all patients, had got their way.

'A new contract for hospital consultants, agreed by a Haughey government, gave them the best of both worlds – state salaried, pensionable posts, with the right to unlimited private practice, inside or outside public hospitals. This consultants' contract turned heavily state subsidised, private medicine into a growth industry, encouraged the development of private hospitals staffed by consultants on state salaries and consolidated the two-tier health system of preferential access for private patients in public hospitals.'[11]

In the contract, consultants were expected to work a thirty-three-hour week in the public hospital system, but they could also do and earn as they liked in their private practice. When there was some opposition from consultants to the contract, the Department of Health reassured them that their time involved in public work would not be measured – a situation that remained in place until 2008.

The 1980s – the era of cuts

The first two years of the 1980s witnessed much political upheaval, severe economic constraints and three changes of government. While spending on health remained stationary, hospitals experienced cutbacks. By 1983, most consultants and all hospitals had signed up to the new consultants' contract.

Barry Desmond was the Labour Minister for Health from 1983 to 1987 in a Fine Gael-Labour coalition. Like many of his predecessors, he took up office with a zeal to reform. He promised the introduction of 'a full comprehensive health service available to all, with priorities based on people's medical needs rather than on their ability to pay for services', to be funded by a national health insurance system which would incorporate the VHI. This European-style model of healthcare he described as 'basic democratic socialism applied to our health services'.[12] Although the then Taoiseach Garret FitzGerald was supportive, Desmond did not have the rest of his cabinet's support for such radical developments.[13]

Sill remembering the reaction to previous attempts to introduce free healthcare for all, Desmond's Department of Health was cautious to proceed. Meanwhile, Ireland's poor economic situation and massive national debt dispelled such developments and the emphasis changed from expansion to cuts in public services.

Desmond was Minister for Health when private practice in healthcare moved into a new era in Ireland. The first two private hospitals were built and for-profit healthcare entered the Irish market. Desmond stuck to his socialist principles and took a firm stance against private hospitals, preventing any public hospitals from developing a separate private hospital. He also made sure that a new category of insurance was required to cover care in private hospitals and tried unsuccessfully to ensure that the full cost of practising private medicine in public hospitals was reimbursed to the public hospitals. However, he justified private practice in public hospitals as the public hospital's income was subsidised from private fees.

Desmond advocated a move towards community and primary care and tried to implement some of the recommendations of the 1967 FitzGerald Report. During his tenure, 704 hospital beds were closed down. However, it was left to the incoming Fianna Fáil government to carry out the real cutbacks.

Rory O'Hanlon, a doctor from Monaghan, was appointed the new Fianna Fáil health minister after the 1987 election and oversaw the most radical cuts in health services ever witnessed by the state. In two years, the number of hospital beds was cut by one-fifth, although O'Hanlon evaded the issue announcing 'changing roles' for hospitals rather than closures.[14] But hospitals did close and access for public patients became increasingly problematic, with long waiting times and poor quality care in a public health service under escalating pressure.

An embargo was placed on health service staffing and charges, and minimal charges were introduced for outpatient and inpatient hospital care. O'Hanlon, unable to reform because of economic constraints, set up a Commission on Health Funding to map out the future of health services in Ireland. Fianna Fáil, whose 1987 electorate slogan had been 'Health cuts hurt the old, the sick and the handicapped'[15], now became the executors of the cuts in the health service they had promised to oppose.

The unions responded to the cutbacks with strike action – even junior hospital doctors went on strike. The cutbacks were not carried out in any planned way and hit the Dublin hospitals most. Fianna Fáil, playing to their populist vote, cut few rural hospital beds. 'The cuts were in public, not private care. Of the one in six acute hospital beds closed in the greater Dublin area in 1987 and 1988, virtually all were public.'[16]

Those who could afford to took out private health insurance which assured them speedier access to hospital beds. Every year, more and more people signed up for it and, by 1993, one-third of the electorate had private health insurance.[17] The Department of Health actively encouraged hospitals to convert public beds into private beds so that they could get additional income from them.[18] By 1987, 20 per cent of public beds were being used for private patients, most of them insured through the state-subsidised VHI. The government was actively cutting public health services, while, at the same time, encouraging and subsidising private healthcare and insurance.

'The deepening public–private divide in hospital care was mirrored in primary care'[19] as the government agreed a new deal with the GPs, paying them a capitation (flat rate per year) for GMS patients and allowing them to continue to charge a fee-for-service to private patients. The government created a two-tiered GP service on top of the two-tiered hospital service. Apartheid in Irish healthcare was official government health policy.

In 1989, an election was forced after the government lost a Labour Party motion on the low level of compensation for people with haemophilia who were infected with HIV through contaminated blood products.

Once again, health, out scored the economy, as the primary election issue. Not surprisingly, Fianna Fáil felt the hit of reduced spending on health and lost four seats. As a result, for the first time Fianna Fáil entered a coalition – with the Progressive Democrats – and responded to the election angst by increasing day-to-day spending on health by five per cent and hospital spending by nine per cent.[20] However, hospital bed numbers continued to be reduced and, in February 1990, winter flu caused chaos as there were insufficient beds in hospitals to meet the needs of the old and the sick.

Beside the cutbacks in health expenditure, there were two other significant health policy developments in the late 1980s. More and more people took out private health insurance. VHI, the only health insurer in operation lost money in two consecutive years. This resulted in increased premiums for subscribers, reduced benefits and a refusal to cover any new private hospitals. The VHI also agreed maximum fees with consultants.

In 1988, there was increasing public discontent with consultants when the VHI revealed that consultants earned on average £24,000 for their private fees on top of their public salary of £33,000, at a time when the average industrial wage was £18,000.[21] In response to this, some consultants broke away from the union, the Irish Medical Organisation, to form a new Irish Hospital Consultants Association (IHCA). The IHCA promised to campaign on public waiting lists, to defend private practice and said it would never go on strike.[22]

Since its inception two decades ago, the IHCA has been a strong voice in medical politics, most notably in its defence of the consultants' contract and consultants' right to practice medicine privately alongside their public salaried work.

The Commission on Health Funding published its report in 1989. It was critical of the two-tiered system of care and recommended a common waiting list for all, a fixed-term contract for consultants and the monitoring of consultants' public work. However, the commission's report was contradictory on some issues. For example, it stated that private insurance should not entitle people to more rapid access to hospital care, yet it 'did not consider it inequitable for private patients to gain more rapid access to care in the private sector provided the public sector delivered care "within a reasonable period of time".'[23] Furthermore, the commission recommended free consultant care to all and recommended hospital charges. 'The Commission listed impressive arguments for excluding private practice from public hospitals yet nonetheless recommended its retention.'[24]

The commission was consistent in its view that private healthcare should not be subsidised by state money. It did not recommend free GP care and was in favour of continuing to pay for health services through the tax system. However, critically for the time it was published, it did not say how much should be spent on health. It believed the primary issue was how the health services were run, not how it was financed, and recommended the establishment of a single Health Service Executive in the place of the health boards. It did not recommend universal access to healthcare without payment in either the hospital or GP setting. Wren concludes, 'had the key recommendations been implemented ... they could have turned the rising tide of the demand for private medicine and rationalised the organisation of health services'.[25] Many of the commission's recommendations remain unimplemented twenty years later.

The 1990s – discontent amidst economic development

The timing of the publication of the Commission on Health Funding's report was significant. There was huge public discontent with the health services, increasing concern about private care and, unusually, a general consensus across political parties, unions and the Catholic bishops that health services should be available to all, without preferential access for private patients. Amidst the consensus, there were diverging views as to how a universal system should be paid for and little action followed to give effect to the rhetoric for a fairer health system.

The government responded with a package of 'reform', to entitle everyone to free consultant care in hospitals, to regulate the public–private mix in hospitals and amend the consultants' contract.[26]

O'Hanlon defended the public–private mix on the basis that everyone got the same quality medical care no matter what their status, a point contradicted by the medical profession who admitted that public patients often got poorer quality care from less qualified trainee doctors.[27]

The Health Amendment Act 1991, stipulated that public hospitals designate a proportion of their beds as private which, according to the minister, protected the numbers of public beds and thereby public patients. At first, the proportion of beds allocated to private practice was 19 per cent. This increased to 20 per cent in 1993.

However, the government failed to introduce the common waiting list proposed by the Commission on Health Funding, the National and Economic and Social Council and the Irish Congress of Trade Unions. In doing so, 'the government's legislation was providing private patients with designated private beds, which they could occupy even if public patients were in greater medical need. It offered public patients equitable access to public beds rather than equitable access to care ... Private beds remained a state-subsidised vehicle for queue jumping by private patients'.[28]

A new consultants' contract was negotiated but with little real change. Efforts to measure the amount of time consultants spent on public care came to nothing. The new contract dropped the section in the previous contract that stated that access to hospital care should be based on need. A 'public-only' contract was introduced so that some consultants could have 'public-only' practice, but this was dropped again six years later, as hospitals were dependent on income from private care. If anything the new contract was a retrenchment by the state leaving more power and control of health services delivery to the consultants.

By the 1990s, Fianna Fáil was firmly a staunch supporter of the two-tier hospital system and although Fine Gael and Labour spent Dáil time pointing out the system's inequities and the impact of the cutbacks on public health services, they failed to come up with any real alternative to the public–private mix. When Fine Gael and Labour returned to government in the Rainbow Coalition in 1994, they 'were ill-prepared to dismantle this new edifice of privilege'.[29]

The 1990s in Ireland was a decade devoted to economics and determined by a cosy consensus. The social partnership agreements between government, unions and other social partners ensured a consistency across governments despite their varied make up and regular changes. When the health services were hitting the headlines, it was in relation to infected blood products and the failure of social work services to protect children from child abuse. The eye was taken off the running and delivery of the health services, and the status quo of overcrowded public hospitals, that privileged private patients over public patients, was allowed to prevail.

Brendan Howlin became Minister for Health during the two-year Fianna Fáil–Labour coalition from 1992 to 1994. Under his leadership, the first Irish health strategy was published in 1994. 'Shaping a Healthier Future' committed to 'maintain the position of private practice which is well established in the public mix'.[30] Even with a Labour minister in government, no attempt was made to deconstruct the unequal two-tier system of healthcare.

Howlin failed to see the relationship between the public–private mix and the pressures on the public system.[31] Instead he put his efforts into reducing waiting lists in the public system through a waiting-list initiative that paid staff to work overtime to get the lists down. He realised that as well as the effort to reduce the lists, there needed to be more beds and services within the system to meet these needs on an ongoing basis. And while the initiative was successful in the short term, it failed to address the structural inequality in the system and the long-term capacity issues – a shortage of beds and doctors in the hospital system and an underdeveloped primary care system.

Much of Howlin's health policy was adopted by the new Rainbow Coalition, made up of Fine Gael, Labour and Democratic Left which came into office in 1994. Taoiseach John Bruton appointed Michael Noonan of Fine Gael as Minister for Health.

By this time, there was a firm consensus that the public–private mix was an inherent part of health services in Ireland. No political party in Dáil Éireann in the early and mid 1990s was offering the alternative of a universal health system based on need, not ability to pay. It seemed to make sense to political and health policy leaders that those who could afford to pay for private health insurance contributed to the system. Public hospitals were reliant on the payments from private health insurers.

Much of Noonan's ministerial time was taken up with the blood products scandal. Demands for justice and compensation by people who had been infected with Hepatitis C and HIV through blood products from the Irish Blood Transfusion Board were met with obstacles at every turn. By the end of the Rainbow government's tenure, health had slipped down the public and political agenda. Infected women and abused children were not the concern of voters.

Fianna Fáil returned to government in 1997, again in coalition with the PDs, with Bertie Ahern as Taoiseach and Brian Cowen appointed as Minister for Health. With the economy booming, the focus was on economics, tax reductions for the middle classes and tax breaks for the rich.

Cowen kept his head down in the Department of Health. Infamously during his ministerial term in health, he made reference to the Department of Health as comparable to Angola – a war zone, full of land mines – a comment he has never lived down. But unlike his predecessor and successor, he avoided many of the potentially fatal missiles that lie in wait for most ministers for health.

Early on in Cowen's tenure, a revised consultants' contract was agreed. Public-only contracts were discontinued as recommended by the group set up to review consultants' pay, as public hospitals were dependent on private fees for income. This contract tried unsuccessfully once again to introduce measures so that consultants' thirty-three-hour weeks could be monitored.

The late 1990s was a time of much strife amongst health service workers with twelve industrial disputes in four years. Cowen was keen to get the consultants' contract sorted without hassle, which he did but 'the contract was a victory for the IHCA and like its predecessors, would soon provoke critical review'.[32] Soon after the contract was agreed, Cowen set up a Forum on Medical Manpower to examine why so many Irish doctors went aboard to work. In 1999, Cowen increased charges for private patients in public hospitals in an effort to decrease state subsidies of private healthcare. This move was followed shortly after by the publication of a White Paper on health insurance, which allowed the health insurance market to be opened up and the VHI to privatisation 'if deemed desirable'.[33] The White Paper acknowledged the extent of state subsidy of private healthcare and recommended, once again, the ending of public subsidy of private care in public hospitals. It did not recommend stopping tax relief on private health insurance. It acknowledged the downsides of the public–private mix of care, yet ensured its continuity, by endorsing adherence to the 80/20 public–private mix.

Another significant policy development during Cowen's time in health was the establishment of the Eastern Regional Health Authority, whose role was to co-ordinate all health and social care services in the east of the country. For the first time the voluntary hospitals were brought under state control to try to ensure continuity of care for patients between home, the hospital and their community.

While the unions were actively campaigning for better terms and conditions for healthcare workers, the issues of the two-tier health system, the underfunding of the public health system and the inability of the Irish health service to meet the growing needs of an increasing population, were not the priority. There was no mention of any of these in the 1996 social partnership agreement negotiated with the Rainbow Coalition. On paper, the Irish Congress of Trade Unions (ICTU) still advocated for equal access to a free health service, but, in reality, it did little to progress this agenda.

In the late 1990s, as the economy boomed and the values of the Celtic Tiger got a firm grip on the Irish life, the public health system was collapsing under increasing pressure, unnoticed by those in positions of political power. While expenditure on health was increasing during this time, it was insufficient to undo the damage done to the public health service by the cuts of the previous decade.

In 1998, a report generated by Howlin's waiting-list initiative found that Ireland's bed occupancy was amongst the highest in Europe. The cutbacks of the 1980s and 1990s were having an impact; hospitals were unable to manage, with too few beds and staff to cope with demands. The winter flu hit once again in January 2000, grinding already lame hospitals to a halt.

A new century, a new health strategy ...

While there was incremental modifications made to the Irish health system during the last two decades of the twentieth century, it was a time of policy continuity not change. As the year 2000 dawned, the health system was about to embark on change not experienced before in Irish health services. In a cabinet reshuffle in January 2000, the able Cork TD Micheál Martin was moved to health. At this time, Martin was seen as a potential Taoiseach-in-waiting, with 'time' to do in health, to prove his worth.

Within days of his appointment, Liz McManus, the Democratic Left spokesperson on health and soon to be Labour spokesperson (after Labour merged with Democratic Left), tabled a Dáil motion on the 'crisis' in the hospitals.[34] During

1999 and 2000, as the economy boomed, Liz McManus consistently raised the overcrowding of hospitals, their inability to meet demand and the inequity of the two-tier health system in the Dáil.

The health debate in Ireland was reawakened and health once again rose up the public and political agenda. A myriad old groupings and new called for health service reform, the old political hot cake of health politics returned to take up centre stage in the critical forum of public concern – a place where it firmly remained for the first eight years of the twenty-first century.

Slow to pick up on it, but always fast to respond to populist trends and worried about the impending election, Fianna Fáil under Micheál Martin, oversaw the development of a new health strategy. Driven by the minister and departmental officials, a large, expensive public consultation was carried out, with numerous in-house committees and forums being established in the development of the new strategy. The health boards, health service staff and unions were involved at all levels. Politicians who sat on local health boards had their say. Peter McDonagh, the Taoiseach's social policy advisor sat on the steering group for the new health strategy. This was being led from the top but informed by all quarters.

The health strategy, 'Quality and Fairness – A Health System for You', was launched in December 2001 with much fanfare and expense in the Mansion House in Dublin. The Taoiseach was front of house, closely aided by Micheál Martin, who many believed could be the minister that could really reform the health system. At the launch, Martin delivered a convincing speech promising short as well as long-term measures. He promised the 'largest ever bed capacity expansion in the history of the health service. In the next 12 months, 650 beds will go in to areas that need them. 3,000 extra beds will go into the system by 2011. And all new beds will be designated for public patients'.[35] He also promised that 'by the end of 2002, no adult will wait more than 12 months, no child more than 6 [months], for treatment. By the end of 2003, no adult will wait more than 6 months, no child more than 3. By the end of 2004, no public patient will wait more than 3 months'.

Martin promised improved services for people with disabilities, older people, children, and people living in poverty – specifically committing to 7,000 additional day-centre places and 1,370 additional assessment and rehabilitation beds for older people. Martin concluded his speech with an impassioned call for support of the new health strategy saying 'it [the health strategy] says to the Irish people, all of whom, in one way or another, are affected by the health service: this is doable. This is deliverable. This will effect changes for the better – changes you will be able to see and measure over the coming years. At the end of this decade, Ladies and Gentlemen, the publication of this Health Strategy will be seen as marking the point from which a good health service was developed into a great health service, the point at which a systems-based system became people-centred, the point where a Government committed to equity, accountability, fairness and people-centredness embedded these principles in the way we plan and deliver Ireland's health services'. Time would prove that this hope and conviction was unwarranted.

But this was not evident in the first six months of 2002. The message was loud and clear from government, as health was one of the key election issues. 'Just re-elect us, give us four more years and we will reform the health services' was the mantra from Fianna Fáil and the PDs. The public, although unhappy with the health services, were pleased with the economy, and ready to give the government more time to sort out the health system. There was a consensus that the health services needed change, and that change takes time and 'Quality and Fairness – A Health System for You' was an impressive blueprint for change in the Irish health services[36].

Like the previous health strategy, 'Quality and Fairness' did not recommend a total overhaul of access to health services; it did not propose a universal healthcare system, free at the point of delivery. It did not seek to change how health services were financed and reinforced the public–private mix which had become the acceptable form of Irish health service provision.

But it did have 'quality' and 'fairness' in its title and equity as one of its core principles. It outlined the need for additional hospitals beds, the need to build up a comprehensive primary care system, the need for organisational reform.

It sowed the seeds for more substantial reform in the organisation of health services, evident in the establishment of the HSE in 2005, the reconfiguration of hospital, efforts to transfer care from hospital to the community, the increased dependency on private for-profit health and social care providers – each of which became the hallmarks of reform in the first decade of the twenty-first century.

Eight years after its publication, outcomes are still poorer for those who have to wait longer for what can be life-saving healthcare, evident in the early and unnecessary death of Susie Long. Private patients are privileged over public patients, evident in the different waiting times to see a consultant. There has been a dearth of action to promote fairer access for public patients in the health system. No review of progress made in the strategy has been published since 2003. The illusive, much assured primary care system is not yet in place. The welcomed mental health policy, A Vision for Change, remains largely unimplemented.

Instead, after the health strategy was published, more strategies were published, more committees established and more management consultants commissioned to produce reports on the structures and functions of the health service, on medical staffing and on hospital location.

And while these committees were meeting, while the private management consultancy companies were thinking and talking, while reports were being written, there was one major reform taking place in Irish health policy that did not even warrant a section of its own in the department's own strategy, the private sector was being incentivised, through tax breaks, to enter the healthcare market. In 2005, this dependency on for-profit hospital care was further institutionalised by Mary Harney's plan to co-locate for-profit private hospitals on the grounds of public hospitals.

But in 2001 and the first half of 2002, there was enough in the health strategy – or at least in the spin and publicity that surrounded it – to convince Irish voters to re-elect the Fianna Fáil–PD Coalition to government in 2002. Although voters brought back in the same Fianna Fáil-PD coalition and thereby a mandate for their health policies, some areas voted in their own local 'health' candidate. Controversy over 'local' hospitals assisted the election of a handful of candidates – Wexford based GP Liam Twomey was elected as an independent (he subsequently joined Fine Gael, for whom he became their health spokesperson), Paudge Connolly was elected in Cavan Monaghan, Gerry Cowley in Mayo. All lost their seats in the 2007 general election. And while they raised their local health issues in Dáil Éireann, they failed to mobilise a consensus on an alternative health policy.

Between 2002 and 2004, Micheál Martin did not live up to his mantle to reform. He delivered the health strategy, the Primary Care Strategy, Hanly, and many more reports and reviews. Change began under Martin, but that change was to prove more time consuming, more expensive and more difficult than originally envisaged. His great legacy was not reform or restructuring the public health system. Instead his legacy is the only real Irish public health innovation – the introduction of the smoking ban. Less than four years after his appointment to health, Martin was moved to Enterprise, Trade and Employment, and was replaced in Health by Tánaiste and leader of the Progressive Democrats, Mary Harney.

The PDs had doubled their number of seats in Dáil Éireann to eight in the 2002 election. Mary Harney held considerable influence on the government, and in particular on the Taoiseach and Minister for Finance Charlie McCreevy. Mary Harney brought to the health portfolio, her political ideology and belief in the free market solution to all ills, including the ills of the ailing health service. Meanwhile, seemingly harmless changes made by Minister for Finance Charlie McCreevy to the 2001 and 2002 Finance acts were having a seismic, unplanned impact on health services in Ireland.

The timing was perfect. In an Ireland of plenty, of booming economic growth, of low taxes and multiplying millionaires, the aims and promises of the health strategy were abandoned and unregulated, unplanned, politically motivated reform was to be driven from the top. The Irish public health system was deemed expensive, yet failing, the solution lay in the reform and privatisation of healthcare, or so Mary Harney believed.

On the day of her appointment, in September 2004, Mary Harney declared, 'I do not take my politics from any ideology. I am not an ideologue ... The one thing I want for the country I love is to have a health service that is accessible to every citizen, regardless of their wealth.'[37]

In the run-up to the 2007 general election, while the economy was creeping back up the political agenda, much focus remained on health. Fianna Fáil and the PDs went to the country looking for time to introduce more of the same, to realise their reforms. Fine Gael, although critical of government policy were unclear about a policy alternative, often avoiding the central issues by campaigning on issues such as a preventative health checks for everyone. They too were happy to maintain the status quo of the public–private divide. Labour and Sinn Féin stood out in the lead up to the general election, each campaigning on the basis of introducing a one-tier health system. Labour advocated a social health insurance model, while Sinn Féin used the UK model of a tax-based national health service. The Greens were close to a universal model, advocating the gradual introduction of universal healthcare, starting with under six year olds. All the oppositions parties opposed the plan to co-locate hospitals on the grounds of public hospitals.

Conclusion

Despite the rhetoric, no recent government in Ireland has even attempted to introduce equitable access to healthcare. In fact, contrary to commitments outlined in the health strategy in 2001, in both Programmes for Government in 2002 and 2007, measures introduced since then have escalated inequalities.

The official response to criticisms on Ireland's unequal healthcare provision during the eight years since the publication of the health strategy is to avoid the issue by responding with a completely different point or to blame inefficiencies in public services. There is a regular mantra from senior politicians about the increased money that has gone into the health budget without any apparent results – the so-called 'black hole'. Ministers avoid the key issue of inequality by talking about seeking mechanisms to ensure the 80/20 public–private designation of beds in public hospitals, placing unfounded hope for an equitable health system in the new consultants' contract and the drive to reform. Since 2005, the focus has been on the establishment of the HSE, the 'transformation' of care from the hospital to the community, the co-location of private for-profit hospitals on the grounds of public hospitals. All of these issues cloud the central injustice in the Irish health system – that access to some essential services is based on ability to pay not need.

The rest of this book deals with these issues in turn, looking at their development primarily during the years 2001 to 2008/9.

Chapter 3

The HSE: did we create a monster?

As governments changed and health policy upheld the status quo during the last quarter of the twentieth century, Irish society witnessed the collapse of many of its central pillars. The public grew ever more disillusioned with the Catholic Church, gardaí, judges and politicians as scandal upon scandal came to light.

Since the turn of the twenty-first century, the health services, and the HSE in particular, have become one of the most criticised elements of Irish society. Is this warranted? Is the HSE, its own worst enemy, badly communicating its weaknesses and failing to show its strengths, at any given opportunity? Or is the HSE just another fall guy of a more individualised, less caring, tabloid culture, where everyone is looking for anyone but themselves to blame for the dilemmas of modern living?

The answer is not straightforward, nor perhaps fully available at this early stage of its existence. However, the story of the creation of the HSE, its uncertain beginning, its murky relationship with the Department of Health, and its continued struggle with finances, mismanagement and unaccountability lay bare some of the difficulties it still faces. Even at this early stage of analysis, what is clear is that the HSE was troubled before it even existed.

The 'old' health boards

The regional health boards, established in 1970, were long overdue for reform when they were disbanded and replaced by the Health Service Executive (HSE) on 1 January 2005. For 35 years, the health boards were the statutory bodies responsible for the delivery and provision of health and social care to the Irish population. Much of this was provided directly by public health services, the rest was contracted out to voluntary and other independent organisations, increasingly to the for-profit sector in the years after the publication of the health strategy in 2001.

Each of the eight health boards had a CEO, responsible for the day-to-day operation of the services, who was answerable to their own local health board. The boards of the health boards were composed of elected local representatives, ministerial nominees and health professionals employed by the board and were expected to execute policy as formulated and decided by the Department of Health. Each had control over their own budgets, as allocated to them by the Department of Finance via the Department of Health.

During the three and a half decades of their existence, fundamental change took place in the demographics and economics of Irish society, and the health and social services struggled to keep pace with the change. Health service developments did take place, but most of them were incremental and insufficient to stay abreast with the healthcare needs of the Irish population.

The only major organisational change in health board structures before 2005 was the establishment of the Eastern Regional Health Authority (ERHA). In 1999, the old Eastern Health Board became the ERHA – an overarching authority made up of three new boards – the East Coast Area Health Board, the Northern Area Health Board and the South Western Area Health Board.

By the time the HSE was introduced in 2005, pretty much everyone agreed radical reform was needed. What was not so clear was the exact nature of the reform required.

When Liam Doran, the outspoken general secretary of the INO for over a decade, reflected on establishment of the HSE three years after it was set up, he summed up general feeling, saying, 'Setting up a Health Service Executive seemed to make sense. In 2003 and 2004, most people said 'yes, it's worth a go'.'

Deciding the new structure and roles

In the 2001 health strategy 'Quality and Fairness – A Health Service for You', action 114 committed 'an independent audit of functions and structures in the health system' to be carried out by the Department of Health and Children and independent consultants with a completion date of June 2002[1].

Prospectus Strategy Consultants were awarded the competitive tender for the contract and Vincent Barton, an ex-Department of Health employee, by then a director in Prospectus, led the audit process.

The Prospectus Report – an Audit of Structures and Functions in the Health System – was one of three major reviews carried out by the Department of Health following the publication of the health strategy.[2] It was published in June 2003, alongside the report of the Commission on Financial Management and Control Systems in the Health Service.[3] This report was also known as the Brennan Report, after its chair Niamh Brennan, a Professor of Management in UCD and wife of the then Minister for Justice and prominent PD politician Michael McDowell.

Minister Martin launched the Brennan and Prospectus reports alongside the 'Health Service Reform Programme' in June 2003. The 'Reform Programme' drew on the commissioned reports' findings and detailed for the first time the 'abolition of the existing health board/authority structures'. It also announced 'the reorganisation of the Department of Health and

Children, the establishment of a Health Service Executive which will be the first ever body charged with managing the health service as a single entity'.[4]

The website set up specifically to keep staff and patients informed of the reform process stated:

> The Reform Programme is focused on improving patient care, providing better value for money and improving healthcare management. Key programme elements include: rationalising health service agencies to reduce fragmentation, including abolition of health board/authority structures; establishing a Health Service Executive (HSE) as a single national entity to manage the health services.
>
> The Health Act 2004 provided a legal framework for the establishment of the Health Service Executive on a statutory basis. With effect from 1 January 2005, the HSE took over responsibility for the management and delivery of health services from the Eastern Regional Health Authority, the health boards and a number of other agencies.[5]

As per the Health Act 2004, the objective of the Executive is 'to use the resources available to it in the most beneficial, effective and efficient manner to improve, promote and protect the health and welfare of the public'.[6]

The 'Reform Programme' was followed by the publication in October 2003 of Report of the National Task Force on Medical Staffing, known as the Hanly Report after its chair, David Hanly[7]. The Hanly Report set out how to improve patient care by reducing the working hours of non-consultant hospital doctors (junior doctors), employing more consultants and reforming medical education and training. It was drawn up in the context of European legislation which required Ireland to reduce its dependency on the excessive working hours of junior hospital doctors. The Hanly Report also made recommendations, like many previous reports on the contentious issue of the location of hospitals.

It is still too soon to tell exactly what stymied the health strategy and the health reform programme referred to by Minister Micheál Martin as the 'blueprint to guide policy-makers and service providers towards delivery of the articulated vision … to guide the planning and activity in the health system over the next seven to ten years'.[8]

Many people involved in the process will talk off, but not on, the record about why health strategy was left to sit on a shelf, unimplemented and apparently redundant. There are varying schools of thought on what happened and why, but common to all are the issues of structures, roles, funding, accountability and leadership.

In the run-up to its establishment, the HSE was heralded as the new, accountable, integrated health system, that would cure many of the dysfunctional ills that existed in the health system. Everyone acknowledged the system was fragmented, uncoordinated, made up of too many disjointed elements and, failing to provide a seamless service for patients.

The old health boards lacked consistency and standards and were overly influenced by local politicians who sat on their boards. They were under increasing pressure to provide more services for a growing, ageing population with increasing costs of drugs, medical equipment and health service staff. Each year, the health boards and voluntary hospitals ran over budget. Each year, they were rescued by some juggling of finance from unspent capital or current budgets, without any real penalties for failing to work within budgets being imposed. The Prospectus, Brennan and Hanly reports were consistent in the view that radical reform and reorganisation was needed in relation to structure, funding and management.

The Hanly Report proved the most controversial of the three reports as it made recommendations on the establishment of regional networks of hospitals that would require decisions on which hospitals would become regional hubs and which would not. If Hanly's recommendations were followed through, the bullet would have to be bitten on which hospitals should be developed and which would be 'downgraded' to become community hospitals or step-down facilities. It was rightly felt that as long as locally elected politicians sat on health boards, no brave decisions would be made in this regard.

Prof Orla Hardiman, commenting on the old health boards said, 'each health board area was an independent fiefdom – politicians liked them as they could get medical cards for constituents'. Local politicians also guarded (and still do) their local hospitals, like their most prized possession.

Leadership

Micheál Martin, as minister, rarely missed a chance to refer to the health service reform as 'the most comprehensive and ambitious ever produced in this country'.[9] From the publication of the health strategy in 2001 to the implementation of the reform programme in 2004, there was a lot of rhetoric about how leadership was crucial to successful reform first by Martin and then Kevin Kelly, as interim chair of the HSE.

Martin's mantra was accurate, as the proposed reform of the health services was the biggest public sector reform in Ireland. Change of such size requires leadership. However, Martin's tenure in health is not now remembered for its leadership, or its reform agenda but for his continuous commissioning of consultants, the publication of their reports and, critically, the failure to act upon their central proposals. His biggest success, altogether removed from the health services, was the smoking ban, which is looked at in Chapter 7.

So who was providing leadership for the implementation of the health strategy during this crucial time of major reform?

In September 2004, in a mid-term cabinet reshuffle Mary Harney, PD leader and a firm believer in free-market economics had replaced Martin as Minister for Health. Following the June 2004 local elections, politicians were not reappointed to the local health boards. The interim HSE board tried, unsuccessfully, to recruit a chief executive. While some of the old health board chief executives applied, Aidan Halligan, an Irish-born and educated Deputy Chief Medical Officer in the NHS in England, was appointed to the position. Just before he was due to start, in November 2004, he decided not to take the job.

In the absence of any other candidate, Kevin Kelly who had been the interim chair of the HSE board, was appointed interim chief executive and Liam Downey, already a member of the interim HSE board, was appointed the first chairman of the HSE board. Kevin Kelly, an ex-banker, was managing director of AIB Bank from 1996–2001.

The make-up of the first and subsequent HSE board is interesting reading. Downey was a former chief executive of a medical technology company, Becton Dickinson Ireland, a member of the national executive council of IBEC and of the Labour Relations Commission.

Other members of the interim HSE board, which became the first HSE board were: Niamh Brennan, who chaired the Commission of Financial Management and Control Systems in the Health Service and UCD Professor of Management; Donal de Buitleir, general manager in the CEO's office in AIB Group, previously an assistant secretary in Revenue Commissioners and a member of the Commission of Financial Management and Control Systems in the Health Service; Professor Anne Scott, Head of School of Nursing in Dublin City University; Michael McCloone county manager in Donegal since 1994, also a member of the Commission of Financial Management and Control Systems in the Health Service; Michael Murphy, Dean of Medicine in NUI, Cork and chairman of the Health Research Board; P.J. Fitzpatrick, ex-CEO of the Eastern Health Board who moved on to become Chief Executive of the Courts Service; John A. Murphy, Professor of Business in Trinity College Dublin, president of the Marketing Institute of Ireland and a member of the Steering Committee of the Audit of Structures and Functions of the Health System (the work undertaken by Prospectus); Maureen Gaffney, chair of the National Economic and Social Forum, a psychologist formerly working in Trinity College Dublin; and Eugene McCague, a solicitor and partner in Arthur Cox and Associates.

Under the 2004 Health Act, five members of the HSE board had to retire by a lottery mechanism in January 2008. Mary Harney as minister reappointed three members – McCague, Scott and Fitzpatrick – and two new appointments were made: Joe Mooney ex-Department of Finance official, and Pat Farrell, chief executive of the Irish Banking Federation and ex-board member of the VHI. In July 2008, Willie O'Reilly, the chief executive of Today FM, Ireland's leading national commercial radio, was appointed to the HSE board, replacing Joe Macri, Managing Director of Microsoft Ireland who had sat on the board since 2005.

What is most interesting about the membership of the interim HSE board and the two boards since is the predominance of men and private-sector finance people, and the distinct absence of health policy and health service/public service management expertise. There have been 16 people sitting on the HSE boards, three of whom have been women. Nine of the 16 have come from a finance/private/management perspective. Two are medical doctors, one a professor of nursing, while just three of them have 'pure' public sector experience – one a county manager, one an ex-health board CEO and one department of finance official. There was no board member who worked in frontline health services.

In particular, the most recent changes to the board are interesting. Farrell is known to be close to Fianna Fáil and a master of all things banking, while Joe Mooney was the Department of Finance mandarin who looked after the health vote. Having the two new members of the HSE board so close to the government indicates some shift in political efforts to rein in the HSE.

There was also a major shake up in personnel at a senior management level within the Department of Health and the new HSE.

In late 2004 and early 2005, Michael Kelly, who had been a well regarded and energetic secretary general in the Department of Health for five years, was totally sidelined. Kelly had got on well with Martin during his time in health and both were determined to reform, to invest more in health. Kelly was supportive of Martin's attempt to stand up to Charlie McCreevy in the Department of Finance. But relations between Kelly and Harney, an old ally of McCreevy's, were not so amicable.

Kelly left the post in the Department of Health when a head needed to roll in the wake of the Travers Report on the nursing homes controversy. The Travers Report found that the main responsibility for illegal charges imposed on nursing home residents lay with the Department of Health, where it said there was a long-term systemic failure to deal with the issue. Travers details the failure of ministers, as far back as Charlie Haughey in 1979, to legislate for charges. However, Kelly was the fall guy and was appointed the chair of the Higher Education Authority on his departure from health.

In May 2005, Michael Scanlon, who had been an assistant secretary at the Department of Finance, was appointed secretary general to the Department of Health and Children.

Up to 2003–04, the ten health board CEOs and the CEO of the ERHA provided a cadre of chief executives and provided both experience and leadership for Irish health and social services. They also worked together under the remit of the Health Board Executive (HeBE), which was an effort to work together in a strategic way at CEO level.

When it was announced that the boards would be abolished with no clear roles for the CEOs, this core group of leaders was lost. Although all of the CEOs were kept in place until July 2005 to assist with the transition from boards to the HSE, just two (Sean Hurley and Pat Donnelly) of the ten remained in the HSE eighteen months after its inception.

Sean Hurley, ex-CEO of the Southern Health Board (SHB) became acting Director of Information and Communication Technology in the new HSE and was responsible for the HSE review of PPARS debacle, appearing before the Dáil Public Accounts Committee on the issue. He was head of the HSE's Corporate Pharmaceutical Unit

Pat Donnelly, formerly CEO of the South Western Area Health Board (SWAHB) is still with the HSE, working in Primary, Community and Continuing Care.

Michael Lyons, was CEO of the ERHA until the establishment of the HSE. Prior to that he was CEO of the East Coast Area Health Board (ECAHB). Before working for the ECAHB, his working life was in the Department of Health. In 2005, he became CEO of the hospice in Harold's Cross and, eight months later, became CEO of Our Lady's Children's Hospital, Crumlin, where he was one of the chief critics of the government decision to locate the new children's hospital on the site of the Mater. In November 2007, he retired from Our Lady's Children's Hospital for 'personal reasons'.

Denis Doherty, who was CEO of the Midland Health Board (MHB) left to become an independent consultant and heads up his own consultancy firm Denis Doherty & Associates, Healthcare

Consultants. His former positions included Director of the Health Boards Executive (HeBE), Director of the Office for Health Management and Chief Executive Officer, MHB and the Mid-Western Health Board (MWHB). He is the health advisor to Tullamore-based Flanagan Group in their development of a 60-bed private hospital, a 30-bed convalescent home, a 70-bed nursing home and a 20-bed hospice. The group is also building a large primary care clinic and childcare facility on the site.

Stiofán de Burca, former CEO in the (MWHB) is now Director of the Health Systems Research Centre, in the University of Limerick.

Pat Harvey, former CEO of the NWHB, is now involved in the development of a new private Wyndale Clinic, located near Letterkenny General Hospital.

Others who had long-term institutional knowledge on the workings of the HSE were there for the initial stages of the HSE but left within the year. Pat McLoughlin who was CEO of both the Eastern and South Eastern Health Boards and then Director of Planning and Commissioning and Deputy CEO in the ERHA was appointed head of the new National Hospitals Office in the first few months of the HSE's establishment, however, he left in early 2006 when agreement was not reached on his contract. In November 2008, he was appointed as an advisor to the Special Group on Public Service Numbers and Expenditure Programmes, known as 'An Bord Snip Nua', by Minister for Finance, Brian Lenihan.

Maureen Browne who had been director of communications in the old Eastern Health Board and the ERHA was appointed Acting National Director of Communications for the initial months of the newly formed HSE. Her contract ended in June 2005, when she left to establish her own media and communications consultancy. At this point it was known that Prof Brendan Drumm was becoming CEO and that he wished to bring his own media advisor with him.

While many would not praise the quality of leadership in the old health boards and ERHA, the most senior people in them did know how to run the system and had a huge amount of organisational knowledge, particularly in relation to complicated financial arrangements. That organisational wisdom was lost very early after the establishment of the HSE.

Kevin Kelly acted as interim CEO until August 2005. Two months earlier, in June, Prof Drumm, a consultant paediatric gastroenterologist based in Our Lady's Children's Hospital, Crumlin, and a UCD professor, was named as the new CEO of the HSE.

Yet, within weeks of the announcement that he would take up the helm of the biggest public sector body in the country, Prof Drumm held a press conference in Our Lady's Children's Hospital to make known he would not be taking the job. According to Mary Harney at the time, 'Drumm had been offered the job, but a failure to reach agreement on one aspect of his contract led to negotiations with him irretrievably breaking down.'

Two weeks later, after much political persuasion and a rescue package being put in place, including a €400,000 pay package, Prof Drumm was back in line for the post and came into office in August 2005.

Although Drumm was considered an excellent physician specialising in paediatric gastroenterology, his absence of large-scale, public service management must be a disadvantage in the biggest public-sector post in Ireland. He had experience outside of his children's hospital work. Between 1995 and 2000, he was Chairman of Comhairle na nOspidéal, the statutory body responsible for regulating consultant appointments in the public sector and advising the minister and health agencies on the organisation of hospital services nationally. This position enabled him to become familiar with the workings of the health service. In this role, he was a member of the Forum on Medical Manpower.

In May 2006, the media leaked details of a bonus of €32,000 awarded to Drumm, although he was in office less than a year. In September 2007, again through media leaks, it emerged that Drumm was awarded a bonus of €80,000, on top of his basic salary of €369,713. In response to the media reports, the HSE chairman issued a statement saying that the 'board of the HSE, on the recommendation of its Remuneration Committee, has approved a Performance Related Pay Award of €80,000 to Professor Drumm, in recognition off his achievements during 2006'. The statement went on to say that the board believed it was 'fitting given Professor Drumm's performance and accomplishments ... along with the energy, drive and commitment he has applied to his responsibilities and the leadership he has brought to the HSE'.[10] It said the arrangement offered, which was agreed by the government, included a performance-related award of up to 25 per cent.

Drumm's pay package was negotiated independently of public-sector pay. As it is a contracted salary, it does not come under the Review Body of Higher Remuneration. However, in its 2007 report, the body stated that 'the serving CEO is being remunerated at a level established on a personal basis. Accordingly, the existing remuneration will continue to apply to the serving CEO but the remuneration we recommend will be treated as the definitive rate for the job'.[11] The Higher Review Body recommended a salary of €303,000 for the next HSE CEO.

Alongside his personal pay package, Drumm got agreement to bring with him a special 'cabinet' of six to spearhead reforms, and €1 million a year to spend on these advisors. When announced, Drumm's team of advisors were known as the 'strategic apex team'. Drumm's decision to bring with him a coterie of advisors has led to confusion and frustration within the HSE. Staff at middle management and on frontline services believed that key decisions were being made by Drumm's 'kitchen cabinet' rather than by the management team made up of the national directors. 'In the INO's experience, there is a genuine disconnect between Drumm and his immediate advisers, and the senior management grades,' says Liam Doran.

Drumm's advisors included:

- Maureen Lynott, who had formerly worked in senior management in BUPA Ireland and Focus Ireland and was working independently as a consultant in the run-up to the establishment of the HSE. Her consultancy work included work with the National Treatment Purchase Fund and Breastcheck. Lynott took up the post of advisor on performance management. A HSE briefing on the reform process in December 2005 named her as Chairperson of the Steering Group and the Strategic Planning, Reform and Implementation Unit (SPRI).
- Sean McGuire, a Carlow GP became Drumm's advisor on primary care. McGuire set up one of the first GP co-ops in the southeast and was advising Drumm on the roll-out of the Primary Care Strategy.
- Maura McGrath was appointed his advisor on human resources. In 2008, Sean McGrath was appointed National Director of Human Resources.
- Karl Anderson, was appointed by Drumm as strategic communications advisor. Previously, he headed up Parents for a New Crumlin Hospital, which was opposing the location of the new Children's Hospital in the Mater site.
- Tommie Martin, came from Comhairle na nOspidéal which was subsumed into the HSE under the new structures. He became National Director of the Office of the CEO under Drumm's regime.
- John O'Brien, formerly the CEO in St James's Hospital was brought in by Drumm to act as his advisor on hospitals. He became acting National Director of the NHO when Pat McLoughlin stood down from the position.

In July 2008, a rather ugly public image of those close to Drumm emerged when the *Sunday Tribune* newspaper had a front-page story on the 3 August 2008 which detailed an alleged fight in a public house between two of Drumm's most senior advisors. At the going away party for Alex Connolly, who had headed up the media relations office, a fight spilled out on to the street outside the Nancy Hands pub on Parkgate Street, opposite HSE headquarters. Apparently, no ambulance was called but one of the advisors later presented in hospital with an arm broken in three places – not a good sign of working relations among the most senior personnel in the HSE team.

The advisors are contracted to work a three day week and receive €1,350 a day, and have five weeks' holiday. Overtime pay ranges from €1,207 to €1,350 a day.

Figures released to RTÉ in May 2008 showed that Maureen Lynott had received €637,273 since her appointment in August 2005. Maura McGrath received €606,887 since her appointment while Anderson had received €544,074 for work over the three years. McGuire, who left the HSE in 2006 and went back to work in the private sector, had received €379,608 for his work. O'Brien and Martin are on salaries.

Unions, in particular, have been critical of the role and power of Drumm's advisors. Kevin Callinan, national secretary of Impact trade union speaking at his annual conference in May 2008, said, 'Since Prof Drumm took up his post in August 2005, he had surrounded himself with a team of advisors, and that this had tended to blur structures. It had also led to a bunker mentality where it seems that the primary purpose of the advisors is to protect their leader at all costs and to reaffirm rather than challenge. Indeed there are increasing reports that this management style does not welcome challenges and is slow to tolerate questioning or alternative viewpoints.'[12]

The new structure

Between the publication of the health strategy in December 2001 and the coming into being of the HSE on 1 January 2005, much of the time and energy of senior management in the Department of Health and the health boards went into planning the reform of the structure and administration of the country's health services.

Inexplicably, amid this rush for reform, there was no move to address the fundamental structural inequality in the health services – the fact that people who can afford private care can access medical services quicker than those who cannot.

The Department of Health led a slow process through the second half of 2003 and the first half of 2004, combining the Prospectus, Hanly and Brennan reports into one coherent strategy. According to Donal Duffy of the Irish Hospital Consultants Association, 'it was like they [the department and interim HSE board] threw the three reports in the air, and what came back down was the HSE'.

Both the Brennan and Prospectus reports recommended reform through the establishment of one central executive, although they differed on the strategy and objectives. According to the Prospectus Report, commissioned by the Department of Health, the purpose of reform was to create 'a consolidated healthcare structure, putting in place a single Health Service Executive to replace the existing health boards', delivering 'value for money and managing ongoing change' and ensuring 'simpler governance and greater accountability'.[13]

The Brennan Report, commissioned as a 'Value for Money Audit of the Health services' by Charlie McCreevy's Department of Finance, found that 'many of the problems [of the health system] are fundamentally structural ... we believe that just improving the systems of financial management and control will do little to improve the efficiency and effectiveness of health expenditure unless there is fundamental reform of how the system is organised and managed'. It concluded that: '... the management vacuum at the heart of the health service must be addressed urgently. We believe that national management of the health service would best be delivered outside the structure of the Department of Health and Children and are recommending the establishment of an executive at national level for this purpose. This would allow the Department of Health and Children to focus more fully on health policy.'[14]

The new structure selected for the Health Service Executive (HSE) was closer to the Prospectus than the Brennan model. Brennan had recommended a single authority to manage the health boards, although the number and configuration of the boards could have changed. Prospectus recommended one single executive, with four regional offices but no health boards (and therefore no politicians).

In November 2003, when Micheál Martin appointed banker Kevin Kelly as chairman of the interim HSE board, the use of the language of the market in Irish healthcare began to permeate: 'patients' became 'clients'; if the public health services were failing, then the private sector could provide some of the solutions.

From November 2003, Kevin Kelly was centrally involved in the reform process. Some senior health sector personnel who worked with him during this time express frustration at his drive to 'commodify health and social care', alleging he 'lacked empathy for the ethos of public services'. Others blamed the lack of planning under his stewardship as core to the confusion about roles, structure and responsibility when the HSE came into being on 1 January 2005.

'It went wrong from day one. The transition period was handled abominably. Even the CEOs were sidelined. There were unnecessary levels of delay and inertia,' says Liam Doran of the INO.

Days before the HSE was due to be established, staff and management were still unclear about new structures and reporting mechanisms. Maureen Browne, who was acting director of communications in the new HSE from January to June 2005, wrote retrospectively in her *Irish Medical News* column that 'it would have seemed prudent to many to defer establishment day to provide time for further measured discussion. However, this was not to be and, with hopelessly inadequate preparation and even less infrastructure agreed, the HSE went live at the beginning of January'.[15]

On 1 January 2005, over forty organisations were amalgamated to form the new HSE. Central to the rationale behind the amalgamation of the old health boards and the myriad other health agencies was to eliminate the duplication of roles and unnecessary waste. Yet, not one person forcibly lost their job. While most of the old health board CEOs 'resigned', they did so with generous packages and most of them went on to other public or private sector jobs.

Senior officials from the unions and the Department of Health say they were encouraging a voluntary redundancy package to be put in place, but government and the Department of Finance were adamant such a package wouldn't be offered.[16] The establishment of the HSE was happening at the same time as the decentralisation of government departments and state agencies and the government was opposed to any voluntary redundancies as part of decentralisation.

On 23 December 2004, Kevin Kelly did a last-minute deal with the public-sector union Impact – which was threatening industrial action due to staff and management having no knowledge of where they would be in the new HSE structure. The deal resulted in a guarantee that all administrator and management staff would have jobs of equal standing in the new organisation. Despite this, tens of thousands of people went into work in the new year of 2005 not knowing to whom they should report, whether their role was to change, what their responsibilities would be, or where they would be based.

Mary Harney, who had taken over as Minister for Health in September 2004, delivered the HSE structure, conceived in Micheál Martin's time. Announcing the Health Bill in the Dáil in November that year, she said that 'the key to the Health Bill is clarity, clarity of roles and clarity of responsibility – the Minister for Health will retain clear accountability for our health services ... Most of all, people will have clarity about who is in charge of policy and who is in charge of the management of the health services'.[17]

The theory of the new structure was simple. Under the 2004 Health Act, the Minister for Health and the department are responsible for health policy and legislation. The minister appoints the board of the HSE. The board appoints the chief executive of the HSE (except for the first one, who was appointed by the minister). The HSE manages and funds all health and social services.

According to Tussing and Wren, who have done the most detailed analysis of the foundation of the HSE, 'The legislation providing for the establishment of the HSE, the Health Act 2004, passed all stages in the Dáil in a guillotined debate in November and December 2004, without time for many provisions to be discussed and fully understood within or outside of the Dáil, even by the then government which promulgated them. There was no White Paper outlining intent of the legislation. The policy–operations divide between minister and CEO leaves great scope for confusion and blame.'[18]

And confusion and blame abounded in its first few years of operation. Commenting on its beginnings, Anthony Staines, professor in the DCU School of Nursing, said the HSE was 'seriously hampered by its origins and the time it has been given to change'. It was made by 'slamming together 11 organisations, some of which were notably dysfunctional. Structural change, as the HSE demonstrates, often paralyses an organisation and its staff for several years. The Minister for Health Mary Harney set it up in haste in 2005. There is no sign that much thought was put into setting it up at the time'.[19]

Kevin Kelly, and subsequently Brendan Drumm, took over a structure that loosely followed the recommendations of the Prospectus Report. The 11 old health boards and a raft of health agencies became one organisation under three different pillars. These pillars were the National Hospitals Office (NHO), Primary Community and Continuing Care (PCCC) and Shared Services.

The National Hospitals Office had a director, four assistant directors and ten hospital network managers. All of those appointed initially came from either Assistant CEO health board posts or senior management positions in the old boards. Pat McLoughlin was the first National Director of the National Hospitals Office. When he resigned in January 2006, John O'Brien, former St James's CEO took up the post as acting NHO director. However, by the end of 2007 when the Portlaoise cancer misdiagnosis scandal was hitting the headlines, O'Brien reverted back to his role as advisor on hospitals and Ann Doherty had become Acting Director of the National Hospitals Office. Doherty, up until then, had been the National Director of Corporate Planning and Control Processes and was considered a safe pair of hands to manage the NHO during turbulent times. She was also assigned by Drumm to oversee a high level group to look at 'integrating' NHO and PCCC.

The Primary, Community and Continuing Care (PCCC) pillar was initially headed by Aidan Browne, with four assistant directors appointed to the four new regions; Dublin/Mid-Leinster; Dublin Northeast; Western and Southern Areas. All of the appointments were made from staff in the health boards. Aidan Browne was the senior HSE person dealing with the Leas Cross scandal. Leas Cross, a private nursing home in North

County Dublin was exposed on a RTÉ *Primetime Investigates* programme as neglecting and poorly treating its residents. Geriatrician Des O'Neill was hired by the HSE to carry out an independent investigation. Des O'Neill's report was given to the HSE in December 2005 but the HSE postponed publication of the report for months after it had been submitted. At its launch in October 2006, the HSE tried to stop family members of people who had died in Leas Cross into the launch of the report. Although no one was ever held accountable for the mismanagement of the Leas Cross Report, Browne left his position in PCCC and moved into a new role as the CEO of Children Acts Advisory Board. Laverne McGuiness who had been National Director of Shared Services took over from Browne in PCCC.

Pat Doorley was appointed national director of Population Health alongside a raft of others who were acting directors of Corporate Services, Communications, IT, HR, Strategic Development. Four regional health offices and 32 local health offices, expert advisory groups and care group directorates were also established, staffed by many assistant national directors.

The combination of the loss of many senior managers from the health boards with the absence of much new blood from the outside and persistent managerial failures of the HSE have resulted in criticisms of the capacity of the HSE management. One person interviewed for this book close to the old and new health service management said, in relation to the calibre of HSE managers, 'If we were talking about football here, we'd be talking about the second division league, and the bottom of it at that.'[20]

The Shared Services pillar, headed up by Laverne McGuiness, was based on the premise that with the amalgamation of a gamut of health agencies, efficiencies could be made through procurement, commissioning and planning, particularly in areas that crossed services, such as recruitment.

Initially, under the auspices of shared services came: population health; finance; information and communications technology; human resources; corporate affairs; change management and organisational change; strategic planning and development; and the four regional health office directors. Subsequently, population health was shown in organisational maps as crossing services of hospitals and primary, community and continuing care.

Just two years after the much heralded structure of the NHO, PCCC and Shared Services, 'the responsibility for the management of all shared services functions and the pursuance of the objectives and implementation of a shared services delivery strategy was transferred from the National Directorate of Shared Services to the appropriate functions Directorates'.[21]

One of the three central pillars of the new, much publicised integrated HSE disappeared from HSE organisational maps during 2007, while its various roles were 'transferred' back to other relevant sections without any public announcements.

According to the report by the Review Body on Higher Remuneration in the public sector published in 2007, 'the post of National Director of Shared Services was abolished and responsibilities in relation to shared services were assigned to the National Director Posts with responsibility for finance, HR, ICT, procurement'.[22]

An attempt by this author to track the changes in the HSE's organisational structure proved impossible. Organisational charts from January 2005 and 2008 are unrecognisable, with new forms, new names of sections, new heads of divisions and new people in posts.

In March 2008, in an interview in the *Sunday Business Post*, Paula Gilvarry, a public health doctor and HSE manager of community services, said, 'The thing that really frustrates me is that, even with an organisational chart up in front of you, you are still totally confused about who is doing what. If you want a decision made who do you talk to?'[23] She describes working in the HSE as like 'swimming in treacle'.

Gilvarry also talked about the difficulty of being a manager in the HSE when compared with the old boards. In past times, as a manager, you could make decisions about new service developments, pitch for budgets and make things happen locally. But under the new system, this is not possible, with everything having to go up and down the line. Plus, as Gilvarry says, 'organisational structures are so complex, she is still not clear who reports to whom'. Her sentiments are reiterated by HSE staff and their unions who talked openly from 2006 onwards about the difficulty in getting decisions made. There was growing criticism of the control and command culture operated from Dublin, and complaints that the excess of centralised management was stagnating key decisions on patient care.

Since its inception, staff and patients complained about the incongruous nature of two service pillars separating primary and community care from hospitals. Upon taking up post, Drumm advocated passionately for the need to build up primary, community and continuing care in order to relieve pressures on the hospital system.

Drumm has championed the Transformation Programme, intended to transform the health service so that patients experience a seamless service from GPs, hospitals and community care. No one could disagree with such aspirations but the structures Drumm inherited, with the two pillars separating care between hospitals and the community, worked against such aims. The Transformation Programme was not launched until January 2007, two full years after the HSE was up and running.

It appeared that HSE senior management was so busy planning to 'transform' the service that the concerns identified by staff and patients were neither heard nor addressed.

Plans to integrate hospitals and primary, community and continuing care were denied in persistent press queries by this author throughout late 2007 and the first half of 2008.

Then, on 3 July 2008, an *Irish Times* article based on a leaked HSE document revealed the planned amalgamation of the NHO and PCCC. Within hours, Minister Mary Harney had to go public and announce that the two central pillars of NHO and PCCC would be amalgamated. She rejected charges of a 'U-turn', 'botched reform' or 'an admission of failure'. However, three and a half years after the architecture at the very heart of the HSE was built, the three central pillars of NHO, PCCC and Shared Services, were planned for extinction. Surely, news that the health services were returning to the regional structures from which they came and that the central pillars of the HSE were to be dismembered and amalgamated was an extraordinary *volte face* by the minister.

Speaking in the Dáil on the day of the leak, Mary Harney said, 'Merging the pillars will mean that, at hospital level, there will not be confusion over whether a home care package comes from the hospital budget or another budget. The merger of the pillars will allow for a more effective response to the needs of patients.' She went on to say the aim of the new structure was 'to have fewer layers of bureaucracy'.[24]

Brendan Drumm, writing on the structural changes in *The Irish Times* a week after the news broke, said, 'I have stressed continuously the need for the HSE to evolve and develop in a way that supports fully integrated care. That is what we are doing as an organisation. The modifications we are introducing do not signal a change of direction for the HSE. They are focused on improving access and delivering better value for patients and clients, and strengthening our capacity to deliver a modern health service.'[25]

The HSE Transformation Staff Briefing for July 2008 is entitled 'National Integration – Local Responsibility'. It outlines the proposed changes emanating from the work of McKinsey consultants who, in the words of Mary Harney, were recruited to help Drumm and the HSE board 'to devise an appropriate organisational structure for the executive',[26] work which was going on since the middle of 2007.

The July 2008 HSE Transformation briefing says: 'We [the HSE] are now introducing some modifications to the way we are organised to support even better service delivery and operational effectiveness. These modifications will mean more local responsibility and authority within defined national parameters, more robust area structures and more clinical involvement in the design and management of patient services.'

Specifically the 'modifications' include:

- The integration of the National Hospitals Office and Primary, Community and Continuing Care in to a single National Directorate of Integrated Service Delivery
- Population health has been reassigned to the planning, integrated service delivery and clinical care and quality directorates
- The appointment of three new national directors of clinical care and quality, of planning and of communications
- New regional area directors will be established.

The number of new regional areas was not yet decided. Four, six or even eight (how many health boards were there originally?) were the numbers floating about.

The briefing says the changes are to be completed by September 2009 and according to Mary Harney, 'this change will involve an increase in neither budget nor headcount'.[27]

Under the plan, new regional directors will be responsible for integrated health and social care services and will have control over their own budgets.

The head of human resources, Sean McGrath appointed in

March 2008, was given responsibility to oversee the implementation of the proposed changes.

The briefing says the exact nature of the change has not been completely worked out as 'further work and consultation is required and we will be providing answers to your questions as they become available'. In February 2009, the new regional structures were still not known, however rumour abounded in the HSE that an announcement was imminent.

So, less than four years after its establishment, the very structure at the centre of HSE service provision was being completely reconfigured.

Commenting in light of the leaked announcement of the structural changes to be introduced in the HSE which hit the public and political radar in the early days of July 2008, Charles Normand, Professor of Health Policy at Trinity College Dublin, said, 'The big lesson from the last [health service] reform was that we did not adequately account for the disruptive effects of the reform ... across Europe the same mistake is made with expectations that reforms will happen quickly ... it takes at least two to three years for reform to bed down properly.'[28] Normand elaborates at any given opportunity on the three-year rule – how if major reform is implemented, it takes at least three years for things to be where they were when the reform was introduced.

While, there was a general welcome from staff and unions in relation to the planned integration of NHO and PCCC in July 2008, staff expressed concern that, after three and a half years of turmoil, they wanted structures and management systems to settle down, that the integration needed to be carried out with as little disruption as possible.

Union leaders welcomed the announcement if it meant that more decisions would be devolved locally and thereby improve patient care. However, scepticism remains. Commenting on the change, Donal Duffy, assistant general secretary of the IHCA said 'it was all about the organisational structure, or to put it another way, the deck chairs on the *Titanic* '.[29]

Despite new management arrangements and significant changes in structures and reporting systems throughout the early years of its formation, to their credit HSE services on the ground continued as before. Day-to-day health and social care services were provided by the same frontline staff, out of the same locations.

The structure of four regional health offices, local health offices and a NHO as outlined by Prospectus was followed. However, many of the required associated actions recommended by Prospectus were diluted or took a long time to happen.

Prospectus recommended the devolution of resources and decision-making to as local a level as possible. In particular, primary, community and continuing care services were to be run by regional directors. While these directors are in place, decision making in this area has been particularly prone to stalling by centralised decision making.

Speaking at the annual Impact conference in May 2008, their national secretary Kevin Callinan said, 'Ordinary health workers felt increasingly detached from influence over services they provided ... in many ways managers face responsibility without power rather than the opposite charge that can sometimes be alleged. But this centralised approach also provides the cover for ideological drive for privatisation and the deepening inequity in our health services'[30].

Michael Lyons, former Department of Health official and ERHA CEO, speaking on his retirement from Our Lady's Children's Hospital, Crumlin in November 2007, said 'there is confusion in the mind of the public, and the public representatives – and even in the mind of the HSE – about whether or not it is a policy-maker or a service deliverer. And there hasn't been any sort of clarity brought to bear on that ... It [the HSE] has driven policy, but it is, at the same time, trying to deliver existing levels of service against a background of diminishing health resources in real terms. It hasn't got that balance right, and this has led to highly centralised decision-making, the disempowerment of the local health office and the network manager system.'[31]

The disempowerment of local health officials referred to by Michael Lyons has been echoed by trade union leaders and health service managers who describe the structure in place as more centralised and monolithic than envisaged at its inception. From the word go, there was confusion about where services fitted into the new structures, who reported to who and who made what decisions, at what level.

Even politicians, like Éamon Ó Cuív and Mary O'Rourke, both members of the government party, spoke publicly during 2007 about the difficulty of findings one's way around the HSE. In November 2007, Fianna Fáil back bencher Ned O'Keeffe became the first government TD to say Minister for Health Mary Harney should resign.

Speaking on *Newstalk* on 27 November, he said, 'the buck has to stop somewhere. I think Mary Harney should resign ... A matter of life and death is involved for many unfortunate female persons across the island of Ireland.' O'Keeffe said he was appalled at the failures of the Health Service Executive (HSE) and indicated Harney had to take responsibility. He resigned from the parliamentary party, before abstaining on a vote on the Labour motion criticising minister Mary Harney's handling of the problems in cancer services. A series of cancer misdiagnosis scandals rocked the Irish health services in 2007 and 2008, these are dealt with in Chapter 5.

While nationally and internationally, the trend in the last decade of the twentieth century and the first decade of the twenty-first was to decentralise public services, the HSE has centralised decision-making. Many middle and senior managers who lived and worked in the regions of the old health boards, spent their time commuting to executive headquarters in Naas and Dublin, until the travel ban was introduced as a cost-saving measure towards the end of 2007. When the HSE was set up, its headquarters were also in Naas, a town 20 miles south of Dublin – all part of the 'decentralisation' programme. However, in effect HSE headquarters firmly remained in Parkgate Street Dublin, from where Drumm, his management team and most senior advisors work.

Four years after its establishment, workers on the frontline continue to be unsure of their exact line management structures and the burgeoning bureaucracy, while the public struggles to find their way around the HSE.

The Prospectus Report also recommended many other developments which were meant to happen alongside the development of a single health service executive. These included the immediate establishment of an independent Health Information and Quality Authority (HIQA) at the same time as the new unified health service. However, the HIQA, an essential part of ensuring quality services and patient safety, was only established in May 2007. As a result, many developments which were envisaged to coincide with the HSE development are years behind, for example, four years after the HSE was set up, nursing homes were still not inspected by the HIQA and private hospitals did not come under its remit. The Commission on Patient Safety and Quality only reported in August 2008 and was formally accepted by Minister Harney in February 2009.

Accountability

In November 2004, when Minister for Health Mary Harney was rushing the new health legislation through the Dáil, she pledged to 'retain clear accountability for our health services'.

The establishment of the HSE on 1 January 2005, was meant to resolve the issue of accountability once and for all. However, what has actually happened in the health service and in health policy post-2005 is the creation of a system which is even less accountable and less transparent than what it replaced.

The 2004 Health Act, which legislated for the foundation of the HSE, did not specify the responsibilities of the Department of Health and the HSE. Amazingly, there is no reference to the role of the department and its secretary general in the act.

While the former health-board system was widely criticised, most notably for political interference, some HSE staff and patients now look back on those bodies as more democratic and more transparent. Although, the health boards were far from perfect, they comprised public representatives, health professionals and political appointees. They held monthly board meetings open to the media and staff, where management had to answer questions. No such accountability exists in current structures.

The HSE board is now appointed by and accountable to the minister. There are no worker-directors. Meetings are held in private. There are no media or public representatives in attendance. Minutes of board meetings are on the HSE website but they don't contain any detail of presentations or documents circulated, so they are virtually meaningless to anyone except those present. If one was conspiratorial, one might think this was on purpose.

New HSE structures, such as a national forum and regional health forums, are in place, but are considered mere window dressing, far removed from decision-making arenas.

The HSE submits service and capital plans to the minister who then lays them before the Houses of the Oireachtas, but the minister is not directly responsible for them. The result of this is that the person in charge of HSE finances and services, Brendan Drumm, is at arm's length from the Oireachtas and the people.

He, along with the minister, makes a quarterly appearance

at the Oireachtas Health Committee. These meetings involve the committee members berating the minister and the CEO over the troubles of the health services and asking detailed questions for over three hours, with just minutes for the minister and HSE CEO to respond.

Other forms of accountability previously in existence have also been weakened. Prior to the HSE, all parliamentary questions (PQs) on health went to, and were answered by, the minister; responses were prepared by departmental officials. There was open debate on PQs in the Dáil with the minister responding directly to questions and criticisms.

In 2005, regulations for dealing with Dáil questions were not in place in the HSE so the majority of questions were unanswered. In 2006, 95 per cent of Dáil questions referred to the HSE remained unanswered. The HSE set a target of responding within twenty days and says that 75 per cent of PQs met the target in 2007. In January 2008, the HSE set itself a new target of responding in fifteen days. From January to June 2008, the HSE Parliamentary Affairs Division set up to deal with PQs had 2,120 questions referred to it for direct reply. Of these, 1,480 were responded to within fifteen days, 143 were answered within twenty days while 266 were not responded to at all.[32]

However, because the vast majority of health PQs are now referred to the HSE for an official response, they are responded to subsequently in writing and therefore gain less prominence than those verbally responded to during PQs which can become the focus of significant Dáil debate and media coverage.

Also politicians who ask a lot of PQs say that it is not unusual for the responses to contain 'gobbledegook'. While questions asked may be specific, responses will only deal with general issues, saying specific cases can not be dealt with – this results in further questions being put in on the same issue.

Central to the issue of accountability is who is responsible for what. The 1989 Commission on Health Funding observed that 'the simple question "who is in charge" cannot be answered'. Every significant health report since has specified the need to clarify who is responsible for what in Irish health services.

The Brennan and Prospectus reports both identified a central flaw in the Irish health services was that no single agency or person had responsibility for the entire system, that services were too fragmented and there was overlap in roles.

Mary Harney on pushing through the 2004 Health Act promised that, once and for all, it would clarify who was responsible for what. But this has yet to be achieved. As a result, confusion abounds between the Department of Health and the HSE, and within the HSE.

The Fitzgerald Report into the management of cancer misdiagnosis scandal in Portlaoise, published in February 2008, found a 'systemic weakness in governance, management and communication' of the events in Portlaoise. Specifically, in relation to the management and governance, Fitzgerald found 'there were too many people involved from different levels and areas within the HSE without clarity about their roles and responsibilities within the process ... The decision making process was fragmented, with insufficient clarity about decisions, who was making them, why they were being made, or when they were signed off'.[33]

The 2004 Health Act, the very foundation of the HSE failed to clarify the differing roles and responsibilities of the Department of Health and the HSE. Why is it that the HSE is driving the cancer strategy and the push towards specialist centres? And yet the Department of Health is driving the plan to co-locate private hospitals on the grounds of public hospitals? In 2008–09, roles still remain blurred within HSE management and between the Department of Health and the HSE, allowing and, in some instances causing, the continued mismanagement of health services in Ireland.

Funding

Money, of course, is at the heart of accountability. Contrary to advice from civil servants in the departments of Health and Finance, the role of the Health Accounting Officer was handed over from the Secretary General of the Department of Health to the Chief Executive of the HSE in the 2004 Health Act. Where the 'accounting officer' is located is significant because in the words of one senior official in health: 'Whoever holds the purse strings, holds the power.'[34]

Prior to the establishment of the HSE, the Secretary General in the Department of Health was responsible for the health vote – the money allocated to health in the annual budget. In the weeks before the executive was set up in 2004, the Department of Finance was in regular correspondence with the Department of Health, expressing concern over the ability of a new organisation to manage such a large and complex budget. An official close to the negotiations between the minister Mary Harney, the Department of Finance, and the Department of Health in the run-up to the introduction of the Health Bill said 'no one in the department ever really believed the minister would hand over control of €11 billion to the HSE. Once she did, the department was left feeling emasculated'.[35]

But Mary Harney was adamant that handing over the health vote to the CEO would clarify lines of accountability, and she got her way. Brendan Drumm, as CEO is the Chief Financial Officer responsible for the health vote. Whoever fills the HSE CEO role after Brendan Drumm will maintain the mantle of the Chief Financial Officer. This is the second largest public sector budget given to any one agency in the state and comprises a quarter of all money allocated by the state.

One of the major reasons for setting up the HSE was to bring hospital and health board budgets under control. Each year, they ran over budget and had to be rescued by creative accounting measures either within the boards or the hospitals or by the Department of Health. Yet, despite the new, much heralded HSE, this overspend of the health service budget has continued. Since its establishment, central government has continued to be concerned over the HSE's ability to manage its budget.

There are two main issues in relation to the HSE's funding. Firstly, does the HSE get sufficient money in the first place? The answer to that question is dealt with in the Chapter 4 and the answer is clearly no. The 2008 HSE Service Plan showed that it provided more services in 2007 than were planned for the year within a very tight budget. It also honestly outlined that there was virtually no room for increased service provision within budget, as the targets for 2008 were set at 2006 levels, despite acknowledging increased demand from an ageing population, 5,000 additional births and higher expectations of health and social care services.

Similarly, in its 2009 Service Plan which was leaked to the media the week before Christmas 2008, the HSE outlined how it planned to provide the same levels of service in the year ahead as it did in 2008 with virtually the same budget[36]. For 2009, the HSE was allocated €14.7 billion, up 1.1 per cent on 2008. However, in reality this was a cut due to a growing, ageing population, increased demand for services, and the high cost of medical inflation.

In the 2009 Service Plan, the HSE outlined how it planned to do this by making savings adding up to €500 million in a range of areas including over time, administration and a cap on staffing etc. However, within hours of the Service Plan being released it then announced that due to the changed economic circumstances, it needed to make an additional €400 million in savings.

The 2009 HSE Service Plan was an improvement on previous efforts. It detailed targets, costs and timeframes for delivering the plan. It earmarked new money to areas such as cancer care, long-term public beds for older people, new therapy posts for children with disabilities, additional staff in primary care.

Just like the detail of the services promised for the year ahead, the savings set out were brave and were possibly deliverable without hurting the quality and availability of patient care. Until an extra €400 million savings were announced, the Monday before Christmas. This is classic HSE financial and communication mismanagement. How could they let the Service Plan go public without managing this budgetary calamity?

Both the 2009 Service Plan and the Minister's accompanying letter of approval to the chair of the HSE board, Liam Downey, provide some answers. In the letter, Harney is bluntly directing the HSE to manage its finances better, to live within its budget and provide the health and social care services as detailed in the service plan.

The HSE, on the other hand, has a section titled 'risks' early in the plan. Here it explicitly lists areas over which it has no control, which may result in the HSE being unable to provide all the services promised within budget. Included here is doubt that €100 million can be saved by the U-turn on over-70s medical cards (as promised by the Taoiseach and the minister), uncertainty as to the final cost of the consultants' contract, and the decline in income that public hospitals may get from private care in the year ahead (due to commitments in the consultants' contract of actually having an 80/20 public–private mix, and decline in health insurance coverage).

The Minister directed the HSE to provide a contingency plan by January 2009 on how it could make more savings (i.e. cuts) so that it could live within budget in the changed economic circumstances. By the last week in April 2009, this contingency plan remained unpublished. While the HSE's financial management for 2009 remained unclear, what was clear early in 2009 was that it would be impossible to provide all the services outlined in the 2009 Service Plan and make savings of nearly €1 billion.

Secondly, does the HSE manage the budget it has adequately? Unfortunately, the answer to this question is probably not, but given that its budget is insufficient in the first place, how can this be determined?

The Department of Finance, like its previous minister Charlie McCreevy, belongs to the 'black hole' school of thought – that the HSE misspends its overly generous budget. However, even with Harney and Cowen in the key ministerial posts for over four years since its establishment, the Department of Finance is still critical of the HSE's financial management.

Documents have revealed that in March 2008 the Department of Finance wrote to the Department of Health expressing concern over the absence of detail in its spending plan for 2008, i.e. the HSE Service Plan. It was particularly critical of the missing detail on how it was going to save €300 million under its value for money initiative. Since then, the Department of Finance has introduced much closer monitoring of HSE spending, looking for meetings every month with the HSE so that it can report on its financial situation and on measures to control its overspend.[37]

There are some other indicators that can be used to assess the HSE's financial accountability and management. One of the most high-profile misspends of the HSE is the PPARS debacle. But, in fact, the HSE inherited this from the health boards. PPARS was an integrated computerised payroll and human resources system, originally intended to service 17 health agencies, including the health boards and some major hospitals. In 1998, the Department of Health sanctioned £9 million – the expected cost of the project – in expenditure on PPARS. By the end of 2005, PPARS had cost €130 million, by which time it was operating in three health service regions and in one hospital. Over a third of this spend went to a consultancy company to assist in rescuing the programme.

The 2007 Report of the Comptroller and Auditor General criticised the HSE for significant unsanctioned spending on PPARS in 2005. The intention was that PPARS would work across the HSE, but that plan was subsequently abandoned by the HSE board. The Comptroller and Auditor General has continually criticised the HSE on its spending on PPARS and ICT.

Another public manifestation of the HSE's apparent budgetary mismanagement is its over expenditure and reliance on administrators. So, are there too many administrators in the Irish health system?

An administrative staff assessment commissioned by the HSE board found that 16 per cent of the 110,000 staff were considered administrative grades.[38] This figure is broadly in line with comparative figures for Northern Ireland, Wales and Scotland and below numbers in England. However, the assessment found that there were too many senior managers (or administrators) and significant differences with how and where different levels were employed in different services around the country. Also, many of the 16 per cent administrative grades are people providing frontline services.

The over abundance of senior management/administration positions are in Grade VIIIs. When the HSE was set up there was 379 Grade VIIIs or equivalents. In December 2008, there were 563. Grade VIII is a relatively new grade introduced as result of an industrial relations agreement between the Health Service Employers Agency (HSEA) and the health boards, before the establishment of the HSE. Many of the posts were in place prior to this agreement but were not called Grade VIIIs.

The establishment of the HSE was the amalgamation of 11

health boards and numerous other agencies including the Health Service Employers Agency, the Office for Health Management, the Primary Care Reimbursement Scheme among many others. Many of the Grade VIIIs came from such organisations and were not new positions. These positions were guaranteed by the last minute deal Kevin Kelly did with the unions, eight days before its establishment when the details of how it would be managed had not been worked out. Despite the fact that over twenty organisations were amalgamated in 2005, many of them with identical posts (e.g. there were 11 Health Promotion Directors in each of the old health boards), not one person lost their job. Health board managers were reappointed to positions in their area, while similar positions were created at a corporate and centralised level, thus multiplying not eliminating roles. By 2008, a Grade VIII salary was high, ranging from €65,919 to €80,787.

As a result of the assessment, and in the context of the financial cutbacks announced by government in August 2008, an early retirement scheme for the HSE was announced. In this, it is envisaged that 1,000 jobs will be culled, 200 at Grade VIII – a senior management position – and 800 at lower grade levels, at a cost of €30 million. One of the reasons that such a similar scheme was blocked at the time of the founding of the HSE was the worry that civil servants being decentralised would seek a similar scheme. Once decentralisation was put on hold, as part of 'urgent budgetary measures' introduced in August 2008, this paved the way for the HSE redundancy scheme. In February 2009, there were still no details of the scheme, however there were indications that it might be three times larger than originally planned and would include major hospitals. The assessment of administrative grades report also recommended the independent assessment of every post above the level of local health manager.

The cost of bonuses paid to senior HSE staff also gains much media attention. Figures released under Freedom of Information to *The Irish Times* in July 2008 show that €1.148 million was paid in bonuses to 99 HSE staff in 2007. The highest bonus of €80,000 went to Drumm.[39]

The issue of staffing is also a constant issue on the public radar. How can the HSE employ so many staff and yet hospitals and community services remain understaffed? As detailed above, and in Chapter 4, the Irish public health system is not overstaffed. It is still catching up on years of cutbacks in the 1980s and also on trying to meet the needs of a growing population with higher expectations.

In response to a Dáil question in May 2008, Brian Cowen, in his role as Taoiseach, told the Dáil that he had sanctioned an additional 1,050 posts in services for older people, palliative care, disability and population health. He said the deal included a commitment by the HSE to redeploy 2,000 staff to frontline community services in line with the Transformation programme. This deal will bring employment in the HSE up to 112,560 by the end of 2008. The transfer of posts will see an increase in those working in primary, community and continuing care, bringing numbers there up to 56,000 whole-time equivalents by the end of 2009, while those in hospitals will be reduced to 51,000 in the same timeframe.[40] Up until late 2007, despite warnings from central government, the Irish health services virtually ignored the staff ceilings that were in place.

Specifically, in relation to their own financial management, a report leaked to the *Irish Examiner* in July 2008 found that the HSE had sloppy banking practices, with multiple accounts leading to unnecessary charges and a badly policed payroll, which cost it more than €20 million a year. Although €20 million is pittance in comparison to the overall budget of €13 billion, it is an indicator of how the HSE manages its money.

The Department of Finance commissioned the National

Treasury Finance Agency to investigate how the HSE manages its cash, bank accounts payroll and private patient accounts. The leaked report of this document said that it found 'nearly 1,000 people manage finances in the health system with many roles duplicated; until recently the HSE was operating 254 accounts in seven different banks; millions of euros were being lost as accounts were not earning interest; banks were creaming off €2 million annually in charges'.[41] It identified ways in which €19.6 million could be saved.

Cutbacks

The most obvious manifestation of the HSE's inability to manage its own budget came on 4 September 2007, when the HSE management introduced overnight cutbacks to make up for a €200 million overspend in its budget. The overspend came mostly from higher than expected costs of the long-term illness and drugs reimbursement schemes. These are demand-led schemes so, unless curtailed, the costs of them are outside of the control of the HSE.

Upon announcing the 'cost containment measures', HSE management said that the cuts would not impact on patient care or frontline services, but many of them did impact on patient care.

Cutbacks introduced in September 2007 included an embargo on staff; a ban on all 'non-clinical' travel; a ban on hiring hotels for meetings and conferences; reduction in journey times by nursing staff; reduced hours or closure of wards and surgery; stopping emergency cover after 8 p.m.; the cancellation of outpatient services in July and August 2008; and the closure of respite wards.

The staff embargo in place from September 2007 was particularly hard hitting on frontline services as people on sick and maternity leave were not replaced. Although the embargo was officially lifted in December, it was replaced by a strict 'employment control process' which only allowed critical frontline staff vacancies to be filled as they arose, in effect an embargo. Figures presented to the HSE board in March 2008 showed that there were 2,000 fewer staff in the HSE than the previous autumn.[42]

The 2009 HSE Service Plan states that the projected staff ceiling at the start of 2009 would be 112,600 whole-time equivalents (WTEs) which was 2,000 higher than the ceiling in place in January 2008. This increase is in line with service developments in areas such as cancer and primary care services. However it also stipulates that the plan is dependent on a reduction of 3,000 WTEs in pay costs 'which will be achieved through actual staff reductions, staff redeployment and pay related savings as a result of changing how some services are provided'[43].

Other figures released show that, in 2005, the HSE spent €82.7 million on travel, in 2006, the figure was €85.2 million, while in 2007 it was €93.4 million. The HSE responded saying that 65 per cent of these costs were on frontline services, such as public health nurses visiting people in their homes.

Cutting services like public health nurses visiting older people in their homes or home-help services or planned surgery just does not make economic sense as, without such services, these people are more likely to end up as more expensive users of the health services in need of hospital care. Although denied by both the minister and HSE management, unions, doctors and patients have reported the consistent negative impact of the cuts from the end of 2007 right through 2008.

In September 2007, Brian Cowen as Minister for Finance expressed his discontent with the HSE using unspent capital money to offset deficits in day-to-day spending. Drumm responded to Cowen saying such an assertion was unfair as the health services had always operated in such a way and 'clearly the HSE cannot conduct its business using a different model until there is agreement on an alternative and we have on several occasions pointed out the lack of clarity and inherent flaws associated with this current model. The suggestions that the use of this practice by the HSE reflects a need for it to achieve better management of its finances is unreasonable'.[44]

Subsequently, it was agreed by government that the HSE could spend €216 million allocated but unspent on the nursing home repayment scheme to shore up its deficits, the very measure which Cowen was complaining about!

In December 2007, Cowen complained again to Harney, expressing his serious concern about the overspend, declaring that it was 'the latest indication that the HSE spending is not being efficiently managed'.

Another criticism of HSE finances is its ability to spend money allocated for one area on another area. For example, €200 million earmarked for spending in 2008 on new service developments in disability, older people and palliative care had not been spent by May 2008. It was being used to shore up deficits in other areas. These budgetary shortages were a result of increased take up of the demand led schemes. In April 2008, more than 10,000 extra medical cards were issued because of the slowdown in the economy, which resulted in more people qualifying for the cards.

In 2006 and 2007, an extra €25 million was allocated annually to fund new developments outlined in 'A Vision for Change', the mental health policy. But according to Freedom of Information documents obtained by the Irish Mental Health Coalition, just €27 million of the promised €50 million was spent on developing new services – the remainder was used to 'shore up budgetary overspends' by the HSE in mental health services. The HSE Service Plan for 2008 shows that no additional funds have been allocated to mental health developments in 2008.

Age Action highlighted the impact of the cuts on older people, with a reduction in the availability of new home care packages for older people. These are essential for keeping older people well at home and preventing them from ending up in hospital unnecessarily. Age Action found that only one of 22 community care areas surveyed had funding available for home helps. In 16 of the 22 areas, there are waiting lists and hours for home help had been cut in four areas.[45]

In May 2008, outgoing president of the Irish Nurses Organisation, Madeline Spears, said, 'Cut backs were in frontline essential services, never in management ... as short sighted policy, it's the worst type of short sighted policy.'[46]

By July 2008, the HSE had over spent by €146 million, despite the cost-cutting measures in place. The overrun was due to increased spending on community drug schemes, medical cards, and long-term illness schemes, plus increased provision of services in hospitals. There was no provision in the 2008 health budget for the extra 100 consultant posts that were advertised, nor for the increased wages of consultants already on the payroll agreed in the new consultants' contract.

As well as seeking to save €250 million in 2008 to prevent budgetary overrun, the Health budget was committed to providing over one-third of the €440 million in cutbacks ordered by Brian Lenihan as Minister for Finance in early July 2008. On announcing the cutbacks, the government said that Health would be excluded from the mandatory 3 per cent cut. However, when details emerged, it turned out that Health would be providing significant amounts of the attempts to salvage the €3 billion shortfall in exchequer accounts: €85 million came from the deferral of the Fair Deal scheme for older people, €21 million through savings in advertising and administration for health agencies other than the HSE, and €38 million was saved through slow roll-out of new projects.

When the news was breaking about the health cuts, Mary Harney insisted they 'would not affect the provision of health services to patients and clients'. Providing more, better quality public health services to a growing, ageing population is just not compatible with cutting costs of an already under funded public health system. This became increasingly obvious during 2008 and 2009 as the economic reality facing Ireland became increasingly bleak.

Communications

The HSE is hardly ever out of the headlines. Bad news stories predominate, people waiting on trolleys in emergency departments, people dying on waiting lists, people being misdiagnosed with cancer hearing about it on the six o'clock news, fights over the location of the children's hospital in Bertie Ahern's constituency, the closure of hospital wards, the downgrading of hospitals, the protracted negotiations of a new consultants' contract, nurses on strike, the list of bad news headlines just goes on and on and on. So does the HSE get overly negative headlines or does it get the image it deserves?

Its CEO, Brendan Drumm criticises the media for focusing on a crisis in the health service when it is not in crisis. And, in many respects, he is right, day-in, day-out hundreds of thousands of patients receive pretty good quality healthcare from tens of thousands of staff on the HSE payroll. However, there are fundamental problems in how the health services are run and provided – most notably, the unequal provision of care and the bad management of the services currently provided under the public health system. However, it is rare for these issues to hit the headlines. It is the personal, human misery stories that do. And it is here that the HSE is its own worst enemy.

Rebecca O'Malley, whose cancer misdiagnosis resulted in her

late diagnosis and late treatment of her breast cancer, has worked tirelessly to ensure that such an event cannot happen to any other women. Speaking to the INO conference in May 2008, the highly articulate O'Malley said that Drumm was 'utilising the dark arts of propaganda and spin' in relation to the report on her misdiagnosis. She said she had yet to receive a reply from Drumm to a letter she had sent to him over three weeks previously. She was angered by Drumm's attempt to turn the report into a good news story when Drumm welcomed the fact that only one diagnosis had been missed. She said it 'demonstrated the culture of spin and lack of openness, honesty and transparency that exists in our healthcare system'. She said she was saddened and angered by the 'climate of fear which hinders nurses from speaking out on behalf of their patients ... that the prevailing culture in our health services needed to change'.

O'Malley's case is just one example. At every given opportunity, the HSE seeks to spin its findings. A leaked report to the HSE board said over 40 per cent of patients were waiting more than twelve hours in A&E departments, the next day the HSE issues a statement saying just 5 per cent of each day's admissions waited over 12 hours in the first four months of 2008. So which is it? It is the 40 per cent which represents the total number of people waiting, or is it the HSE's officially published figure, which shows the numbers waiting who were admitted? Many people who go to A&E are treated but not admitted.

When brave women like Orla Tinsley speak out about the appalling conditions of cystic fibrosis patients, the HSE instead of holding up their hands and saying, you are right, we need more funding for single rooms and home care for CF patients, they bombard the media with spin on progress made on treatment of CF patients.

Meanwhile as local action groups are mobilised all around

the country to stop the 'downgrading' or closure of local hospitals, the HSE say 'people must trust us, you need centres of excellence and better primary community care'. But, at the same time, they downgrade and close local units without providing centres of excellence or primary and community care.

On the cutbacks, the HSE management and the minister insist they will not impact upon patient care, yet, throughout the spring and summer of 2008, there was story after story in the news of staff shortages, of the suspension of surgery, the temporary closure of wards or reduced home-help hours.

The public just does not trust the HSE and, in 2008–09, they have every reason not to. The HSE may be well intentioned but until patients and the public see real improvements in the services they receive, they will not trust the HSE.

HSE commissioned research 'Insight 08' shows that most patients are satisfied with the health services they receive, when they get the service. However, Ireland tends to rate itself high on a whole range of measures that do not reflect the actual situation, e.g. despite having lower life expectancy and poorer health status than many of our European neighbours, we rate ourselves with the best self-reported health in Europe.

Also some critical questions are not asked in the research, e.g. Susie Long or anyone like her waiting seven months or more for diagnosis would not have been surveyed in such patient satisfaction research, as they are not yet in the system. The same way that patients waiting for diagnosis are not included in waiting figures or those in emergency departments are not considered as waiting until a decision is made to admit them.

In many respects, the HSE is their own worst enemy. They outline plans and promises and do not deliver them.

Requests by the media are often met with delayed, unhelpful responses which do not answer the questions asked. And when it comes to dealing with the public, the HSE operates with a hostile, bunker-like mentality which only makes matters worse, compounding the perception of an organisation that delays, obstructs, avoids, and spins difficult decisions and announcements.

There was some dawn of hope for the HSE communications as a significant changeover in staff took place towards the end of 2008. Paul Connors, a public relations consultant who served in the army for many years took over as National Director of Communications. Early indications of Connors' modus operandi were good in early 2009, indicating a significant shift in how the HSE operates, heralding a potential new era of a more transparent, accountable HSE.

Conclusion

A central motive for setting up the HSE was to bring together the 11 health boards, the voluntary hospitals and a score of other health agencies under the management of one unified health service. The aim was to provide integrated, quality health and social care to the citizens of Ireland. While, in theory, the executive was announced in mid-2003, very little was worked out in the detail of roles and structures prior to its establishment in January 2005.

Years on from the establishment of the HSE, day-in, day-out, confusion and blame remain rife within the HSE management and between the HSE, the Department of Health and its minister.

Michael Kelly, the Secretary General in the Department of Health at the time of the publication of the health strategy, has stated publicly that he believes the tensions between Ministers Martin and Charlie McCreevy in the Departments of Health and Finance were central to the withdrawal of support and action to progress the key components in the health strategy.[47]

One senior administrator closely involved in the

establishment of the HSE, who does not wish to be named, says, 'The setting up of the HSE was meant to enable management to make the right decisions in the right place. Instead, it's been a dysfunctional process, it was never meant to centralise services and there's a serious lack of concrete leadership. Portlaoise [the cancer misdiagnosis scandal] demonstrates that at every level of management. The rhetoric is there, but there is no follow through.'[48]

The reports into the misdiagnosis of cancer in Portlaoise found that there were very serious problems with management, governance and communications within the HSE.

When pushing through the rushed legislation to establish the HSE, Mary Harney promised that, once and for all, accountability would be brought to the health services, that public patients would finally know who was responsible for what.

In the aftermath of the Portlaoise debacle, she said no single person, including herself, is responsible for the 'systemic failures' that led to the misdiagnosis of nine women in the Midland Regional Hospital at Portlaoise.

Changing structures, particularly those as big as the HSE, takes time. Vincent Barton, director of Prospectus, who wrote the report that influenced the establishment of the HSE says, 'This is long-haul work, on a larger scale than any other public service redesign programme in the state. International experience shows that changes of this sort take a number of years to bed down and can be hard to sustain in face of the more short-term pressures of political or fiscal cycles.'

This reinforces the Charles Normand three-year rule, that change takes time. In 2009, there are the seeds of progress, the cancer centres are beginning to take form, driven by the leadership of Professor Tom Keane, the shift to primary care is there in rhetoric if not yet in action, the concepts of team working and accountability are being introduced and HIQA is up and running.

However, the ongoing cancer misdiagnosis debacles, the inability to come clean about budgets and spending plans, the new regional structures integrating hospitals and primary and community care, amongst many others, demonstrate that the initial aims of the HSE – a unified, accountable, quality health system – are not yet realised five years on from its foundation. Whether or not these are achievable, in the absence of clearer roles and responsibilities for the Department of Health and the HSE, without greater accountability within the executive, and without more effective and dynamic leadership remains to be seen.

Chapter 4

The 'black hole' myth and hospitals – activity, unequal access, consultants, staffing and 'crises'

There is a public perception that Irish hospitals are in crisis. A weekend visit to an emergency department, a long wait for essential diagnosis or treatment, witnessing a relative die in a public ward, the filth of many hospitals – people's personal experiences combined with relentless media headlines and reporting of hospital crises are enough to make anyone believe that Irish hospitals are in crisis, and that this has been the case for decades. These issues, important as they are, help deflect away the central inequality in the Irish health system – access to specialist and hospital care.

Irish hospitals have always been under pressure. They have never had sufficient money and resources invested in them to be able to treat all patients on the basis of medical need. They have been located and developed in an unplanned, ad hoc way. Furthermore, certain blockages in one part of the system have wide impacts across the system.

Healthcare expenditure

In the 1920s and 1930s, free medical care for all was unaffordable to the new state of Ireland born out of conflict with Britain and then within the island. Money was very tight and, in the 1930s and 1940s, most hospital development money came from outside Ireland through fundraising by the Hospital Sweepstakes.

During the 1970s, progress was made in modernising some of the older hospitals and new regional public hospitals were built in Limerick, Cork and Galway. State funding of the voluntary hospitals was also increased during this time. However, Irish hospitals continuously lived beyond their means, with more demand and increasing costs than their revenue allowed for. In the 1930s, the Sweepstakes money was used to pay for hospitals' budgetary deficits, even though it was strictly meant to be used for capital developments – the practice of using capital spending to shore up over runs in day-to-day spending continued right up to the early years of the twenty-first century.

Progress in medical developments and improved living conditions in the second half of the twentieth century contributed to improved life expectancy alongside increased demands for health services and hospital care. Together with the increased demand for services was the higher cost of medicines, expensive new medical treatments, specialist medical practitioners and allied health professionals.

In the 1980s, the critical economic situation and massive national debt resulted in severe cutbacks in the public money allocated to health services. Between 1980 and 1990, the proportion of money spent on health fell from 7.72 per cent of GDP to 5.72 per cent, critically between 1986 and 1989, day-to-day public spending on health (known as current spending) remained static despite increased demand.[1] This 'static' spending, in effect, resulted in cutbacks because of increased demand and use of health services. Hospitals bore the brunt of these budgetary cuts with ward and, in some cases, hospital closures.

According to Maev-Ann Wren who has written most on this period, 'it would be hard to overstate the effect on Irish healthcare of the 1980s cutbacks. While Ireland was cutting its health spending, other countries were increasing theirs. An

OECD review over the period 1980–1993 found that in Ireland the share of the national income devoted to health had dropped by 23 per cent, when in 13 other OECD countries there had been a 24 percentage increase.'[2]

Since the 1990s, as the economy strengthened, there was increased public money available for public services and a significantly increased allocation to health. In particular from 1997 onwards, more than ever before was invested in health services.

However, the rise in health expenditure often just kept up with rapidly increasing inflation, costs and demands. The increase never had a chance to make up for the impact of budgetary restraints of the 1980s. Also, while Ireland was spending more than ever before on health during the early years of the twenty-first century, we were still spending below the OECD average.

In 1998, Ireland spent, a total of €3.6 billion on health. The year 2001 was the first one that Irish health spending exceeded the EU average. In 2002, Ireland spent €8.3 billion, just half the 2009 budget for health which was projected at €16.3 billion.

There is no question that health spending has increased rapidly over the past decade. However, it was coming from an incredibly low base and has had to make up for decades of underspending. Crucially, capital spending on buildings and critical investments, such as hospitals, primary care centres and long-stay, nursing home units, were still not made by 2008.

The 2001 health strategy 'Quality and Fairness' made the case for the need for significantly more spending on health. While the strategy did not detail the costs of the investment required, the Department of Health was aware of the cost implications.

The Department of Health's management team attended a regional meeting of the cabinet in Ballymacscanlon in May

2001. There the details of the strategy and its cost implications were outlined clearly. Michael Kelly, secretary to the Department of Health in January 2000, writing retrospectively about the health strategy, obliquely mentions the tensions between the Minister for Health, Micheál Martin, and Charlie McCreevy, the Minister for Finance and the reluctance by the latter to pay for the implementation of the health strategy.

Kelly wrote: 'Our internal conclusion [that of the top management team in the Department of Health] was that the meeting had gone well, we had been given the opportunity to present on all the relevant issues and we were satisfied that the Government collectively had been fully briefed on the extent of the problems in the health system and on the underlying policy and resourcing questions. The constructive mood of the meeting itself was somewhat marred by the very different perspectives on its outcome expressed respectively by the Minister for Health and Children and the Minister for Finance subsequently. The tension between these perspectives was to be a constant feature of the policy debate about health over the ensuing years and I believe a key influence in limiting progress that could be made in pushing forward with the development and reform agenda which was adopted by Government but much of which remains unimplemented.'[3]

In 2002, Micheál Martin, the minister who launched the health strategy, appeared on the *Late Late Show* and indicated clearly that taxes would need to be raised in order for the health strategy to be fully implemented. In clear contrast, Charlie McCreevy, the Minister for Finance since 1997, was determined to keep the lid on health expenditure. It was no coincidence that it was McCreevy who oversaw the most profitable years of economic boom, who repeatedly spoke disapprovingly about the 'black hole' in health, referring to the perceived endless amounts of money being invested in health, with little apparent gain to the patients using the system. For political leaders, it appeared that more and more money was invested in the system, with little obvious benefit to them or the public. For McCreevy, the low tax base was central to Ireland's economic development and, ruled by his own neo-liberal ideology, raising taxes to pay for healthcare was simply not an option under his stewardship, even if recommended by both the then Minister for Health and his department.

In 2001, the Department of Health estimated that to fulfil actions outlined in the health strategy would cost €7.7 billion in capital investment and increasing day-to-day spending on health by €5 billion over a ten year period. This was calculated at 2001 prices. Further analysis carried out by Maev-Ann Wren estimated that an additional €5 billion was needed annually between 2001 and 2011 to pay for the day-to-day costs of the new developments planned in the strategy, a rise to approximately 12 per cent of GNP being spent on health by 2007.[4] In *How Ireland Cares*, additional calculations by Tussing and Wren calculated that to reach all the major targets in the 2001 health strategy, €500 million would need to be spent on capital investments annually over seven to ten years, just one- third of what is spent on roads and public transport annually.[5]

Recent costings carried out in 2008 by Trinity College Dublin show that in order to meet basic needs for maintaining and developing the health system, between €3.2 and €6.4 billion additional investment is required. These estimates are based on remedying the under capacity of GPs, consultants, hospital beds and primary care infrastructure in 2008[6].

While health expenditure continued to increase during the years after the publication of the health strategy, it did not increase to the required level to meet the costs of the commitments made in it. The 'black hole' scenario is often reinforced by the ex-Minister for Finance Charlie McCreevy and current Minister for Health Mary Harney, who repeatedly claims Ireland now spends more than the OECD average and has a regular mantra about achieving value for money for the taxpayer's health budget.

On 23 January 2007, Mary Harney stated, 'Over recent years we have grown public investment in health at unprecedented rates. We have increased public health spending at one of the fastest rates among developed countries. Public health spending is now 78 per cent of the total health spending in the country – higher than the OECD average.' And Mary Harney is right, by far the largest proportion of Irish health spending comes out of public money. Despite the fact that over half the population holds private health insurance, less than one-fifth of the entire health budget is funded through insurance.[6]

Comparing the percentage of public spending in total health spending is different to comparing how much is spent on health with other countries. When we look at that, only in 2005 did we equal the EU 25 average of health spend as a percentage of GDP. The 'black hole' is a myth, we have never spent enough on public health services and we still do not.

In 2008, the budget allocation to health was €16.1 billion, an increase of €1.1 billion from 2007.[7] Public health spending represents almost one-quarter of all government spending and, apart from the Department of Social and Family Affairs from where social welfare and pension payments are distributed, it is the biggest spending of all government departments.

In 2005, Ireland spent 8.2 per cent of GDP on health (GNI is used for Ireland as it's a more accurate comparative measure due to inflated GDP figures as a result of foreign direct investment). However, in 2005, Germany, Belgium, Austria, and Portugal were all spending more than 10 per cent of GDP on health, while France was spending 11.2 per cent of its GDP on health.

In 2006, Ireland's comparative health spend dropped again in 2006 to 2004 levels. OECD figures show Ireland's spend on health in 2006 was 7.5 per cent of GDP. The EU 15 average for that year was 9.2 per cent, so money invested in health in Ireland in 2006 was just 83 per cent of EU average and 67 per cent of what the French spend on health.[8]

Capital expenditure on health in recent years has also been analysed by Wren. 'Capital investment, money required to build hospitals and primary care centres, to supply modern diagnostic equipment, or single rooms to control hospital acquired infections, has a long way to go in the game of catch-up.'[9] Wren highlights the difficulties with comparing Ireland's spend on health with other OECD countries as Irish data does not clearly detail differences between health and social spend. Social spend is still often included in comparative figures such as money allocated to social care and services. Wren estimates, 'after making conservative adjustments for this, Ireland's investment in healthcare facilities has been on average under three-quarters of the EU per capita average in the 35 years since 1970, approximately 60 per cent of the German investment.'[10]

Of this increased expenditure on health, over one-third of the day-to-day spending each year goes to hospitals and well over half of capital expenditure is spent on hospitals.

There are difficulties when looking at spending on hospitals over time as the way in which money has been allocated to hospitals and the way that it is counted has changed since the establishment of the HSE. Prior to January 2005, the Department of Health kept and published these figures. Since that date, the HSE keeps them.

Since 2005, all money allocated to hospitals is routed through the National Hospitals Office so it is possible to compare hospital spend since 2005. Prior to 2005, budgets for public hospitals run by the health board and voluntary hospitals were accounted for separately.

In 2004, the NHO was allocated just over €4 billion. In 2005, this rose to just over €4.4 billion. In 2006, it was €4.5 billion. In 2007, it was €4.8 billion. By 2008, it was €5.1 billion.[11] In 2009, it was projected at €5.28 billion. While these are very large amounts of money by any standards, if one takes public service inflation in to account, then hospital's received a rise in spending between 2004 and 2005, a decline in funding of 1.8 per cent between 2005 and 2006. Between 2006 and 2008, hospitals received very small increases, which barely kept pace with inflation and increased activity, while in 2009 many hospitals received an actual cut in budgets even before public service inflation was taken into account for the first time in over a decade.

International and national data clearly shows that the Irish health system is not a 'black hole'; it has been consistently underfunded and is still playing catch up for the financial constraints and underspending of the 1980s and part of the 1990s. Given the increased demand for healthcare, increased costs and relative budgets, hospitals in Ireland still remain underfunded. The majority of health and social care needs can be met outside the hospital system and the non-hospital services get about two-thirds of the health budget. Despite repeated attempts to transfer care and therefore funding to the community, this has not yet materialised. These issues are dealt with in Chapter 8.

Yet, insufficient money invested in Irish hospitals is not the only problem in the hospital system. Unfortunately, there are many, many more. One of the many contentious issues in Irish health politics is whether or not there are enough hospital beds in the system to deal with the needs of the public. In the past 30 years, there has been a marked decline in hospital beds. So do we have enough of them? And if not, how many do we need? If we do have enough, are they the right types of beds in the right places?

Hospital beds

Acute hospital beds are those used for emergency or planned medical or surgical treatment, including intensive care beds. They do not include long-term rehabilitation or nursing home beds. In 1981, there were over 17,668 acute hospital beds. By 2000, there were fewer than 12,000, a huge reduction by any reckoning, even when the increases in daycare are taken into account. The majority of this reduction in bed numbers was in the eastern region, with 2,000 of the 3,397 beds cut during the 1980s coming from the east of the country.[12]

Between 1997 and 2005, there was a one per cent increase in inpatient hospital beds, increasing by, on average, 120 beds per year. In 2005, there were 12,093 public hospital beds in the system, but increases in population meant that the ratio of beds to population actually dropped from 3.14 per 1,000 in 2000, to 3.04 per 1,000 in 2005.[13]

During this same period, there was a more significant increase in day places, in line with international trends of advanced medical practice resulting in treating patients on the same day in the hospital. Day places increased from 609 in 1997 to 1,251 in 2005. In total, in 2005, there were 13,344 inpatient and day places of which 9 per cent were day places. This works out at 2.8 beds per 1,000 in 2005 well below the OECD average of 3.9 beds per 1,000 population. Compared to other European and OECD countries, this figure is very low. For example, Austria and Germany have over six beds per 1,000, Hungary and Luxembourg have over five beds per 1,000 while France and the UK have over three beds per 1,000.[14] So Ireland has significantly fewer beds per head of population when compared with OECD countries, only the United States of America, Turkey and Sweden have fewer beds per head.

Ireland also has very high bed occupancy – the measurement used to determine how many beds in any hospital or region are filled at any one time. Internationally agreed best practice for hospitals to work efficiently and effectively, recommends bed occupancy to be below 85 per cent.[15]

Over 100 per cent bed occupancy means that every single bed in the hospital is occupied plus additional trolleys and temporary measures such as chairs and recliners are being used to accommodate patients. This results in overcrowded wards, emergency departments, corridors alongside over-burdened staff. Quite simply, hospitals operating at over 85 per cent are working way beyond what their occupancy should be. Over occupancy has negative consequences for safety, quality of care and efficiency.

The average bed occupancy in Ireland from 2003, shows that bed occupancy averaged out at 84.9 per cent which 'suggests a sector which is barely able to cope with the demands placed on it'.[16] Only Norway had a higher bed occupancy than Ireland in the 2003 to 2006 period.

Analysis of the bed capacity in specific Irish hospitals shows that of the nine largest hospitals, eight had occupancy over 90 per cent, explaining why many patients and their families experience hospitals bursting at their seams. They also found that 'twenty-six hospitals had general medicine wards running at over 85 per cent occupancy, with nineteen running over 100 per cent occupancy. Geriatric medicine in eight hospitals was running at over 100 per cent bed occupancy. Other specialisations that had serious over capacity were general surgery, psychiatry, cardiology, orthopaedics and obstetrics. Such overcrowding carries additional risks to health and costs associated with treatment of hospital-acquired infections'.[17] This research estimates an additional 1,900 beds are needed to ensure that bed occupancy in hospitals is under 85 per cent. (See below for more information on hospital-acquired infections.)

A report presented to the board of the HSE in the first week of October 2008 stated that 1,200 acute beds in public hospitals were closed or unavailable for new patients because of budgetary restrictions or other reasons. Over half of these beds (682) were unavailable for new patients because of delayed discharges (delayed discharged patients are those who have completed the acute phase of their care and are medically fit for discharge), while the remaining 513 were closed as a money-saving mechanism, or because of infection control or refurbishment. This means that, in October 2008, just under ten per cent of the total beds were unavailable or closed.[18]

Figures from the HSE's monthly Performance Monitoring Reports which are now published promptly on the HSE website show that in December 2008, there were 11,605 inpatient beds, 696 of these were occupied by delayed discharges, while another 374 were closed for refurbishment, change of facilities or infection control measures. These figures confirm that there are 500 fewer inpatient beds in the system at the end of 2008 than there were in 2005 and that nine per cent of 11,605 are unavailable for use for acute patients. The Service Plan for 2009 contains commitments to work within budget by decreasing average length of stay in hospital, increasing day patient cases and reducing inpatient activity. This indicates a further reduction in the actual numbers of acute inpatient beds.

However, it is not simply a matter of a shortage of beds in Irish hospitals. If the beds in hospitals were more wisely utilised would the additional 1,900 beds be needed?

There are a range of studies looking at the issues of bed usage and capacity in Irish hospitals in the past seven years. While these studies differ in the actual number of extra beds they assess is needed in the system, they are conclusive that a significant percentage of current bed usage is a result of deficiencies in other aspects of the health system.

A review of bed usage published by the HSE in 2008 showed that 13 per cent of hospital admissions were inappropriate, meaning that patients in those beds should have been treated in the community or at home and not admitted to hospital in the first place.

It also found that 39 per cent of hospital stays were inappropriate, meaning that patients no longer needed to be in hospital beds and could be receiving follow-up treatment in a more appropriate environment, such as a short-term nursing home placements or at home if the appropriate community supports were available.[19]

Delayed discharges are also known as 'bed blockers'. As the services do not exist at home or in a community setting, the patient, often an older person, remains in hospital, and is considered a 'bed blocker', as they prevent people really in need of hospital care from getting a bed. The term 'bed blocker' implies that the patient is 'blocking' the bed or the system when, in fact, it is the health-system managers that are to blame for not having sufficient beds or community supports so that patients can move into community short-term and long-stay beds or move home.

The 2008 bed usage report carried out by PA Consulting recommended the better management of chronic diseases in the community, increased community care and supports for patients leaving hospitals, and better management within hospitals to reduce the numbers of unnecessary days spent in hospitals by patients, while simultaneously freeing up other beds.[20]

Analysis of lengths of stays in Irish hospitals show that some patients stay too long, because of the shortage of appropriate move on places.[21] Interestingly, one of the main researchers in this area found that, 'nevertheless, there is little evidence from the above analysis that the current hospital resources are on the whole being managed poorly'.[22] This evidence is totally contrary to the political and public rhetoric, often driven by the Minister for Health herself, about our hospitals being badly managed.

Taking into account the growing and ageing demographics in Ireland, as well as the high rates of occupancy, the Trinity researchers estimate that an additional 2,500 beds are needed by 2007 standards.[23]

While the studies on the numbers of beds required differ in methodology, there are pretty clear conclusions coming from them. The ESRI study estimated that between 1,800 and 3,280 additional beds are required between 2007 and 2013.[24]

Previous research carried out by the Trinity research team estimated the number of additional beds required by 2007 at 2,553, assuming the funding and payment mechanism stayed as it is. The Department of Health's own health strategy outlined the need for 3,000 beds by 2011,[25] while the PA Consulting study commissioned by the HSE stated that 8,162 beds would be required with the current system continuing, but there could be 2,826 fewer beds than are currently in place by 2020 if there was a 'fully integrated model with developed community services'.[26]

What is clear from the different analyses is that there are currently too few beds in the system, as it is currently configured. The 2001 health strategy, which is still the government's official health document, 'Quality and Fairness' committed to an additional 2,800 inpatient beds and 200 extra day places. However, fewer than 1,000 of these have been added to the system since the report's publication eight years ago and while numbers of inpatient beds increased between 2001 and 2005, there has been a steady decline since 2005.

The cost of adding a hospital bed into the health services is estimated at between €500,000 to €1 million euro.[27] Given the financial pressure that hospitals have been under throughout the past decade, it is no wonder that so few beds have been added to the system.

Hospital activity

When hospital activity is looked at, it is easy to see where the hospitals' money has gone. Between 1997 and 2006, there was a 13 per cent increase in inpatients and a phenomenal 130 per cent increase in day treatments. Medical practice, which has improved and is less invasive, is responsible for the huge surge in day activity. Also, when at all possible, hospitals are keen to treat patients on a day basis as it is less costly and often less difficult for the patient.

In 2006, there was a 47 per cent increase in outpatient activity compared to 1997, while attendances in emergency departments were up 5.6 per cent, with more than 250,000 attendances at emergency departments each year. In 2006, the average length of stay in hospital was 6.3 days.[28]

The HSE Annual Report for 2007, published in June 2008, detailed increased activity in hospitals between 2006 and 2007. The number of inpatients treated was up 3.7 per cent to 614,291, the number of outpatient appointments was up 5.1 per cent to just over three million, the number of births was up by 11.7 per cent to 70,000, the highest number of births in 25 years.[29] Activity targets for inpatient and day cases were exceeded beyond targets set for 2008 and within budget.

Yet, despite significant increases in the numbers using hospital, OECD analysis of Irish healthcare found that 'the Irish are, with the exception of the Mexicans, by far the lowest users of medical care within OECD countries. For inpatient as well as outpatients' services, international comparisons show that there is no overuse of medical care in Ireland compared to other OECD countries'.[30]

Comparatively, Ireland has a younger population to the rest of the EU and OECD. This, in itself, should result in less demand on the health services and time to plan for the future needs of the ageing population. While this is reflected in a significantly lower doctor–patient consultation rate with 2.5

consultations per person per annum, compared to 5.1 in the UK, 6.6 in France, 7 in Germany, Ireland has fewer doctors than other OECD countries.

Ireland also has a significantly lower number of surgical procedures per annum with 43 per 1,000 compared to 95 per 1,000 in Germany and 144 per 1,000 in the UK. The OECD gives health warnings about the accuracy of doctor–patient and surgical ratios, however, in relation to the latter, it cites cataract surgical rates as an indicator, detailing that in Ireland there are 251.1 cataract surgeries per 100,000 compared with 626.8 per 100,000 in the UK and 751.9 per 100,000 in France and 1,600 per 100,000 in Belgium.[31]

Public patients still wait longer for hospital care

The Irish healthcare system has never been sufficiently funded and is still making up for the cutbacks of the 1980s. While the actual numbers of inpatient hospital beds have declined, hospital activity has increased. Despite some progress made on quality and efficiency in hospital care since the establishment of the HSE in 2005, the fundamental inequality at the core of the Irish health system has remained untouched – public patients still have to wait longer to access a specialist and receive care in many specialities than private patients. At the heart of this dual provision of care is the consultants' contract and the official government policy of an 80/20 public–private mix of care in Irish public hospitals.

The consultants' contract allows and encourages consultants to practice privately and publicly, often in the same public hospital. The 80/20 public–private mix in public hospitals in turn facilitates this dual practice. The result of this two-tier system of care is that incentives are in place to privilege private patients over public patients. This can result in delayed access to life-saving diagnosis and treatment as was the case for Susie

Long. Government decisions have consistently reinforced the dual nature of public and private provision in public hospitals in Ireland despite rhetoric and policy commitments to the contrary. While most European countries have some level of public and private mix, it is unique to Ireland to have large quantities of private healthcare carried out in our public hospitals and that the vast majority of this private care is publicly funded.

Consultants' contract

In Ireland in 2009, the majority of consultants practice privately and publicly. They are paid a generous salary for their public work and charge fees to each of their private patients. Consultants' salaries, before the new contract was agreed in 2008, ranged from €144,000 to €178,000, excluding their private fees. Consultants were obliged to work 33 hours in the hospital under their public contracts, however, how much time and how their time was spent was neither measured nor monitored. No record was kept of how much they earned from their private fees but many earned as much again, if not more, from their private practice. While the majority of consultants work many more than the 33-hour week required, some manipulate the system and see private patients in their public time.[32]

The crux of the unfairness in the Irish hospital system lies in the consultants' contract. This enables private patients to be seen quicker and to be looked after by a consultant for which he/she is paid a private fee, while public patients may take longer to access care and when they do, they are more likely to be seen by a junior hospital doctor. For many patients there are waits of months or, in some cases years to see a specialist in the first place and then to receive treatment in a public hospital. Long waiting times are caused by the shortage of hospital beds and consultants, combined with inefficiencies in hospitals and the healthcare system. No matter what the time frame is or whether or not the public patient is actually treated by the consultant, the consultant will still be paid handsomely for his/her public practice. A minority of consultants, often psychiatrists, geriatricians, public health and emergency medicine specialists practice only in the public system.

According to the OECD, in Ireland 'consultants annual income is 50 per cent higher than France and 80 per cent higher than Germany'.[33] And this was before the significant hike in pay given under the new, long-promised contact finally agreed in 2008. Starting salaries for consultants in Sweden and the United Kingdom in February 2009 were €70,000 per annum and consultants in these countries are required to work public only contracts.

Action 89 of the 2001 health strategy promised that 'greater equity for public patients will be sought in a revised contract for hospital consultants'. It stated 'the terms of the common contract for hospital consultants are central to the establishment of an appropriate balance between public and private care in public hospitals. The forthcoming negotiations on the contract must be undertaken using a developmental agenda which will involve restructuring of key elements of the current system to promote equity of access, organisational improvements and more clinical involvement in and responsibility for management programmes. In addition, the introduction of more flexible work practices, including teamworking, rostering, cover arrangements, competence assurance and accountability initiatives must be addressed. The aim will be to build on the strengths of the present system while also providing the necessary flexibility to implement the improvements which are required in the provision of health services to public patients. In particular, it will be proposed that newly appointed consultants would work exclusively for public patients for a specified number of years. This would mean that consultants would concentrate on treating public patients in the early years of their contract, but would be in a position to develop private practice at a later stage where their contract so permits.'[34]

Consultant contract negotiations did not follow the publication of the strategy but two reports on the funding and structure of the health services (the Brennan and Prospectus reports) both dealt in detail with the consultants' contract.[35,36] They, like many reports before them, highlighted the critical importance of changing the common contract so that equity can be achieved for public patients. But they also highlighted the unaccountability of consultants, the lack of management of them, their ability to act as 'god-like', 'one-man' shows among management and staff in hospitals.

Between 2004 and 2009, Mary Harney, as Minister for Health, oversaw the negotiation of a new consultants' contract. She maintained throughout that the new consultants' contract would resolve many of the problems within the health system in particular the issues of inequality and access.

Under the new contract, which had effect from 1 September 2008, consultants work a 37-hour week for significantly more wages. Salaries for public work ranges between €156,000 and €240,000 per year. The salary for Type A contracts, for public only work is €211,000 to €252,000. For public and private work on site (which will include the co-located hospitals, if they ever happen) is €197,000 to €205,000. The salary for Type B* starts at €156,000 and this allows for public work and private off-site, so the consultant can practice in a private hospital not connected to the public hospital. In February 2009, 80 per cent of consultants had signed up to the new consultants' contract and just 30 per cent of these opted for a public only contract. Under the new consultants' contract agreed by government and contrary to commitments made in the health strategy, the majority of consultants continue to practice publicly and privately in 2009.

Under the new contract, consultants are rostered from 8 a.m. to 8 p.m., and up to five hours at weekends and public holidays. They do not get additional money for working after 6 p.m., but they do for working weekends and public holidays. Also, the ratio of public–private work has changed to 70/30 for existing consultants. This was conceded to as a way of luring consultants who practised privately up to 2008 and for whom their private practice was more than 20 per cent of their workload. For new consultants taking up positions post-September 2008, the ratio of public–private work will be 80/20. This will be closely monitored and measured. For the first time, outpatient work is included in the public–private ratio.

Consultants were wooed into the new contract on the promise that 2,000 more consultants would be hired, the significantly higher wages and new jobs in the form of clinical directors. As a sweetener, those who signed the new contact by 1 September were promised their higher salary backdated to June 2008. Up to 2008, consultants were accountable to no one. Under the new contract, they will be accountable to the clinical directors. Speaking on 28 August 2008, Brendan Drumm said that up to 100 new clinical directors will be appointed, with about one for every 40 or 50 consultants. Consultants will be eligible to apply for the new clinical director posts and will receive an additional €50,000 if appointed to the post. A new national clinical director will also be appointed to the HSE.[37] By February 2009, 80 per cent of existing consultants had signed the new contract, though some of the detail of the contract remains unclear, particularly in relation to consultants in academic posts and in specialities that are traditionally and predominantly public-only contracts, such as geriatrics, psychiatry and emergency medicine, and the impact the public–private ratio will have on the quality and the funding of public hospitals.

The new contract gives greater flexibility in consultants' practice, consultants are now scheduled to be in hospitals on evenings and weekends to admit, discharge and care for patients, the post of clinical director means that consultants are now accountable and the new management role enables them to take on a leadership role within the health services. In theory, it means that consultants cannot spend more than 30 per cent or 20 per cent of their time on private practice, and this will be measured and monitored for the first time.

However, many of the problems of the old contract continue, while it is unclear how it will actually be implemented in February 2009. For example, consultants are still paid a salary for public work and a fee for each patient seen privately. This continues to incentivise private work. It is not clear if the 20 and 30 per cent limit on private work will mean that many consultants will opt for private-only work, to be situated in hospitals with bigger budgets and better quality equipment, where their earnings are not capped although given the high uptake of contracts, this does not seem to be happening.

The new contract introduces a common waiting list for diagnosis. Mary Harney has consistently said that this new common waiting list will end the two-tier health system. No one working in the system agrees. Private patients will still be able to access specialist care more quickly than public patients. Private patients can opt to see consultants in their private rooms outside of the hospital and then opt to get treated as a private or public patient in the public hospital. The list for the waiting times for treatment in the public hospital as a private patient will be shorter than that of a public patient. The consultants' contract has no mention of a common waiting list for treatment. Also, while consultants now have to work evenings, they do not have to provide in-house cover. So this cover will continue to be provided by junior doctors, with increasingly restricted hours and numbers, so there may in fact be a deterioration of standards in night-time cover in public hospitals.

There is no detail either on what happens in co-located hospitals. If a patient is admitted through a common emergency department in the public hospital, how is the decision made on who gets treated by whom and in which hospital, particularly if some doctors have public-only contracts? Under the co-location scheme, the co-located private hospitals are obliged to mirror all services provided for in the public hospital except for national specialities. They are also obliged to take private patients within two hours of a decision to admit being made in the emergency department. How will it be decided who goes where? Will the current two-tier nature of our hospital care be further escalated with wealthier, private patients going to the new shiny, co-located private hospital, with public patients remaining in the old, under-funded, over-burdened public hospital?

Is the consultants' contract really the solution to the troubles in the Irish health services? Or is it a bad, over-priced deal, that will lead to further decline in the public health system with poorer clinical cover, inadequate governance, underfunded public hospitals and an enshrined two-tier system of care? Time will tell but one thing is certain – it reinforces rather than deconstructs the two-tier system of hospital care.

The 80/20 myth – private care in public hospitals

The fact that well over 20 per cent of public hospital beds are used for the care of private patients and this is government policy makes Ireland distinctive in its provision of unequal hospital care. The fact that the private care in public hospitals is subsidised by up to 80 per cent makes our system even more extraordinary and unfair. Consultants are allowed to provide care for both private and public patients because of the 80/20 public–private mix in public hospitals.

Consistent government policy has reinforced this 80/20 public–private mix, while internal documents acknowledged that the 80/20 rule was not sufficient to keep private care at just 20 per cent. Documents released under Freedom of Information to Dale Tussing and Maev-Ann Wren for their book *How Ireland Cares* show that 'the Department's February 2003 bed count concluded ... that "it is clear from the exercise that the designation process [i.e. the 80/20 public–private mix] alone is not sufficient to control the amount of private activity occurring in hospitals".[38]

Analysis of the Hospital Inpatient Inquiry for 2006 found that 23 per cent of discharges for all acute hospital treatment were private patients.[39] While the aggregate figure shows hospitals close to the public–private 80/20 designation, the actual balance in hospitals is quite different. At the end of 2006, the HSE warned Tallaght Hospital about its designation of private beds, having found that over 40 per cent of the beds in the public hospital were being used to treat private patients. The HSE report on Acute Bed Capacity published in 2008 found that 26 per cent of inpatients in public hospitals were private patients.[40]

However, other statistics released subsequently suggest that this is an under-estimation. Figures presented to the Public Accounts Committee by HSE management in February 2008 show that over 50 per cent of planned surgery in some public hospitals was carried out on private patients. In St John's Hospital in Limerick, 54 per cent of elective cases were private in 2006; in Limerick Regional, the figures was 52 per cent; in Mallow, 47 per cent; in Mercy Cork, 46 per cent; in Cork University, it was 43 per cent. Tallaght Hospital was carrying out 44 per cent of its elective work privately while the figure for Cavan was 42 per cent.[41] Holles Street and the Coombe maternity hospitals had particularly high rates of elective procedures carried out privately with 52 per cent and 44 per cent respectively. Just seven of the 60 hospitals listed had less than 20 per cent private elective treatment. Fifty of these hospitals catered for emergency admissions in 2006, and just 18 of these kept within the 20 per cent limit. Ten of them had 30 per cent or more emergency admissions, with four of them exceeding 40 per cent private emergency admissions. The total percentage of private day cases carried out in the public hospitals was 19 per cent which brings the overall private figure down to 23 per cent, but masks the fact that many public hospitals carry out significantly more than the stipulated 20 per cent private care.

Also, during the first decade of the twenty-first century, the definition of a bed was changing, so what was considered a bed by the Department of Health up to 2003 was not the same as what was considered a bed by the Department during 2004 and by the HSE after 2005. Patients treated on recliners, trolleys, couches and chairs began to be counted as 'day places', therefore contributing to increased numbers of day places that are counted as hospital beds.[42]

Essentially, there is still no regular publication of data which enables comparison over time of access, waiting times and outcomes for public and private patients. Persistent requests by this author to the HSE during 2007 and 2008 for information concerning actual numbers in inpatient hospital beds remained unanswered. In a new era of HSE accountability evident to the author early in 2009, actual bed numbers were made available but comparative data on access, use and outcomes for public and private patients is not kept or if it is, it is not readily available.

Public patients wait longer for care

Many of the figures that are available to the public in 2008 are a result of Freedom of Information (FOI) requests and leaked documents obtained by journalists. It is virtually impossible to compare key indicators of equity – such as waiting times for public and private patients to see a specialist, pre and post-2005 – or what comparative data on outcomes of treatment would look like.

However, some figures and documents released by the HSE during 2007 and 2008 show clearly that Susie Long was not an unusual case but, rather, an exemplar of the systematic apartheid experienced by public patients.

In the aftermath of Susie Long's death, government figures and HSE management repeatedly stated that she had been let down by the system, that the new consultants' contract and the National Treatment Purchase Fund (NTPF) would address the inequality in the system.

On 1 March 2008, an article published in *The Irish Times* by Eithne Donnellan revealed that 'data obtained shows patients can wait up to 18 months for a colonoscopy examination in Portlaoise General Hospital, up to 12 months for the test at Tullamore General Hospital or University College Galway, and up to nine months in Limerick Regional Hospital or Kerry General Hospital'.[43] The official HSE response was that patients marked as urgent by their GP are seen within a matter of days or weeks, 'usually seen in less than five weeks across HSE areas ... that only routine referrals have to wait for long periods'. They said that the 'waiting list figures supplied by its hospitals hadn't been validated'; they should be treated with 'caution'.

Doctors working in the system say that someone who is bleeding out of their rectum should be considered a priority. This did not happen for Susie Long and is not happening for other patients, even in 2009.

In the same article, Donnellan cited the case of a woman who 'attended her family doctor last November [2007] and was referred to the Mater Hospital for a colonoscopy ... won't be seen for examination until April [2008], some five months after presenting to her doctor, even though her symptoms include bleeding from her back passage, which would suggest her case could be urgent'. In July 2008, this woman still had not had a colonoscopy, seven months after referral.

In response to the information published in *The Irish Times*, Minister for Health Mary Harney said, 'it's not acceptable to me, and it's not acceptable to the cancer control programme, that patients would have to wait for such long periods before they get their initial diagnosis, because we know with cancer, in particular, that early diagnosis is very important if we are to get good outcomes'.

Figures released in January 2009 show some improvement during 2008 in waiting times for a colonoscopy. They also showed that 435 patients are waiting more than six months for a colonoscopy which according to the Irish Cancer Society is "an unacceptably long time for this crucial test".[44] The Irish Cancer Society advocates that patients should have a colonoscopy within six weeks of being referred by their GP. The figures released by the NTPF show some hospitals making significant improvements in waiting times, e.g. the Mater Hospital reduced waiting times from nine months to one month, Sligo Hospital reduced its waiting times from seven months to one month. However, patients at Cork University Hospital and Naas General Hospital were still waiting an average of seven months for a colonoscopy, while average wait times at Waterford Regional Hospital were six months, and average wait times at Beaumont Hospital Dublin were five months[45].

Other information, obtained by *The Irish Times* health correspondent Eithne Donnellan and published on 31 December 2007, revealed unacceptable waiting times for outpatient clinics. Again, this information is not made readily available by any government body so the journalist had to go through the FOI system to gather it and make requests to each individual hospital. If any state agency does gather such data, it is not publicly available.

Donnellan found that '139,000 patients were on outpatient waiting list in 24 hospitals across the state either last year [2006] or earlier this year [2007]'.[46]

As only half the hospitals in Ireland provided figures to Donnellan, this is a huge under-estimation of how many public patients are waiting for an outpatient appointment. These waiting times represent the length of time a patient waits between referral by their GP and actually seeing a consultant. In some instances, the length of wait was hard to fathom. Figures Donnellan received show that 48 patients, waiting for urology and dermatology appointments, had been waiting up to eight years to be seen in Mayo General Hospital. Other patients in Galway were waiting seven years to see a neurologist. Patients in Ennis and Kerry were waiting four years for an appointment. In Cork, Limerick, Sligo and Letterkenny, patients were waiting three years or more for an appointment.

The NTPF fund began dealing with outpatients in 2005 on a pilot basis. Up to the end of 2007, it had treated 22,549 outpatients and has set itself a target of treating 13,500 outpatients for 2008, less than 10 per cent of the patients known to be waiting.

While significant improvements have taken place in waiting times for hospital care, the figures gathered by *The Irish Times* prove that many public patients still wait years for treatment. 'These could include patients with hip pain, waiting to see if they require a hip replacement operation … They could include patients with bladder problems waiting to see a urologist to determine if their problem could actually be caused by prostrate cancer.'.[47]

Donnellan's figures were ground breaking, as outpatient figures had never been published before. In the words of the journalist who spent months gathering and chasing up this data, 'it's easy to see why [such figures remain unpublished], from the intolerable lengths of time patients are having to wait'.[48]

Contrary to government and ministerial promises since the publication of the health strategy in 2001, public patients in many parts of the country in 2009 still have to wait months and sometimes years for a diagnosis and therefore treatment. Despite the government and HSE mantra that early diagnosis saves lives, it is just not possible for many public patients to access what can be life-saving diagnosis. There is lots of political and policy rhetoric about 'equity' and 'medical care provided on the basis of need', however the reality is very different, and firmly reveals the enshrinement of an apartheid system of hospital care in Ireland in 2009.

The NTPF – a band-aid on the wound of hospital waiting times

One of the two main devices for avoiding critiques of the two-tier health system is the unavailability of data which details and demonstrates the unequal access and outcomes of public and private patients in relation to inpatient and outpatient specialist care.

There has always been a dearth of data comparing public and private patients' access and outcomes but, in the past few years, it has become increasingly difficult to monitor trends over time in access and use of hospital and specialist services.

Up to 2004, the Department of Health kept and published figures on waiting times in the hospital system. Since 2005, the National Treatment Purchase Fund is responsible for data collection and publication in relation to waiting times activity. However, there are significant problems with the NTPF figures. Figures on utilisation are different to figures on access because they do not count people who are waiting for the service or who are denied access. Also, there is an inherent contradiction to allocating responsibility to the same agency for reducing wait times as well as keeping an independent record of those wait times for which it has responsibility. Since the NTPF started to keep these statistics, it has repeatedly stated that it has reduced waiting times from two to five years to two to five months. Yet, it acknowledges in its own report that prior to the new NTPF system being put in place the Department of Health kept figures by speciality not by patient and not all specialities were counted.[49] Quite simply, these figures are not comparable.

The NTPF was set up with the aim of reducing waiting times for public patients. The NTPF organises private treatment for public patients who have been waiting the longest for treatment in public hospitals. Under the NTPF, these public patients can be treated privately in Ireland, Northern Ireland or Britain. In Ireland, the public patients can be treated privately in public hospitals.

Action 81 in 'Quality and Fairness', states that 'a comprehensive set of actions will be taken to reduce waiting times for public patients, including the establishment of a new earmarked Treatment Purchase Fund'. This action 'targets to ensure that no public patient will wait longer than three months for treatment following referral from an outpatient department by the end of 2004'. The strategy document outlined that the Department of Health, a 'National Treatment Purchase Team' and the health boards would be responsible for its implementation.

In responses to criticism of the waiting times since the establishment of the NTPF, both the minister and HSE management are critical of hospitals with long waiting lists that were slow to refer patients to the NTPF. But the waiting times for the NTPF also show that the NTPF has failed to meet government commitments on waiting times for public patients. Many patients still wait significantly longer than the three month target.

Of course, if someone is a public patient waiting for treatment, the NTPF is a welcome development if it means treatment is received sooner. The NTPF annual reports are full of testimonies of content patients. Over 110,000 patients had been treated by the NTPF by the end of 2007. Yet, there are serious concerns about the NTPF being the solution to the access difficulties and long waiting times in Irish hospitals.

The NTFP only carries out routine procedures. Up until 2005, the NTPF only dealt with inpatient cases, so appointments like that of Susie Long who needed an outpatient appointment were not included in their remit. Also, waiting times published by the NTPF do not actually reflect all waiting times. For example, Susie Long would not have appeared as a figure on NTPF data as she had not received an appointment. Also, you only qualify to be counted as waiting when you have been waiting for three months after your initial consultation.

The fact that public patients can be treated under the NTPF as a private patient in the same public hospital that they are referred from seems an extraordinary diversion of money away from the public system into the private system. The NTPF says 'it tries to avoid paying consultants to treat their own public patients but concedes that this may happen occasionally'.[50] In other words, the NTPF tries to ensure that public patients are treated privately in a place other than the public hospitals from which they were referred.

However, a report on the NTPF by the Comptroller and Auditor General found that 36 per cent of cases carried out under the NTPF occurred in the same hospital where the patient had been a public patient previously.[51]

Most importantly, from an equity perspective, the NTPF is like a band-aid on the wound of hospital waiting times. It does not address the causes of the waiting times in the first place (the shortage of hospital beds, of consultants, of an integrated and efficient health system). Vitally, it diverts much needed money for the public system into the private system.

The NTPF budget for 2007 was €91.744 million. This equated to approximately 0.5 per cent of the government's spending on health. Its budget for 2008 was €100 million.[52] Its budget in its first year of operation (2002) was €5 million, so it has had a 20-fold increase in its budget in six years.

However, figures published in its 2007 Annual Report (on 25 June 2008) show that six years on from the establishment of the NTFP, there are still 21,470 patients waiting for more than three months for required surgical or medical care, 16,000 of these are waiting for surgery. It also details that there are still 2,155 public patients waiting more than a year for surgery.

At the launch of the 2007 NTPF annual report, NTPF chairman John O'Dwyer said that more than half the patients waiting more than a year were coming from just a small number of hospitals. The report named Tallaght, Letterkenny, Sligo, Tullamore and Cork University hospitals as the chief offenders.

It is estimated that if you include people who have not been waiting three months, then the numbers waiting for medical or surgical procedures in Irish hospitals is closer to 40,000 people.

Mary Harney, at the launch of the 2007 NTPF Annual Report in June 2008, warned of financial penalties for hospitals that failed to refer patients to the NTPF. She made reference to Norway, where a similar scheme is in place and where hospitals are statutorily obliged to refer patients to the fund, and said she had not ruled out going down such an avenue if hospitals continued not to refer to the NTPF.

Similar to her response to the publication of waiting times for colonoscopies, she said there was no excuse for patients having to wait, 'the capacity exists, the money exists and there is no justification for having 2,155 patients waiting over 12 months'.

Hospitals considered the main offenders of not referring patients to the NTPF responded to ministerial criticisms saying that patients referred to the NTPF had turned down treatment offers, preferring to be treated in their 'local' hospital.

It just does not make sense that at times when hospitals have constraining budgets to give €100 million to the for-profit private health sector instead of investing that money in the public health system.

In terms of value for money, it is hard to determine if the NTPF provides value as it refuses to publish what it pays for procedures claiming this information is 'commercially sensitive'.

The 2004 Annual Report of the Comptroller and Auditor General (C&AG) published in 2005 found a huge variation in the rates paid by the NTPF for procedures, with the highest rates for similar procedures sometimes two or three times higher than the lowest rates paid. Given that consultants are paid a fee-for-service for private patients and a salary for public work and that 36 per cent of treatments of NTPF occur in the same hospital, there must be an incentive for consultants to see patients privately under the NTPF, rather than in the public hospital system.[53]

Patients groups have also highlighted that patients treated privately through the NTPF may not be entitled to the free follow-up care that they would be entitled to if they were treated in the public hospital system.

While there is a lot of murkiness around the waiting times of public and private patients, there is one clear fact: the government has failed to meet the targets it set itself in 2001. Its commitments to reduce waiting times for inpatient public patients for medical and surgical procedures to three months and under by the end of 2004 has not been reached.

Also, the government response to unequal waiting times in the form of the NTPF is flawed. Not all procedures are covered. People are not considered as 'waiting' until they have waited for more than three months. There are perverse incentives for consultants to treat patients privately rather than in the public hospital system. Patients who are treated through the NTPF may not get the follow-up treatment they require. In 2009, the

NTPF only covered outpatient appointments on a pilot basis and, therefore, many people waiting for initial appointment or diagnosis are not counted as 'waiting'. Public hospitals lose out on the revenue that is being invested in the NTPF instead of assisting to remedy the public hospital system.

Health sector staffing

Much of the increased expenditure on health from 1997 onwards has been on increased staffing levels. Between 1995 and 2007, the number of people employed in the public heath service increased by 73 per cent. Much of this growth occurred in the health and social care areas, which accounted for a 164 per cent growth during this time. Health and social care professionals rose from just under 6,000 to over 15,700. The number of medical staff grew by 61 per cent, the numbers of nurses went up by 43 per cent, management and administration was up by 104 per cent, while general support staff dropped by 38 per cent. Details of the administration staff is dealt with in Chapter 3, and demonstrates that many of those classified as administrators are working in front line services such as outpatient clinics, the reception of a hospital or an emergency department.

Total health and social care employment in the public sector in Ireland is 30.8 staff per 1,000 inhabitants, just below the OECD average, rating above the United Kingdom, the USA, Canada and New Zealand but lower than Germany, France, Italy and Spain.[54]

The OECD concludes that despite the high increases in medical professionals in Ireland, there are still fewer physicians in Ireland per capita than many other OECD countries. In 2005, Ireland had 2.8 physicians per 1,000 compared to the OECD average of 3 per 1,000.[55]

Hospital consultants

As well as too few hospital beds, Ireland also has too few hospital consultants. While there have been substantial increases in the number of hospital-based consultants in recent years, it is still well below comparative international rates. In 2001, there were 1,500 consultants, this had risen to 2,100 by 2006. In December 2008, according to the HSE there are 1,833 consultants in the public health system, according to the Health Service Employers Agency, there were 2,200.

A Department of Health commissioned report on medical staffing published in 2003 as a follow-up to the publication of the health strategy found that in order to be in line with the European Working Time Directive (EWTD), there should be 3,100 consultants employed by 2009, rising to 3,600 by 2013. This report estimated this would cost €52 million.

The number of consultants in Irish hospitals has been restricted because of cost constraints but, up to 2004, consultants themselves kept a stronghold over the location and appointment of specialities through their involvement in Comhairle na nOspidéal where they held a majority position. They were one of the many health agencies amalgamated into the new HSE in 2005, so responsibility for the appointment of consultants now lies with the HSE. From 2004, there were protracted negotiations between consultants and government over a new consultants' contract and long-promised additional consultants post were delayed until the new contract was agreed.

Hospital doctors

Traditionally, Irish hospitals have always been over-reliant on non-consultant hospital doctors (NCHDs) because of the shortages of consultants. In 2008, there were over twice as many NCHD as there were consultants.

NCHDs are qualified doctors who work in a trainee's post

for a speciality alongside consultants to get their post-graduate qualifications, which enables them to become consultants too. NCHDs work very long hours and often provide care for public patients. Private patients are more likely to get treated by consultants than NCHDs.

The European Working Time Directive (EWTD) signed up to by the Irish government means that NCHDs can no longer work the very long hours that they have practised to date. There is a commitment from government to reduce the working hours and the numbers of NCHDs and increase the numbers of consultants, however, this was delayed for years by the protracted consultants' contract negotiations.

Many Irish doctors go abroad to get their further training, as a result of which, there is a high reliance on recruiting foreign-trained doctors in the Irish health service. In the HSE, 33.38 per cent of staff working as medical and dental personnel are from ethnic minorities, most of whom come from overseas.[56] It is estimated that 30 per cent of medical manpower are foreign-trained doctors, the majority of whom are NCHDs. Ireland has attracted significant numbers of foreign-trained hospital and medical staff in the past 20 years, most recently because of the relatively high wages available. However, globally there is an increased awareness of first world countries bleeding developing world countries dry of one of their most valuable assets, their doctors and nurses. Some European countries, such as Norway, have tried to address this issue by introducing ethical hiring practices for medical and nursing staff.

Nurses

Another politically driven mantra about the Irish health services is that we have too many nurses. While this is true in terms of overall numbers, it fails to take other factors in to account and, like most other aspects of the health system, it is more complicated than it may appear.

There are 38,000 nurses working in the public health system, which gives Ireland a higher number of practising nurses when compared to other OECD countries. There are 15.2 per 1,000 which is twice the OECD average, higher than both the UK who have 9.9 per 1,000 and France (who have 7.7 per 1,000).[57] Ireland also has a higher number of graduating nurses, who now have to qualify with a nursing degree to get a nursing position.

However, the comparisons are problematic as they do not take in to account the fact that 40 per cent of Irish nurses work part-time and the skill mix in Irish hospitals is different to other countries.[58] In France, every nurse has a nursing assistant working with her/him, while, in Ireland, the number of nursing assistants is low and nothing like a one to one ratio pertaining in other countries.

There has been difficulty in Ireland in attracting people into nursing posts, especially in Dublin and Cork where house prices and the standard of living are very costly. As a result, in the first five years of the new century, 'immigration was the main source of supply of general nurses' in Ireland. In 2007, 15 per cent of the 38,000 nurses working for the HSE were from ethnic minorities, the majority of whom come from Asia.[59]

Mary Harney, as Minister for Health, and the HSE management often makes reference to the fact that there are more nurses in Ireland than elsewhere, but they decline to take in to account 40 per cent of nurses are not full-time and the fact that there are significantly fewer doctors and nurse assistants in Irish hospitals.

Anyone who spends any period of time in an Irish public hospital can vouch for the fact that nursing is understaffed and nurses are under huge pressure, with increasing administrative duties and extensions of their medical responsibilities. In line with international trends, some Irish nurses can now prescribe medicines, and often it is the nurse specialist who bears the majority of the responsibility of clinical care for sick patients.

In 1997 and 2007, nurses in Ireland went on strike and, on both occasions, they had significant public support. Two of the key issues behind the strike were pay and conditions. It is no coincidence that nurses are a predominately female profession who are on average paid 14 per cent less than their male counterparts. Part of the resolution to the second nurses' strike was agreement to introduce a 37.5-hour working week with effect from June 2008, in line with other allied health professionals. The deal was agreed on the condition that it was cost neutral and did not affect patient care.

By mid-July 2008, only half the nurses in the country had had their working times reduced to the promised 37.5 hours a week. While the remainder of nurses working hours were being agreed, the National Implementation Body, the trouble-shooting mechanism in place under social partnership, recommended transferring funds used to pay for overtime or agency nurses to pay for more full-time positions so that the 37.5-hour week could be achieved.

Aspects of hospital care

With insufficient budgets, shortages of hospital beds and consultants, and inadequate provision of care outside of the hospital setting, it is no surprise that it is hard to get into hospital. As a result of these combining factors, there are a series of hurdles to overcome in order to get into the hospital system, and the more unwell, or indeed the poorer you are, the harder it is to get over these hurdles. Sometimes, it can even be hard to get out of a hospital, as there is nowhere appropriate for patients who are not well enough to manage at home to go. (See Chapter 8 for more on community and continuing care.)

Emergency departments – a microcosm of the troubles in the wider health system

Anyone in need of urgent medical attention enters the hospital system through the emergency department (ED), renamed from A&E in 2006. While conditions and waiting times in A&E departments had been an issue since the mid to late 1990s, it was not until the winter of 2003–04, that they became a such a high-profile public and political issue.

The 2001 health strategy including Action 86 stated, 'a substantial programme of improvements in accident and emergency departments will be introduced'.[60] Specifically, it promised additional A&E consultants, assessment units in A&E departments to channel patients quickly to appropriate care, and increased use of nurse practitioners. The health strategy also committed to ensuring 2,800 more acute hospital inpatient beds and 5,600 extended bed/community nursing units. Progressing each of these commitments was central to alleviating pressure on A&E departments.

In 2002, Micheál Martin announced the building of seventeen 50-bed community-nursing units. However, without the co-operation of the Department of Finance, progress on hospital beds and community hospital beds was not achieved.

By the winter of 2003–04, there were scores and sometimes hundreds of people waiting in A&Es around the country, sometimes for days on end, some of those waiting were the sickest and most vulnerable in our society. For example, if an older person needs to be admitted to hospital, because of the shortage of beds and the delays in accessing a specialist, entering hospital through A&E can be the only way in. However, if that older person is really unwell, waiting in A&E may be the worst environment for them to be in, the seats are uncomfortable, there may be disruption in the waiting room and the chances of infection is high.

Within weeks of taking office in September 2004, Minister

for Health, Mary Harney announced a ten-point plan to resolve the crisis in A&E. A major part of the ten-point plan was to divert people attending unnecessarily away from A&Es. The ten-point plan included the development of minor injury clinics; increased numbers of higher dependency beds in private nursing homes; additional home care packages; an audit of cleanliness; and diagnostics in private hospitals. Some of these actions were introduced but not at a sufficient level to alleviate growing pressures on A&Es.

In the same month as Mary Harney took up office, two mothers, lay side by side on trolleys for five days in the Mater Hospital. The conditions were awful. Janette Byrne, the daughter of Kathleen Byrne, one of the women involved set up a campaign to highlight the inhumane conditions and waiting times in A&E. Her mother had experienced a series of strokes, but had to wait five days for a hospital bed, in the meantime she acquired the hospital vomiting bug and bed sores from being on the trolley for so long. Patients Together was formed in October 2004 'to highlight the horror of A&E and to work for change in the A&E departments all across this wealthy nation'.[61] Five years on, in 2009, Janette's campaign is alive and well. She runs a voluntary organisation called Patients Together acting as a support and advocate for people who receive poor and unfair treatment by the public health system. The stories of people who have contacted Patients Together could fill the pages of this book by themselves.

Some A&E departments have particularly intractable problems, these include the Mater, Beaumont and Our Lady of Lourdes, Drogheda. In protest to the conditions and waiting times in the Mater Hospital, local Labour TD, Joe Costello has been holding a vigil outside the hospital each Saturday since Autumn 2004.

In October 2004, Mary Harney's ten-point plan coincided with Janette Byrne's very effective media campaign, and politicians and the public began to pay attention to the chronic conditions faced by patients in A&Es. In September 2005, just a month after he took office, Brendan Drumm the new HSE CEO admitted it would take at least two years to solve the problems in A&E, acknowledging that the causes of the problems lay in the wider health system.

A month later, in October 2005, the Irish Nurses Organisation (INO) started collecting and publishing daily counts on how many people were waiting in each A&E department across the country.

'Trolleywatch', as their count is known, which is emailed to anyone interested in receiving it and on the INO website is still a bleak daily reminder of the number of people waiting in hospitals for emergency care. On 7 October 2008, there were 280 people waiting on trolleys around the country. That same day the INO issued a statement highlighting that there were 44 patients waiting overnight for admission from the emergency department of Galway University Hospital. It said that 'ten of the patients were moved into the Surgical Day Ward, while seven were nursed in the public waiting room. There were still 30 patients on trolleys in that department this morning awaiting admission'. Spokesperson from the INO said 'according to our members, conditions in the department overnight were akin to third world conditions. A record 252 patients went through the emergency department during this 24-hour period and staff were under severe pressure trying to cope. The department can neither accommodate nor cope physically or from a staffing perspective with this ongoing unacceptable situation'.[62]

But like many other important issues in Irish society, it took time to permeate the public's psyche and it was an appearance on *The Late, Late Show* that copper-fastened the concern of the poor conditions in A&E.

Brendan Gleeson, a well-known and liked Irish actor, raged against the Irish health system in a extraordinary television appearance in March 2006. Gleeson unleashed an unprecedented political tirade about his parents' treatment in A&E, what he described as 'like a military field hospital ... the place is a disgrace ... it's a war crime what's happening in there'.

> Old people particularly are being left on trolleys ad nauseum until they, you know, some of them have died ... My dad was there for four or five days a number of years ago. It was such a hideous experience [for him] that the last time we nearly lost him because he was so reluctant to go through the A&E experience. He very nearly went, he was very close to dying because he could not face what was going on in there [A&E].
>
> My mother was in there for three or four days and there was one toilet in the A&E in Beaumont Hospital. The indignity of it was unspeakable, but there were two other people there. The three of them got together and at one stage, one of them had gone to the toilet, and a nurse came up and tried to sweep away the trolley that this woman had been on for two days. My mum had to put down her hand and say, 'You're not taking that trolley because she's only gone into the toilet.' Now this is [a country] where we're making billions. This has been going on and on and on for years and years.
>
> There are people here whose parents are going to die in disgusting circumstances. The staff are keeping the people as much as they can in some sort of humane situation but this is absolutely disgusting ...
>
> I want to ask here and now, that anybody, if they don't sort this thing out in three to six months, anybody who votes for this crowd to get back in next time, might as well kill themselves. I'll be honest with you, I don't think much of the other crowd either.

> It's disgusting that we are allowing people to die when we have billions, we have billions. A baboon could sort this bloody thing out ...

Two days after Gleeson's 'baboon' outburst on 19 March 2006, the HSE announced the opening of admission lounges in A&E departments. Eleven days after Brendan Gleeson's now famous tirade, Minister Harney declared the A&E crisis to be a 'national emergency' and set up a task force to find solutions.

A year after a national emergency was declared, on one day in April 2006, there were 495 people recorded on trolleys, the highest ever figure in the Trolleywatch count.

While the emergency department task force were busy doing their work, the HSE announced the introduction of other short-term practical measures, such as avoiding hospital admissions through enhanced GPs out-of-hours, more GP access to diagnostics, chronic illness management and home care packages, many of which were familiar mantra to the 'crisis' in A&E. Actions also focused on reducing hospital stays through access to beds and facilities, discharge planning, more availability of diagnostics, more consultants. The HSE set targets so that no patient would wait more than 24 hours for admission, that no department should have more than ten people waiting, and that those waiting should be guaranteed privacy and dignity.

The emergency department task force produced its report in December 2006, but, conveniently for government, it was not published by the HSE until after the May general election on 1 June 2007, the Friday before the June bank holiday weekend. The Task Force Report was welcomed by all in the health sector as it acknowledged, as HSE chief Drumm had done previously, that blockages in A&E were a result of trouble in other parts of the health system. The report clearly outlined the causes, consequences and responses required to address the difficulties in emergency departments. The report identified the 'core problem' as 'hospitals routinely do not have beds available to meet patient need. This results in those patients who require admission to hospital spending significant periods in emergency departments'.[63]

It recommended the introduction of targets in relation to waiting times in emergency departments commencing with a 12-hour target, from decision to admit, in 2007. It recommended a 'total wait time target of six hours from admission to discharge from the emergency department is to be set for all patients'.

Nevertheless, the waiting time target in place does not reflect the actual waiting times of patients. It measures the amount of time a patient waits from when the decision to admit has been made (not when a patient arrives in hospital) and it ends when a decision to move the patient is made (not when the actual move happens, which can be hours later). The report also admits such 'gaming' is taking place – the manipulation of figures so that targets are achieved or real waiting times are not realised.

In the UK, a four-hour maximum wait time was introduced. This was achieved because of the huge level of political pressure to do so. However, research in the UK has shown that the four-hour wait time significantly increased hospital admission and costs. While a UK Audit Commission report found that the targets were in direct competition with achieving financial balance.

Given that the emergency department targets were set in the same year that the HSE introduced cost-cutting initiatives, a freeze on new appointments and a ban on hiring agency staff, achieving them will be very difficult.

Delayed discharges or 'bed blockers' have been consistently identified as one of the main problems for backups in A&E.

However, progress is slow in this area and the introduction of freezes in nursing home subventions and in home care packages as part of cost-cutting measures introduced in September 2007, have only exacerbated the problem. In December 2008, there were 696 people resident in acute hospitals because there were no alternatives, a figure that has been increasing consistently since the publication of the Emergency Department Task Force Report.

In order to incentivise hospitals to achieve their targets, reward schemes in the form of a 'Patients Experience Fund' and the '100 Plus Scheme' were put in place. These reward hospitals for meeting targets but punish the poor-performing hospitals without providing them with the assistance required to address the cause of the problem in the first place. On August 2007, the HSE announced that 60 additional posts would be provided in 24 hospitals under this scheme, with another 40 posts to be announced. However, their announcement was immediately followed by cost-cutting initiatives and the posts were not delivered. By December 2008, not one of these posts had been filled.

Christine O'Malley, who is an outspoken geriatrician in Nenagh Hospital and former president of the Irish Medical Organisation has stated publicly the impact emergency department targets have on the rest of hospital admissions. Because hospitals do not want to be punished and lose much needed money, they prioritise less sick emergency patients over more urgent planned admissions. O'Malley has also spoken about how patients are kept unnecessarily in very expensive Intensive Care Units to keep general wards free for emergency admissions, 'one of many ways of keeping the trolley count down'.[64] Also, the scheme does not assist the hospitals where persistent problems remain in EDs, thereby unfairly penalising hospitals for difficulties that may be outside their control.

The ED Task Force Report highlighted how seven hospital

EDs are unfit for purpose. Fergal Hickey, chair of the Irish Association of Emergency Medicine (IAEM) at the time of the publication of report in June 2007 said 'no EDs are fit for purpose, even the new ones are deficient'. The report also found that most EDs had inadequate physical infrastructure and the key causes of delays were inadequacies in hospital and community services.

In June 2008, a year on from the publication of the Task Force Report, the IAEM noted that many EDs have experienced record numbers of inpatient boarders (patients on trolleys) in the first quarter of 2008, that seven EDs were still 'unfit for purpose' and that most EDs still have inadequate physical infrastructure. It also comments that despite a commitment in the report to zero tolerance for trolley waits, there still remains a culture of acceptance of trolley waits that extends right up to the Minister for Health and Children who stated in the Dáil that waiting on a trolley could be 'a pleasant experience'.[65]

While the six-hour target has been officially in place since February 2007, the IAEM was critical that the HSE has failed to set a date from which hospitals will meet a performance target of six hours or less wait time from the time of decision to admit, nor has the HSE set out a timeframe from which a total maximum wait of six hours from arrival at the ED to admission or discharge will apply. The IAEM statement on 1 June 2008 said, 'On the first anniversary of publication of the Task Force Report, the single biggest issue facing EDs in Ireland continues to be the persistent and excessive overcrowding with boarded inpatients, i.e. patients who have completed their episode of emergency care and are awaiting an inpatient bed.'

The IAEM calls on the HSE to implement the ED Task Force Report in full as continued delays only further compromise patient care. 'International evidence confirms that ED overcrowding results in excess mortality. International and Irish evidence confirms that ED overcrowding produces worse clinical outcomes with this risk being greatest for elderly patients.'[66]

The IAEM points out how the overcrowding of EDs was eradicated in the NHS in England and Wales over a three-year period. In 2008, 98 per cent of patients who attend an ED in England and Wales were treated and admitted or discharged within four hours of attendance.[67] This initiative was extended to Scotland and Northern Ireland with similarly impressive improvements in the patient experience. The IAEM question why it should be acceptable for patients in Ireland to suffer the indignity and clinical risk associated with ED overcrowding? 'For how much longer do patients have to suffer and die unnecessarily before those charged with political and operational accountability for the Health Services take their responsibilities seriously?' [68]

One such case is 39-year-old Beverly Seville-Doyle, a mother of three with diabetes who went to the Mater after complaining of pains in her chest and arm. She went to see her consultant in his clinic at 2 p.m. where the doctors decided she should be kept overnight for observation. However, even though she was a private patient there was no bed for her. She was referred to the ED at 5 p.m. where she was seated in a chair and put on a drip. At 6 a.m. the next morning, 22 January 2008, she went, unaccompanied, to the toilet and collapsed. She was found shortly afterwards by nurses. Her family was called but by the time they got there, after being delayed finding car parking spaces, Beverly was dead.

The Mater Hospital refused to comment on the death but said it accepted that the excellent work of staff was not matched by 'limitations of the A&E [ED] department'. The Mater spokesperson admitted that the ED facility is outdated, in need of replacement and that a new ED department is 'at an advanced stage of planning'.[69]

The HSE responded by saying it was concentrated on

improving emergency departments around the country and reducing waiting times.

Since becoming a high-profile public and political issue, there have been improvements in conditions and waiting times in some emergency departments. However, significant problems remain. Hospitals are still understaffed and have an insufficient number of beds to cope with the number of people presenting to EDs. Community and continuing care services have not been sufficiently invested in, leading directly to patients being kept in hospital for longer than is required. Primary and community-care services are inadequate and, therefore, people go to EDs for care that should be provided in the community – and therefore keeping people out of hospital.

In October 2008, people are still waiting unacceptably long times in what can be horrific conditions sometimes resulting in the unnecessary deaths of patients. Others are known to have died having left EDs because of the conditions or the long wait. How many more have died out of fear of going into the ED is an unknown quantity.

Orla Hardiman, consultant neurologist in Beaumont Hospital and spokesperson for Doctors Alliance, writing in February 2008 stated: 'Hospitals are now being penalised if people have to wait too long in A&E [ED]. But this is really because there are too many people, waiting for too few hospital beds, and because there is a shortage of long stay units for those who can't go home, and a shortage of professionals in the primary care system that could facilitate a safe transfer for those who might otherwise manage at home. The problems in our public hospitals are now compounded because all the clinical departments are now short staffed since the employment embargo in September 2007.'[70]

The 2009 HSE Service Plan published in December 2008 set a target of 100 per cent of emergency department patients to be treated and discharged or admitted within six hours of registration for 2009. In the early weeks of 2009 when the weather was extremely cold and delayed discharges in hospitals hit a record high, the numbers waiting on the INO's trolley count reached the 400 plus patients waiting on trolleys for the first time since spring 2006. Despite political media and public attention alongside a range of efforts to reduce waiting times in EDs, evidence of progress real progress was in short supply.

MRSA and Hospital Acquired Infections

One of the many issues of public concern with the healthcare system in Ireland is the poor hygiene in many of our hospitals. For decades, matrons, who were usually sisters from religious orders, kept hospitals spotlessly clean. However, as the numbers of religious has declined and as fewer of them are in positions as matrons, hygiene conditions have deteriorated. There has also been a changeover from staff cleaners to contract cleaners and there is some international evidence showing how this has a negative impact on hygiene standards.

And while patients have been critical of hospital hygiene for years, it is only in the past few years that poor hygiene has been linked to higher death rates in hospitals.

Two particular hospital related infections – MRSA (methicillin-resistant staphylococcus aureus) and C Diff (clostridium difficile) have been the cause of unknown numbers of deaths in Irish hospitals.

MRSA is a bacterium, which is highly infectious and resistant to many available antibiotics. It thrives in hospital, where people are being cared for in close quarters and where immune systems are low. MRSA has been reported in Ireland since 1999 with increases found annually from 1999 to 2002. There was a slight decrease between 2003 and 2005.

Ireland has been slow to recognise and react to the threat of MRSA and only in 2005 did the HSE request all Irish hospitals to publish figures on MRSA on a regular basis. Poor hygiene, over-crowding and the over-prescription of antibiotics (leading to chronic resistance to antibiotics) are a lethal combination when it comes to MRSA and are central to the high levels of MRSA in Ireland. Increased reliance on antibiotics has led to an increased resistance to them, which means that bacteria, such as MRSA, are more likely to survive and thrive and are more resistant to the antibiotics that are used to combat them.

As stated earlier, various reports have found that hospital occupancy in Ireland is close to or over 100 per cent occupancy. Well-established international evidence shows that 85 per cent occupancy is the optimum level for hospitals. The ED Task Force Report found the 'recently published studies from Australia, Spain, the USA and other countries show an association between overcrowding in hospitals and emergency departments and increased mortality and morbidity'.[71]

In March 2007, the HSE published an 'Infection Control Action Plan', which detailed how MRSA accounts for only one in ten healthcare-associated infections (HCAI). The plan sets three five-year objectives:

1. To reduce healthcare associated infections by 20 per cent
2. To reduce MRSA by 30 per cent.
3. To reduce antibiotic consumption by 20 per cent.[72]

Ireland participated in a cross-country comparison of the prevalence of healthcare associated infections, which found Ireland had the lowest prevalence when compared to England, Wales and Northern Ireland. Ireland had a 4.9 per cent prevalence of hospital infections. This means that 25,000 of the total number of inpatients 500,000 have a HCAI, so one in 20 Irish patients get a HCAI.[73]

However, this same research found Ireland had a higher prevalence of MRSA when compared with Norway, Sweden and the Netherlands. Ten of the people who get HCAI get MRSA, so 2,500 patients, which is 0.5 per cent of all inpatients, or one in 200 inpatients, contract MRSA.

The two key measures to reduce the risk of contracting a HCAI and MRSA are to diminish the potential for infections and alter people's use of antibiotics. While a range of actions are outlined by the HSE, the measures simply ignore the over-occupancy in Irish hospitals, the need for lower occupancy, the need for single rooms and the need for more acute hospital beds.

The actual number of MRSA-related deaths is not known, as MRSA is not often included on the death certificate. MRSA support groups have accused hospitals of failing to record MRSA on death certificates though, increasingly, coroners are including it as one of the contributing factors to death. The Dublin City Coroner, Dr Brian Farrell, deemed it necessary in early 2007 to ask hospitals to refer MRSA-related patients' deaths to his office so that he could consider whether or not to hold an inquest.

The MRSA Families Support Group is critical of hospitals and the HSE for trying to cover up MRSA-related deaths by failing to be honest with families about their relative's infection. The numbers of inquests returning verdicts of death as a result of MRSA increased during 2007 and 2008.

In January 2008, the HSE launched a 'Have you washed your hands?' campaign, encouraging patients in hospitals to ask their healthcare practitioners if they have washed their hands in advance of being treated by them. There are a range of public-information campaigns, limited visiting hours and the widespread availability of gels for preventing the spread of infection in place in Irish hospitals and healthcare facilities.

In May 2008, the Health Protection Surveillance Centre in the HSE published figures on the numbers of people infected with MRSA in Irish hospitals.[74] It found that 526 people were infected with MRSA compared to 572 in 2006. St James's had the highest numbers of infections at 61, followed by 50 patients infected in Beaumont, 40 at the Mater, 39 in Cork University

Hospital and 20 at UCH Galway. However, it expressed caution with citing just the total numbers of those found infected, as number reflected the size of the hospital, the number of beds and the frequency of testing. When the number of beds used in a hospital is compared to the infection rate, the report found that Beaumont, the Mater, Mayo General, Bantry and Nenagh hospitals had higher rates of infection than some of the hospitals with the highest numbers of infections.

The figures reflect previous year's findings which show a levelling off of MRSA infections in Ireland. Also it is important to take into account that patients who test positive for MRSA may have contracted it in the community. The HPSC report found that the overall level of antibiotic consumption was higher in 2007 than in 2006.

The other HCIA to gain recent public attention is C Diff as it is known commonly. Almost everyone who develops C Diff is taking, or has recently taken, antibiotics. It usually hits people who have a serious health issue, often with a critical disease, a worn-down immune system and older people, often with the above conditions, are the most vulnerable. C Diff is a particularly virulent infection and spreads easily in a hospital-like environment. It causes serious discomfort and diarrhoea and can result in serious illness or death of very sick or old patients. In May 2008, it became a notifiable disease. As it was not notifiable before this, it is hard to know how prevalent it has been. Like MRSA, there have been increasing numbers of inquest verdicts finding deaths related to C Diff infection in the patient.

Like MRSA, C Diff became a public issue through patients' groups and relatives of people who have died from it, many of whom were not even informed of the fact that their relative had the infection in the first place.

The most high-profile C Diff case was in Ennis General Hospital, an 88-bed hospital. In the first six months of 2007,

46 patients in Ennis were infected with C Diff, 39 were women and seven were men. Of these, 15 patients died within 30 days of being diagnosed. The review of the presence of C Diff carried out by the HSE found that C Diff was 'not the primary cause of death of these patients'. Although it was noted as an antecedent cause in eight of the deaths. Of the 46 patients, six additional patients had died by December 2007. Of these, one had C Diff mentioned on their death notification.

The report made detailed recommendations for improving hygiene standards and infection control processes in Ennis. The HSE set up a National HCAI Governance Committee chaired by Dr Pat Doorley, HSE Director of Population Health, supported by local implementation teams at regional level. The HSE has also appointed 32 additional healthcare professionals with responsibility for infection control.

In May 2008, the HPSC published a new report 'Surveillance, Diagnosis and Management of Clostridium difficile – associated disease in Ireland'. It recommended that the Department of Health and the HSE need to make the prevention of this potentially fatal infection a high priority. It said special funding needed to be set aside to help hospitals and nursing homes meet new national guidelines on controlling the infection. In particular, it called for the isolation of patients in a single room with en suite facilities for those with confirmed or suspected C Diff. It also recommended hospitals adequately monitor C Diff, have enough hand-washing sinks and infection-control staff to deal with what it warns has 'a high epidemic potential'.

Although individual cases were not notifiable until May 2008, the report said that there were 11 outbreaks here between 2004 and 2007, seven in hospitals and the remainder in nursing homes.

C Diff was also linked to 16 deaths at St Columcille's

Hospital in Dublin in 2007 and 15 deaths at Ennis General Hospital but was not found to be the primary cause in all cases. The report recommended that a national laboratory be set up to monitor strains of the infection, especially some of the more virulent strains that are emerging and which are related to deaths. It also stated that education on infection prevention and control should be mandatory for all hospital staff.

Within the first three weeks of C Diff becoming a notifiable disease, the director of the HPSC, Dr Darina O'Flanagan said that 101 cases had been notified but more were expected as not all HSE areas had reported yet. Consultant microbiologist Fidelma Fitzpatrick said the HPSC expected 40 cases per week. Ireland was the first country to make C Diff a notifiable disease and it is hoped that this will assist monitoring and combating the disease.

In November 2007, the Health Information and Quality Authority published the first independent audit of hygiene in National Hygiene Services Quality Review 2007. It found that no Irish public hospital has 'very good' hygiene standards. Seven hospitals were rated with 'good' hygiene, 35 as 'fair' and nine as 'poor'.

The seven best performing hospitals, which received a 'good' rating, were at Tallaght, Beaumont, St James's, St Vincent's and the Rotunda each in Dublin, Naas General and St Luke's in Kilkenny.

The nine worst performing hospitals in the audit, which received a 'poor' ratings, were the Mid Western Regional Hospital in Nenagh, Our Lady of Lourdes in Drogheda, Our Lady's in Navan, Mallow General, Portiuncula in County Galway, Roscommon County Hospital, St Mary's Orthopaedic in Cork, Wexford General and St Michael's Hospital in Dún Laoghaire, Dublin.[75]

Mary Harney responded to the results saying she was 'very disappointed' and said that every chief executive officer and every hospital board would have to take the findings very seriously. HIQA said the message to hospitals is that they can, and should, do better. The HIQA audit includes unannounced visits by the authority's assessors, as well as interviews with staff, managers and patients.

The 2007 HIQA audit bucks the previous trends of improvement found in the HSE-conducted National Hygiene Audit. The HSE audit in 2005 found hygiene standards were inadequate in 91 per cent of hospitals. The 2006 audit found improvements, with 32 of the 54 hospitals getting a 'good' hygiene rating. However, the 2007 audit clearly indicated that much remains to be done in relation to ridding our hospitals of infection.

A second HIQA audit published in December 2008, found some improvement, one hospital – Cappagh Hospital got the 'very good' rating, while 11 were rated as 'good', 29 as 'fair', while nine hospitals obtained a 'poor' rating[76]. Private hospitals are not included in the HIQA audit.

Dying in public wards

One of the most stark manifestations of the apparent 'crisis' in our hospitals is the lack of dignity with which many patients are left to die in the public hospital system.

Each year, almost 30,000 people die in Ireland. Many of these deaths are associated with old age and chronic illness. Although the majority of people wish to die at home, approximately two-thirds die in hospital, 40 per cent of whom die in acute hospital wards. Most people who die in hospital pass away in overcrowded, public wards because of the shortage of single rooms and the over occupancy in Irish public hospitals. Often there is just 16 inches between the beds, not enough room for a chair on either side of the bed of the dying person. The patient has just a curtain around their bed, with the day-to-day activity going on around them.

This author witnessed the death of a close relative in a public ward in St Vincent's Hospital in Dublin in February 2006. All my uncle wanted before he died was to be returned to the nursing home where he had lived during the last years of his life or at least to have the dignity of a single room to die in. No matter what we tried, this just was not possible. He was too sick to be moved. There were no single rooms available in the public hospital. He had private health insurance but the neighbouring private hospital would not take him because he was so sick.

During the last eight hours of his life, family members and close friends gathered around his bed, talking and praying. There was hardly enough room for a chair on either side of his bed. In the last hour before he died, it was a busy lunch-time in the ward. Staff came in shouting, 'Chicken or beef?' There was nothing but a dirty curtain separating us from the rest of the ward. The nurses and care staff could not have been kinder but they were obviously under pressure dealing with other patients.

No sick person should be in a ward where another patient is dying. No person should have to live the last moments of their life so publicly, without dignity.

In the USA, not known for its patient-focused healthcare, 44 out of 50 states insist that hospitals build only single rooms. In Sweden, Norway, Australia and the Netherlands, new hospitals have only single rooms.

The Irish Hospice Foundation has set up an initiative called Hospice Friendly Hospitals which is campaigning for better conditions in hospitals for people when they are dying. Speaking at the launch of their campaign for single-bed hospitals in June 2008, Mervyn Taylor, programme manager of the initiative, said, 'In Ireland we are still building hospitals that offer wards for public patients and private rooms for patients with insurance. Research commissioned has shown that single bedded rooms are more cost-effective as well as being more humane. They reduce stress for patients, their family and staff. They also reduce the likelihood of infection, and disturbances from noise and interruptions and increase privacy.'[77] International research also shows that the benefits outweigh the costs as single-bed hospitals are cheaper to run.

Well-known Irish actor Gabriel Byrne, who launched the single-room campaign for the Hospice Friendly Hospitals in June 2008, said 'It is a moral imperative that we face up to the conditions that our most vulnerable citizens are living and dying in. It is simply unacceptable that someone dies in a crowded ward with 22 people in one room. It is a disgrace that the only privacy offered would be a flimsy curtain around the bed and the next bed is as little as 13 inches away. They should not have to endure the indignity of being forced to use a commode by the bed in a bustling ward. Those important last conversations with loved ones should not be interrupted by a blaring TV on the ward or the laughter erupting from people visiting other patients. We need to create a sense of sanctuary for the dying person and their family as death approaches.'[78]

Given the decreasing numbers of acute hospital beds, the shortage of services in the community and scarcity of single rooms, it is likely that many Irish people will continue to die in busy wards without dignity for the foreseeable future.

Conclusion

In Ireland, despite a quadrupling in health spending between 1998 and 2008, we have never spent enough on the health services to provide good-quality public health services for all on the basis of need. There are shortages of hospital beds, of consultants and allied health professionals. Buildings are in poor condition, wards are overcrowded. The new consultants' contract seems like a bad deal for the state and patients. Consultants will be paid more and continue to be incentivised to carry out private care without any guarantee of an improved public health system. The new contract reinforces the two-tier system of hospital care where public patients wait longer to access diagnosis and treatment.

The crisis in emergency departments, the widespread infection of patients in hospitals and the lack of dignity afforded to patients who die in hospital wards are microcosms of the difficulties across the health system – of the inadequate primary, community and continuing care services, of underinvestment in hospitals, of inadequate planning and delivery of health and social care.

Every Irish person, may at some time in their lives, no matter where they come from or what their income, find themselves in an emergency department, or with a hospital-acquired infection, or dying in a public ward. But it is public patients who are more likely to end up in these situations as they are less likely to be able to afford to go to a private emergency department or to pay privately, which could secure a private room where they are less at risk from infection and have more privacy in their dying hours.

Some people receive high-quality public hospital care when they secure access to it, but as documented in this chapter, there are real difficulties in public patients accessing that care. There are also problems for patients with the increased privatisation of healthcare in Ireland, the location of hospital services and the quality of care provided for the main causes of ill health, such as cancer, heart disease and strokes. These issues are dealt with in Chapters 5 and 6. Many more people could receive the care they need outside of the hospital system, these issues are dealt with in Chapter 8.

Apart from the establishment of the HSE, the main reform agendas driven by Mary Harney since 2004, have been the new consultants' contract and the co-location of private hospitals on the grounds of public hospitals. Despite the promises of both these developments, the likelihood is that Mary Harney's tenure in health will be remembered as one which drove increased privatisation, strengthened the two-tier nature of hospital care. Such moves were incompatible with the provision of a really good quality, universal public health system of care.

Chapter 5

The thorniest issue of all – the location of specialities and hospitals in Ireland

The location and type of hospital available to each patient, community and region in Ireland is probably the most contentious issue in Irish health politics. Decades of political and administrative intention and legions of reports have attempted to rationalise and strategically plan where hospitals should be located and, critically, what type of services they should provide. Yet, government after government has systematically failed to provide leadership and act on this important issue. From 2007 on, Mary Harney as Minister for Health began to take a strong line on this issue, championing the location of the eight cancer 'specialist centres'. Also during this time the HSE began to rationalise hospital services in the North East and Mid West.

It seems that once every generation, a minister plucks up the courage to bite this political bullet, soon to realise the onslaught of obstacles and unpopularity that comes with it. Almost immediately, the well-intentioned but naive minister realises that pragmatism must prevail. Plans are abandoned, as political survival becomes the priority with another election looming. Up to the local elections in June 2004, local politicians, often double-jobbing as TDs, sat on local health boards that had responsibility for all health and social services in their region, including the public hospitals in their area. These politicians saw themselves as the local guardians of their nearest hospital and effectively defended their position at a regional level and lobbied for more resources for them at a national level.

The population of Ireland is relatively small, smaller than many European cities, yet on the HSE website in 2008, there are 50 'acute' public hospitals listed in September 2008, just one fewer than 40 years ago.[1] This means that there is one hospital to every 80,000 people. The type of hospital and the services provided varies enormously between hospital and location.

In 1936, a hospital commission set up to advise on funding the hospital system proposed the rationalisation of hospitals. Instead, Hospital Sweepstakes money was used to build and develop more hospitals across the country, the hospital commission's findings were firmly rejected.

In 1968, the FitzGerald Report recommended that there should be a radical reconfiguration of Irish hospitals, centralising specialities in four regional hospitals, which would be supported by 12 general hospitals. Other hospitals would become community hospitals and health centres. The report generated a lot of opposition in the communities where hospitals were to be 'downgraded', as well as from voluntary hospitals, which had no intention of losing their autonomy or status. The proposed reconfiguration was ignored in the 1970 Health Act and never happened.

In the 1980s, when day-to-day health spending remained static and capital expenditure was cut, hospitals bore the brunt of the 'cutbacks'. Barry Desmond, Minister for Health from 1983 to 1987, tried to implement some of the recommendations of the FitzGerald Report, with 704 hospital beds 'cut' under his tenure.

Fianna Fáil's Rory O'Hanlon, who took over from Desmond, supervised a greater drop in the numbers of hospital beds, reducing their over all quantity by one-fifth but did so by announcing a 'changing roles' for hospitals rather than closures. O'Hanlon effectively won the public opinion battle – it is

Desmond not O'Hanlon who is remembered for the ferocious cuts in health. However, the cuts that took place under Desmond and O'Hanlon were largely for financial reasons and were not orchestrated to best meet the medical need of the local and regional populations they were there to serve. Between 1981 and 1999, over 6,000 hospital beds were taken out of the system, a majority of them in Dublin, where the pace of population increase was at its greatest.[2]

Hanly's reforms

In June 2003, under the stewardship of Micheál Martin, the report of the National Task Force on Medical Staffing was published. Known publicly after its chairman, David Hanly, the primary remit of the Hanly Report was to make recommendations about how the European Working Time Directive (EWTD), which required significant reduced working hours by Non-Consultant Hospital Doctors (NCHDs) could become effective on 1 August 2004. It was acknowledged in the report, that NCHDs worked on average a 75-hour week, often for continuous periods of more than 30 hours, with minimal rest.[3]

The Hanly Report made the case for consultant-provided care (rather than consultant-led care as was, and still is in 2009, the status quo) in the interest of patient safety, as well as a mechanism for reducing working hours of NCHDs, a necessary obligation for Europe. NCHDs who work 75 hours during the week, often without adequate supervision and training, are more likely to make mistakes than more qualified, better supervised and well-rested trainee doctors or, indeed, consultants. Some smaller hospitals are disproportionately dependent on NCHDs because of a shortage of consultants. In essence, Hanly was about providing safer hospitals for patients and staff, but no one was prepared to say that explicitly, because, to do so, would imply that the hospital system in place was not safe.

In order to make detailed recommendations on medical staffing, the task force had to 'carefully examine the configuration of acute hospital services'. The task force found it 'was not possible to specify the number and distribution of medical staffing required to meet the EWTD without understanding the volume and type of services that each hospital would provide'. In order to do this, they looked at two regions – the former East Coast Area Health Board (ECAHB) covering parts of south Dublin and north Wicklow, and the Mid Western Health Board (MWHB).

It found there was 'convincing evidence that the best results in treatment are achieved when patients are treated by staff working as part of a multi-disciplinary specialist team, and that better clinical outcomes are achieved in units which have the required numbers of specialist staff, high volumes of activity and access to appropriate diagnostic and treatment facilities'.[4]

In simple terms, the task force outlined how the higher the number of cases dealt with by larger numbers of surgeons/specialists, the better the outcome for the patient. They found 'the cost of providing a full spectrum of services throughout the current acute hospital system would be unsustainable in terms of maintaining adequate standards of medical practice and fiscal prudence'.[5]

In this context, Hanly made recommendations on the reorganisation of acute hospital services. Most importantly, the report recommended, 'in the pilot regions studied, acute hospital services should be delivered by an integrated network of hospitals, currently serving populations of about 350,000. A small number of more specialist services should continue to be provided on a supra-regional or national basis'.[6]

It concluded that in order for a hospital to provide emergency care, it needed a team made up of a minimum of 21 consultants, seven in acute medicine, seven in surgery and seven in anaesthesia. In order for hospitals to provide 'comprehensive acute care' a minimum of 45 to 50 consultants was required. In other words, it recommended that many hospitals currently providing emergency and acute care – such as complex surgery, emergency departments, obstetrics and specialised treatment for particular conditions – should not be doing so. This sort of activity should take place in bigger hospitals while the local hospitals should provide community-based care, increasing volumes of day and outpatient activity, including elective procedures, diagnostics, minor injury clinics and community nursing home facilities.

In the pilot areas examined by the task force, they proposed that the hospitals in Nenagh, Ennis, and Loughlinstown were too small to continue to provide emergency and acute care. And it is for this proposal that 'Hanly' became a household name in many communities around the country.

Apart from the pilot areas considered, Hanly did not recommend which hospitals in the rest of the country should become the major hospitals providing emergency and acute care. Neither did it recommend where the supra-regional and national services should be located for treatment not provided by the regional networks. There was no implementation plan, no timeframe and no budget to match its central proposals. It recommended the publication of a second report, quickly, that would detail the location of local and major hospitals across the rest of the country.

Speaking at its launch on 15 October 2003, Micheál Martin said, 'What I am announcing today is the beginning of a new way of organising hospital services. Firstly I want to emphasise that the government will not close any hospital, nor does the task force recommend the closure of any hospital. Secondly, the process is not about "downgrading" hospitals. Instead we need to bring services closer to patients while ensuring that those services are both safe and sustainable. The process will be one of transformation and development. It is about harnessing the strengths of every hospital so that they can best meet the needs of patients.'[7]

Within days of its publication, local hospital action groups had sprung up around the country. While the government tried to put a brave face and a good spin on it, very quickly communities in the pilot areas realised which hospitals were to be 'downgraded'. Local residents, politicians, doctors and GPs in the named areas were up in arms. The letters page of *The Irish Times* was lined by pillars of society opposed to the 'downgrading' of their local hospital. The Hanly plan was to stop the provision of A&E and 24-hour acute care in Ennis, Nenagh and Loughlinstown hospitals. While others from communities close to other small hospitals across the county were also concerned. Mallow, Bantry, Roscommon, Ballinasloe, Monaghan, each suspected that they were next, so they too began to organise.

The plan was that project teams would be put in place in the pilot areas to implement Hanly to their areas. The minister asked David Hanly to chair another group that would draw up a blueprint for the rest of the country, but, significantly, it would not be published until after the local elections in May 2004.

The politics of Hanly

Actions on Hanly's recommendations were stalled from the word go. There was political opposition from all sides. In response to the publication of the report, Fine Gael's health spokesperson Olivia Mitchell, said, 'Given the government's record of mismanagement and its failure to deliver on promised health reforms when budgets were in surplus, Fine Gael has no confidence in the government's ability to effect such an enormous change without endangering lives.' She also said that her party was 'opposed to the reduction in the number of hospitals delivering A&E services envisaged in this report. A reduction from 40 such hospitals to 12 is not equitable, it is not safe and is not acceptable'.[8]

She was joined in her criticism by Labour Party health spokeswoman Liz McManus, who said 'Micheál Martin and his ministerial colleagues may feel that it is safer for them to kick the issue of the new configuration of the hospital service into touch until after next year's local and European elections, but further delays are not in the interest of the health service or those who depend on it. Change is needed but informed public debate about the nature of that change is also essential.'[9]

Micheál Martin, as minister, stood by the report, so did front bench Fianna Fáil and PD TDs. But sooner rather than later, Fianna Fáil backbench TDs and senators began to voice their opposition to it. While they all welcomed some of the proposals in the report, such as the significant increase in consultants, most insisted 'their' local hospital should not be 'downgraded'.

In a Dáil debate on Hanly in November 2003, Marie Hoctor, a Fianna Fáil backbench TD for North Tipperary told the Dáil, that they should retain accident and emergency services as they had them and they needed to enhance ambulance services, 'We want to keep our services in Nenagh.' She said it was 'unthinkable and unacceptable that, in the long term, a doctor would not be on duty at Nenagh Hospital between 9 p.m. and 8 a.m.'.[10] After the general election in May 2007, Bertie Ahern appointed Hoctor as Minister of State at the Department of Health with responsibility for older people.

Tony Killeen, a Clare-based Fianna Fáil TD, stated his 'grave concerns' for Ennis Hospital, making the case for it to remain a major hospital. In September 2004, he was promoted to a Minister of State position, holding three different portfolios between then and September 2008.

Minister for Defence and sitting TD for Tipperary North,

Michael Smith joined the chorus of opposition and spoke out against the Hanly Report. He was reprimanded by the Taoiseach and then apologised for his comments. He lost his seat in the May 2007 election.

It seems that it was not all right to speak out against government policy if you were a member of the front bench, but if you were a backbench TD, speaking out did not hinder your subsequent promotion to a Minister of State position.

Doctors working in local hospitals campaigned against the reorganisation of hospitals as detailed in the Hanly Report condemning it as 'anti-rural' and 'socially destructive'. Rallies were held in Nenagh and Ennis to object to the proposals. Senior officials in the Department of Health and politicians tried to reassure the public. On 19 November 2003, Jim Kiely the chief medical officer in the department, issued a statement in support of the Hanly Report, making the case that if implemented in parallel with the promised 3,000 hospital beds, the Primary Care Strategy, the resourcing and reform of the ambulance services, it will result in 'equitable and rapid access to high quality emergency and elective care' .[11] True to old-school, parish-pump politics, the following week, Taoiseach Bertie Ahern promised in the Dáil that no hospital would close as a result of the government's health strategy.

But the momentum had begun. Local communities were mobilised. In November, tens of thousands turned out to rallies in Nenagh and Ennis. They wanted 24-hour medical cover and A&Es to be retained in both hospitals.

In December 2003, appearing before the Oireachtas Committee, David Hanly said that he thought that it would take three to five years to implement the report's recommendations in the pilot areas and said that the Department of Finance has well aware of the financial commitments involved in achieving its recommendations.

The week before Christmas 2003, Clare County Council

adopted a Fianna Fáil motion rejecting the report's recommendation to downgrade A&E services at Ennis Hospital. The main opposition to Hanly was this key issue. People firmly believed that closing down local A&E departments would cost lives. The concept of the 'golden hour' became common parlance among hospital activists.

The 'golden hour' is the term used to describe getting critical care to a person within the first hour of having a heart attack or an accident or an urgent medical situation. If a person receives treatment in that golden hour, short and long-term results are substantially better. Removing A&E from Ennis would mean that many Clare residents would be outside the golden hour distance from Limerick Regional where the regional A&E was to be located. The motion was unanimously passed. Speaking after the meeting, the leader of the Fianna Fáil group said that 'the message to the top must be clear. Any downgrading of the A&E at Ennis is unacceptable'. [12]

On 24 December, Minister Martin admitted there had been a delay getting the project teams in place in the East Coast Area and Mid Western Health Board areas.

In January 2004, he set up a national steering committee to oversee the Health Service Reform Programme, and David Hanly was appointed to that eight-person group. Central to the role of the group was to pull together the different strands of the reform programme – the establishment of the HSE, the restructuring of health services and many other health-related agencies and, most controversially, the crucial issue of hospital location and type of hospital. Appointing Hanly seemed an obvious statement of intent.

However, it was proved to be a statement of intent that was practically impossible to deliver on. By February 2004, eight local health services action groups from Ennis, Nenagh, Monaghan, Roscommon, Athlone, Ballinasloe, Mallow and Mullingar came together to form a National Hospital Defence

Campaign. Their remit was to oppose plans to centralise acute hospital services in the run-up to the local and European elections of June 2004. Their spokesperson was Labour senator Kathleen O'Meara, who had stood unsuccessfully as a candidate in the North Tipperary constituency.

The Fianna Fáil Ard Fheis, held on the first weekend of March, was more carefully managed than usual. There were no motions from local cumann, no votes on any contentious issues. Polls carried out in constituencies in the run-up to the Ard Fheis showed government parties fairing badly. The forthcoming elections were the first time that the dual mandate was effective, so elected TDs were not running for seats in the local election. A whole new cadre of local politicians, not known on the national landscape, was emerging. They hoped that the division of roles between local councillor and TD might insulate them from the unpopularity of the Hanly reforms. On his Friday night opening address, an Taoiseach Bertie Ahern made a commitment to 24-hour medical cover in all hospitals, in one fell swoop, undermining a central pillar of the Hanly reform process. The word Hanly was never mentioned in the keynote address made by the Taoiseach on primetime television on the Saturday night.

When the u-turn was put to Minister Martin, he said he had taken on board the concerns of local people and directed that 24-hour cover be provided in all hospitals as a basic principle. Clearly, political pragmatism still thrived in Fianna Fáil and the Hanly reforms were shelved in the interest of votes in local and European elections of June 2004. In April, the minister went to Ennis to meet the local action group and gave his personal commitment that 24-hour A&E services would be retained at Ennis, denying that such a statement undermined the key recommendations in the Hanly Report.

A week later, speaking at the unveiling of plans for a new health centre in Nenagh, the minister said that there would not be an end to A&E facilities at Nenagh. Speaking in response to the announcement that the two A&E units would remain open in Nenagh and Ennis, David Hanly said to *The Irish Times*, 'I think you will find a lot of what is going on here is very political in the context of the June election and its certainly something I'm not going to get involved in.'[13]

Changing political landscape

Fianna Fáil's concessions on Hanly were too little, too late. The government parties did badly in the 2004 local elections. Fianna Fáil lost 80 seats and were left with 302 seats, while the PDs lost six seats and were left with 19 sitting county councillors. Meanwhile, the opposition parties, in particular those who took a strong line on Hanly, did very well. Sinn Féin's vote totalled 54, an extra 33 seats, Independents won an additional seven seats, holding 92 county council seats in all. Labour was up significantly to 101, while Fine Gael won sixteen extra to reach a high of 293 seats. The Greens nearly doubled their county councillors going from ten to 18 seats.

In the aftermath of these dreadful results for the two government parties, differences began to emerge between Fianna Fáil and the PDs about what sort of change was needed to win back the support it had lost.

Brendan Smith, TD for Cavan–Monaghan spoke about the need for 'less Progressive Democrat policy, and that is a view widely shared throughout Fianna Fáil by elected representatives and others. Fianna Fáil has to drive and implement policy that reflects the views of people who support us'.[14] Fianna Fáil backbenchers, and political commentators across the political spectrum, cited Hanly and the government handling of the splitting up of Aer Rianta as the reasons for the poor showing of government parties in the election.

And, very significantly, after the local elections, local county councillors were not appointed to their local health boards. In preparation for the establishment of the HSE, an interim board of the HSE was established with Kevin Kelly as chairman. Part of the rationale for the establishment of the HSE was to take the politics out of local healthcare, so that better quality healthcare could be planned and provided for the whole country. The health boards had some positive attributes, but most people agreed they enabled too much parochialism in health service planning that was not always in the best interest of the communities they were there to serve.

In the second half of 2004 and the first half of 2005, leadership in the health services and the Department of Health were predominantly preoccupied with getting the HSE up and running as a single entity. The eye was taken off the 'Hanly' ball as Fianna Fáil and the PDs regrouped. But another significant change that would fundamentally alter the health scene was on the horizon. The cabinet was reshuffled. Micheál Martin, the architect and driver of health services reform and the Hanly report, was moved to Enterprise, Trade and Employment and Mary Harney, Tánaiste and leader of the PDs became Minister for Health in the last days of September 2004.

So what happened? 'Hanly II' was never published. In fact, it hardly got up and running as consultants refused to engage with it until the issue of medical indemnity was resolved for them. There never was a second report making the contentious call of detailing which hospitals around the rest of the country were to be local hospitals, general hospitals and regional hospitals. Speaking at an Oireachtas health committee in February 2005, Mary Harney, as minister responsible for Hanly's implementation and 'Hanly II' said, 'I agree we need hospital reform, regional autonomy, more consultant-led services and that hospitals be appropriately used. I will not say what should happen in one hospital or another as I am not an expert.'[15]

However, just three months earlier, in November 2004, when Mary Harney was rushing the Health Act through the Dáil, she committed to retaining clear accountability for the health services. She made reference to the plethora of health agencies that existed pre-HSE, the unnecessary numbers sitting on the health boards, the need for reform, and the necessity for ministerial leadership and responsibility.

'It [speaking about arrangements pre-2005] has become a jumble and it has led to below par results for patients and below par value for money for taxpayers. Those are the two reasons we are proposing this legislation and the two ways government policy should be judged: better outcomes for patients and better value for taxpayers' money. To achieve them, we badly need clarity of roles and accountability – political responsibility for the Minister and management responsibility for the management. The lines of responsibility and accountability are clear in this legislation, the clearest they will ever have been in health administration in this country. That will make a real difference to the quality of health services provided for our people. The need for reform of our health management structures has been well known for a long time by anyone with an interest in public administration.' [16]

Surely ministerial involvement and direction in the most contentious issue of all in Irish health services – the location of hospitals, was one such area where clarity and political responsibility were required. The minister seemed to have changed her mind in three short months and that hot potato was passed to the HSE.

In April 2005, Kevin Kelly, acting CEO of the HSE, told the Oireachtas Health Committee that 'the current position as regards the Hanly Report is that the Tánaiste and Minister for Health has asked the National Hospitals Office to take it on board. Hanly II is on hold because of the current dispute with consultants around the issue of insurance cover. Although we cannot move forward with the report for that reason, the brief has been given to the Health Service Executive to take it up when we are in a position to do so'.[17]

Pat McLoughlin, a hugely experienced ex-health board CEO who was appointed head of the National Hospitals Office went on to say in relation to Hanly, 'The principles in the report are fine. It proposes additional consultant manpower, reduced reliance on junior doctors, a more structured system of training for junior doctors and greater regional self-sufficiency and capacity ... In the coming year, we will begin a consultation process with the profession and community on the issue of configuration. The principles are in place and, as a planning unit, we now need to examine how the report will impact on each individual area, which will differ from place to place.'[18] By January 2006, McLoughlin was no longer in the NHO, he left when difficulties in agreeing terms and conditions in his contract could not be resolved by HSE management.

Between November 2003 and June 2006, no reports were published on the configuration or location of hospitals either regionally or nationally. No decisive action was taken. No leadership given.

The North East experiment

The plans for the Mid West and East Coast areas did not materialise, the national report was not commissioned, let alone written. Once the HSE NHO was up and running, it decided to start with the northeast.

The northeast had experienced a disproportionately high quota of healthcare scandals the most high-profile of which were: Michael Neary's excessively high rates of hysterectomies in Our Lady of Lourdes in Drogheda up to 1997; the death of baby Bronagh Livingston after her mother was refused admission to Monaghan Hospital; the death of Pat Joe Walsh, who bled to death in Monaghan Hospital when he was denied urgent surgery; and the cancer misdiagnosis scandals.

The report published in June 2006, 'Improving Safety and Achieving Better Standards: An Action Plan for Health Services in the North East' was commissioned in response to these series of crises in the region and found that the existence of five hospitals in four counties, Navan, Cavan, Drogheda, Dundalk and Monaghan 'is exposing patients to increased risks and creating additional risks to staff. This had to change'.[19]

A private consultancy firm, Teamwork, who were commissioned by the HSE produced the report which proposed a three-stranded action: 'The development of local services, with the existing five hospitals and primary and community care providers playing central roles; the development of a new regional acute hospital; [and] binding these local and regional services together through a series of clinical networks, which are centred around the needs of patients.'[20]

The Neary case

In December 1998, *The Irish Times* ran a story based on a leaked document, which showed that the consultant obstetrician, Michael Neary in Our Lady of Lourdes Hospital in Drogheda, had carried out over one hundred avoidable hysterectomies. Many of the women directly affected, who had their wombs unnecessarily removed, found out about the situation through the publication of *The Irish Times* article. The investigations that followed supported the claims made by the midwife who had blown the whistle. The North Eastern Health Board, which had taken over the running of the hospital from the religious order which had run it since its inception, the Medical Missionaries of Mary, the previous year, acted promptly when they were made aware of the case.

The subsequent inquiry found that between 1974 and 1998, Michael Neary carried out 129 hysterectomies. During the same period, his colleague, Finian Lynch, carried out forty. Their rates were twenty and ten times the national average respectively. Neary carried out one hysterectomy for every 17 caesarean sections he performed, often telling the women or their spouses that he saved their lives. Comparative figures for two of Dublin's maternity hospitals are significantly lower, in the Coombe there was one hysterectomy for every 600 caesareans, in Holles Street, there was one for every 405 caesareans.[21] It was extraordinary that such high rates could continue unnoticed in any modern health service.

The maternity unit in Our Lady of Lourdes Hospital was typical of many maternity units around the country in the last decades of the twentieth century; busy, short staffed and underfunded, its practices unregulated and unmonitored. Neary was a hard-working, hugely respected clinician. When the story broke, colleagues and patients, mostly women, marched in protest to Dáil Éireann, in support of Neary. He held god-like status in the hospital and in the region. Initially, when the health board responded to concerns expressed about Neary's behaviour, they asked three Dublin-based obstetricians to review some of his cases. Neary selected the cases to be reviewed. His colleagues, nominated by the Irish Hospitals Consultants Association, found that Neary had no case to answer, saying the women of the northeast were lucky to have him looking after them. It was only when the health board sent a selection of his files to a Manchester-based consultant obstetrician, Dr Maresh, who found Neary's rate beyond all international norms, that they could act decisively. Neary was put on immediate leave on 11 December 1998. In February 1999, he was suspended from practice. In June 2000, the Irish Medical Council, the regulatory body for doctors in Ireland, began an inquiry through its fitness to practice committee. It took them an extraordinary three years to complete their work when they sought a high court order to have Neary struck off the medical register for medical practitioners.

In April 2004, a well-known judge, Maureen Harding Clarke was appointed to carry out a non-statutory private inquiry into the circumstances surrounding the high number of hysterectomies at the hospital. Harding Clarke reported in March 2006, after a long difficult inquiry, often hindered by missing files. In her report, she concluded that her work was obstructed by people close to Michael Neary. She said, 'A person or persons unidentified, who had knowledge of where records were stored and who had easy access to those records, was responsible for a deliberate, careful and systematic removal of key historical records which are missing, together with master cards and patient charts.'[22] These women, whose files were removed, will never know whether their hysterectomies were required or not. Harding Clarke made a series of recommendations to ensure that such a horror story could never happen again. Three years after the report's publication, many of the key recommendations remain unimplemented. In 2007, the government agreed a compensation package for the women affected by Neary. However, some women, who either did not have hysterectomies but did have other unnecessary surgery by Neary or who were deemed 'too old', have been excluded from the compensation scheme. In 2008, they are still campaigning to be included.

In August 2008, RTÉ broadcast a two-part drama series entitled *Whistleblower* based on the Neary case. An audience of nearly 500,000 viewers watched the programme both nights, nearly one-third of the entire viewership, indicating that, in 2008, ten years after the Neary story first broke, the Irish public is as engaged as ever in this shocking episode in Irish healthcare. Michael Neary has never been prosecuted for his negligence. Neither is there any obvious explanation for his actions.

Rationalising hospital services in the North East

The HSE June 2006 Action Plan for the North East recommended the provision of acute hospital services in just two locations in the region by 2009 and in one regional centre by 2015. The report concluded that the current system of patients being either treated in local hospitals or in hospitals in Dublin is not serving the community well and has to change. It said the northeast is characterised by small populations producing low patient numbers, insufficient to provide 24/7 consultant-provided services in each county. The report also identified huge difficulties in recruiting and retaining staff in the region, a lack of clinical governance and unsuitable staffing arrangements. It recommended that, in the future, local hospitals should provide care for chronic conditions, diagnostics and minor injury clinics in co-operation with GPs and other community health workers. It proposed that a further report should be commissioned to advise on the actual location of the new 'regional' hospital.

In the meantime, acute services were being withdrawn from some of the region's hospitals, e.g. maternity care was stopped in Dundalk and Monaghan hospitals, the intensive care unit in Cavan was closed, while 24-hour acute care was withdrawn from Monaghan. The withdrawal of these services coincided with the high-profile deaths of a young baby (Bronagh Livingston) and an older man (Pat Joe Walsh) which fuelled the fear of the local community to the changing roles of hospital services in the region.

The HSE argue that leaving acute services in the smaller hospitals is dangerous and puts people's lives at risk, while those opposing the closure of acute services argue the same outcome, that removing services from local hospitals is putting people's lives at risk. In effect, what was happening in the northeast was 'Hanly' in action, just not in name. Yet, even this was proving fractious as it was happening without the required development of other services, critically ambulance, transport and high-quality, accessible primary, community and continuing care.

Brendan Drumm, CEO of the HSE, heralded the future of the HSE in their three-year Transformation Programme 2007–2010, launched in December 2006. The Transformation Programme outlined 13 different 'transformation priorities', number three of which was 'to configure hospital services to deliver optimal and cost effective results'.[23]

The northeast was identified as the prototype where hospital governance and management were to be reconfigured; emergency department, maternity and paediatric services were to be transformed; and the HSE Transformation Programme piloted. Throughout the Transformation Programme the emphasis has been on providing services in primary, community and continuing care setting rather than in acute hospitals. However, central to this is the building up of primary, community and continuing care so that local people see that their health needs can be met outside of the acute hospital.

The track record of high profile deaths and mistakes associated with hospitals in the northeast, combined with the closure of certain services in acute hospitals, has resulted in a complete absence of trust among the public and the patients of the region in HSE management and the Minister for Health. There are active campaigns in each county to safeguard the status of their local hospital. Understandably, without the development of primary, community and continuing care services, good ambulance and emergency care, communities are angry and uneasy about what is happening before their eyes – hospitals are being 'downgraded' without the corresponding development of services to meet the majority of their healthcare needs outside of the acute hospital sector.

In June 2007, the HSE published an Acute Hospital Bed Review.[24] This found that 39 per cent of those in acute hospitals could be cared for in another setting, many more patients could be treated as day patients rather than as inpatients and patient stays in hospitals could be shortened if there were appropriate places and supports for patients in the community. In this survey, the northeast had the highest numbers of patients – 47 per cent – who could be treated outside of the hospital setting.

The HSE then published a further report called 'An Integrated Health System' drawing on the findings of the Acute Hospital Bed Review in January 2008.[25] This recommended a reduction in the number of emergency department admissions with more patients being treated in the community, in medical assessment units and outpatient clinics; increased day patient cases; a reduction in length of stay in hospital; and increases in non-acute, rehabilitation and therapy beds. This is consistent with the Transformation Programme whereby more patients are to be treated in the home or in their community.

However, the conundrum remains – the public will not buy into any of these plans if their experience is that of the 'downgrading of local services' without the beefing up of primary, community and continuing care. Particularly in the northeast, where their experience is that of closure of certain services within the acute hospitals without alternatives being put in place.

Also when government policy is inconsistent, this reinforces the scepticism of both local communities and patients. For example, in the past few years, Navan Hospital has been reducing its services, yet the North East Hospital Location Study published by the HSE in April 2008 recommended Navan as the location of the new 'regional' hospital.[26]

Inconsistent policy is being further subverted by political interference. The same day as the publication of the North East Hospital Location Study, the then minister of foreign affairs and local TD for Dundalk, Dermot Ahern, said that there was no money earmarked for the new 'regional' hospital and that it simply just would not happen. He commented that it was likely the consultant's report on the issue 'would sit on a shelf', that there was 'not a red cent in the government coffers to fund the hospital'.[27]

The recommendation for Navan to be the location of the regional hospital was a surprise, particularly for those in Louth who had hoped it would be located near Drogheda. The new 750-bed hospital would effectively replace the five existing hospitals in Drogheda, Dundalk, Navan, Cavan and Monaghan, which would become day hospitals for minor operations. For those living in north Monaghan, Cavan and Louth, Navan is a long distance to travel, particularly given the poor quality of the roads.

Even the OECD was critical of what was happening in hospital location and planning in Ireland. Its review of public services published in April 2008 used the northeast as a case study for its examination of health services. It broadly welcomed the approach being taken but it was critical of the absence of reforms in primary care while the downgrading of acute hospitals was already taking place alongside the sidetracking of primary care budgets to hospitals. It strongly recommended the transfer of staff from hospitals to a community setting, the establishment of primary care teams and adequate provision of nursing homes and step-down facilities in advance of 'reconfiguring' hospital services.

The OECD Report was also critical of the shortage of GPs and nurse specialists; the 'general lack of awareness and information among the medical profession' in the northeast of the Transformation Programme. Drawing on international evidence, the OECD suggested that there could be two not one 'regional' hospital in the northeast. The HSE commissioned report found that there should be one hospital for every 350,000 to 500,000 people, however, the OECD suggested there could also be a hospital for every 150,000 to 300,000, thus potentially allowing for two hospitals in the northeast. The population in the area is 400,000.

In relation to budgeting, the OECD said, 'The reconfiguration project is taking place within existing budgetary allocations. The total cost of reform needs to be anticipated, and the necessary funds and resources made available to support the appropriate sequencing of reforms.'

In fact the 'reconfiguration' was taking place in 2008 and into 2009 amidst cutbacks, with ward closures, a staff recruitment embargo and, in particular, a reduction in staff in community services. A financial report presented to the HSE board in early May 2008 found that there were over 2,200 more jobs in the hospital sector in March 2008 compared with August 2007 (when the cutbacks were introduced). But, significantly, there were over 2,500 fewer staff in the community sector. And the OECD criticism of budgeting reflects the experience of the communities in the northeast. Money has not been invested sufficiently in primary and community care or in transport to give the communities the confidence to trust the HSE plan.

The northeast is a microcosm of what is to happen around the country. There were, and continues to be in 2009, significant gaps between rhetoric and action, between policy and practice, between plans and reality in relation to policy governing the where and what of hospital location in Ireland.

The 2006 HSE commissioned report on the northeast lists 48 reports, reviews and proposals for acute hospital services in the northeast published between 1998 and 2006 alone. It lists another 81 'documents relating to the wider health system including the northeast'. Yet, apart from the diminution of services in the counties' hospitals and cutbacks in frontline services, very little has happened to implement the plans for the northeast.

The OECD report concludes: 'It is possible that the HSE is

trying to do too much at once and is not actively looking at what it can achieve and deliver on in the short term, to improve consumer/public confidence in the health system in Ireland generally, and the reform programme in the northeast specifically. As indicated in the case study on Managing Agencies, the governance and management structures that exist between the agency [HSE] and its parent Department [Health and Children) should be examined to ensure that there is a shared understanding and agreement on how the HSE is working to advance implementation of government policy.'

Even the OECD has observed the deficiency of any obvious gains for the population and their low confidence in the HSE, particularly in the northeast. Also, it names the lack of clarity on leadership, policy and executive roles between the HSE and the Department of Health as problematic and contributing to the confusion and torpor.

The OECD Report also reinforces the Hanly model and the model proposed (but not yet carried out) in the northeast. It explains how the reconfiguration of acute hospital services is happening internationally – with medical care and practitioners becoming increasingly specialised, an exponential growth in knowledge, and increasingly team-based care meeting patient needs. 'Specialisation implies a larger demographic base and is the reason why medical teams – and by association hospitals – have to merge all over the world.'[28] However, the evidence in this area is not definitive. For example in some cases such as cancer and vascular surgery, outcomes for patients are better for hospitals which carry out high volumes of work. Nevertheless, making hospitals too big where there are high numbers of patients receiving diverse types of care can be more expensive and may not ensure better patient outcomes.

In January 2009, the HSE published its plan to reorganise hospital services in the mid west. The Labour Party received a copy of the report which had been completed the previous summer and were about to publish it when the HSE did so on a Sunday night.[29] Up to early 2009, four hospitals in the mid west – Ennis, Nenagh, Limerick Regional and St John's in Limerick were providing 24/7 acute hospital care each with an emergency department, all providing acute surgery and medical care for patients from the region.

In essence the plan for the region is to shift emergency, acute medical and surgical care to Limerick Regional, with less complex care to be provided in the other three hospitals. The plan is for Nenagh, Ennis and St John's each to have a medical assessment unit. The report carries a detailed assessment of who is presenting with what type of needs in each of the hospitals. It concludes that many of the patients attending emergency departments could be dealt with more effectively by their local GP. The plan envisages a significant development of primary and community care services, the expansion of paramedics and ambulance services. Also the three hospitals having acute care removed from them will provide diagnostics, day surgery, and other ambulatory care.

In contrast to the Hanly announcements nearly five years previously, local Fianna Fáil TD and Minister of State with the Department of Health stood by the report and the removal of certain services from the three smaller hospitals. Opposition parties had a field day. Labour Party senator, Alan Kelly who received the report prior to publication said that an earlier version detailed how €370 million was required to implement the changes in the report. No such detail was in the final document published by the HSE. The local consultant surgeon, Paul Burke, who is the project director for 'integration of services in the mid west', went on the airwaves saying that they had learnt from previous mistakes (obliquely referring to the North East), that no service would close before other services would be put in place, and that he was confident the funding was there to realise the plan. HSE management viewed the mid west as the template for how to reconfigure services in the rest of the country in order to ensure patients safety. They saw it as a natural laboratory. In February 2009, it was too soon to tell whether the plans for the mid west could be realised, especially with the ever increasing constraints on the HSE's budget.

Cancer care in Ireland

Similar to the opposition in the northeast to the 'downgrading' of services in three of the five hospitals located there, the location of cancer services has resulted in the mobilisation of communities across the country to keep cancer services in their local hospital. Comparable to Hanly, cancer services are being planned so that there will eight specialist centres, operating in four networks, out of which services will be provided. Controversially, there are no planned specialist cancer centres north of Dublin or Galway and four of the eight centres are in Dublin. In 2007 and 2008, in response to the proposed centralisation of cancer services, local 'save our cancer services' were established in Sligo, Castlebar, Portlaoise, Drogheda, Tralee, Kilkenny and Wexford, while services were being transferred to specialist centres.

Up to 2007, over 30 hospitals in Ireland provided cancer diagnosis and treatment. At the heart of the decision to move to eight specialist centres is the fact that outcomes are better for those treated in bigger, more specialised centres. In these centres, there is triple assessment of diagnosis and multidisciplinary teams that provide diagnosis and treatment. However, the move to such specialist centres is not a popular one and has been plagued by similar parochial politics to Hanly. Mary Harney as Minister for Health has taken a very firm line on it and demonstrated leadership on this issue. She persistently reinforces the issue of patient safety needing to take precedent over hospital location. Tom Keane was appointed interim director of the cancer control programme in spring 2008. Keane committed to ensuring 60 per cent of women receive optimum care by the end of 2008 and 90 per cent by the end of 2009. Optimum care means diagnosis and treatment under the supervision or in one of the eight specialist centres. Speaking in February 2009, Keane said the plan was ahead of schedule and that by Summer 2009 all Irish women would be receiving care for breast cancer through one of the eight specialist centres.

The cancer misdiagnosis scandals

As Neary rocked the public confidence in the hospital system, so too did the cancer misdiagnoses scandals that hit the headlines in 2007 and 2008.

Rebecca O'Malley's misdiagnosis

Rebecca O'Malley went public with her cancer misdiagnosis story out of frustration and the lack of an appropriate response from the HSE. She told her personal health story in the hope that it would lead to better patient care for others by exposing the poor quality care she received and the obstruction and cover up of her case by the HSE.

Rebecca O'Malley, a 41-year-old mother of one living in Tipperary, was referred to Limerick Regional Hospital in March 2005 by her GP because of an observed abnormality in her left breast. She had a mammogram and an ultrasound both of which were reported as normal. A fine needle biopsy was also done and sent to the laboratory in Cork University Hospital for analysis. In April 2005, she was told the result was normal.

Just under a year later, Rebecca attended her GP for another reason and the GP referred her back to Limerick, having examined her breast. In May and June, she had two further biopsies and was informed that she had invasive cancer and that a mastectomy was recommended. She travelled to London for the operation, having lost confidence in her local health services in Limerick. Between October 2005 and April 2007, she requested an explanation as to her misdiagnosis and asked for her original tests to be re-examined. In April 2007, ten months after the misdiagnosis was confirmed, she was told that a mistake had been made. She looked for an independent inquiry. When she failed to get a response on this, she went public with her story.

Eventually, after a meeting with Minister Mary Harney, an independent inquiry was announced and carried out by HIQA. The report, published after some delay in April 2008, found that her misdiagnosis was the result of a one-off error by the locum consultant pathologist in Cork University Hospital.[30] The HIQA report was also very critical of the HSE, Limerick Regional and Cork University hospitals' handling of the misdiagnosis and highlighted significant management and communications deficiencies in and between all the agencies involved. It was particularly critical of the absence of triple assessment and a multidisciplinary team in Limerick Hospital, which could have prevented the misdiagnosis. The report has a detailed list of what needs to happen to ensure such a misdiagnosis does not happen again. In 2008, O'Malley was still campaigning to ensure that the recommendations are implemented.

The Portlaoise debacle

On 31 August 2007, the HSE told the women using the breast cancer diagnosis services at Portlaoise Hospital there was 'no need for concern' after a consultant radiologist was sent on leave and a review of radiology practice was set up.

The HSE commissioned Dr Ann O'Doherty to review all mammograms carried out in the hospital since November 2003. Having consulted experts in England, she advised the HSE against reviewing the ultrasound scans. The HSE went ahead locally getting Dr Peter Naughten to review the scans. Nine women who were originally given the all clear for breast cancer, were then told they had cancer and started their treatment late due to the misdiagnosis.

On Thursday 22 November 2007, it emerged at the Oireachtas Health Committee, that a further 97 women who underwent ultrasound scans were being recalled for examination amid fears that they were wrongly given the all clear. The first any of these women knew of being called for examination was through the national media. Because of the public and political outcry, the HSE and Mary Harney acted swiftly to inform these women and to ensure the reviews were carried out as soon as possible. Some of the women were referred to Dublin hospitals for further checks.

Minister Mary Harney and HSE chief Brendan Drumm said they did not know about the review of ultrasounds by Dr Peter Naughten until hours before the Oireachtas Committee meeting. However, Dr Naughten had told the HSE months earlier, that some of the women needed to meet cancer surgeons after he had reviewed their ultrasound scans. And, in July 2005, over two years before the HSE went public on the crisis, Dr Naughten wrote to Mary Harney describing the breast cancer services at Portlaoise as a 'shambles' and that he would not want his wife to have to use the breast cancer services there. Mary Harney passed the letter on to the HSE. There was no follow up to the letter as far as Dr Naughten was aware.

In 2000, Niall O'Higgin's report on national breast cancer services had suggested the centre for the midlands be situated in Tullamore.[31] In 2001, the then Midland Health Board located breast cancer services in Portlaoise. In 2006, hospital staff expressed concerns to HSE about the age of the radiology equipment. It was not until the hospital's Director of Nursing raised concerns of over the high numbers of false positives in the hospital in August 2007, that the HSE began to act.

Portlaoise Hospital stopped providing care for any new cancer patients in 2007.

Three reports were commissioned on the Portlaoise misdiagnosis. The O'Doherty Report found the quality, safety and standard of main aspects of the breast cancer service at Portlaoise well below best practice, the quality of the mammograms was patchy, and there was no triple assessment at the hospital.[32] The Fitzgerald Report in a review of the handling of the cancer misdiagnoses found that there were systemic weaknesses in the management, governance and communication in the HSE, there was a deficiency in the review of the mammograms, and there was confusion in relation to responsibility and communication.[33] The Portlaoise breast cancer misdiagnoses were a result of a 'systems failure'. No one was responsible, no one person to blame.

The Barrington's Hospital case

In August 2007, another Tipperary woman was misdiagnosed with cancer. She was a patient in Barrington's Private Hospital in Limerick, She had two biopsies in Barrington's, both were sent to University College Galway for analysis, both came back all clear. As a result of her misdiagnosis, her cancer treatment was delayed by 18 months. An independent review of care given to all breast cancer patients in the hospitals was carried out and Barrington's Hospital was asked to stop treating breast cancer patients.[34]

The review found that there were two cases where patients had been given false positives, i.e. they were told they were all clear when in fact they had cancer. Both women started their cancer treatment late as a result of the misdiagnosis. It also found 'inappropriate clinical care in more than half the women (285) who consented to have their cases reviewed'. The report was critical of the lack of triple assessment in Barrington's which, in some cases, may have led to unnecessary surgery and removal of lumps. It also found there was a lack of multidisciplinary care for cancer patients in the hospital. Concerns about cancer care at Barrington's had been raised by Limerick Regional Hospital's consultant oncologist in 2005 with the Department of Health and Children. These were passed on to the HSE in early 2006, but nothing happened until August 2007 when breast cancer treatment was suspended at the hospital.

Cancer misdiagnosis in the North East

In March 2008, another cancer misdiagnosis scandal hit the headlines. Again, emanating from the northeast. A review of the work of a locum consultant who had worked in Navan, Dundalk and Our Lady of Lourdes hospitals, was initiated by the HSE when a doctor complained about a small number of lung cancers that had gone unnoticed in x-rays by the locum doctor. Initially, the HSE said that the review did not relate to breast services, mammograms, ultrasounds, CT scans or MRI scans, however, two months later, it emerged that these scans would be part of the review. Over 6,000 chest x-rays and seventy CT scans were subsequently reviewed. Six patients were misdiagnosed by the locum consultant. Although the HSE was made aware of the concerns about his diagnoses in November 2007, no public statement was made until a leak appeared in the press in March 2008.

Learning from the mistakes of the past and present – putting patient safety first

So what can be learned from all these crises in the health system? And will the lessons be acted upon? Will there ever be a network of hospitals in Ireland where patient safety is paramount and risk is at a minimum?

Maureen Harding Clarke's inquiry into the Neary scandal

recommended independent audit and peer review, adequate resources, rested and unstressed hospital staff, team working, ongoing staff training and education, and greater management accountability. Since then Harding Clarke has publicly criticised the HSE for failing to implement her recommendations.

The reports into the various cancer misdiagnoses reiterate Harding Clarke's findings, that team working and clinical audit are still not in place in many Irish hospitals delivering acute care in 2009. They also highlight the state's failure which allowed major breast cancer services to continue in many smaller hospitals without adequate funding or staffing, and the failure to act on previous reports, such as the O'Higgins Report, on services for symptomatic breast disease. They show that cancer diagnosis and care is inconsistent and in some hospitals it is well below what can be considered quality care. In effect, they support the policy of having eight cancer specialist centres. In the middle of the Portlaoise cancer debacle, in November 2007, Mary Hynes, Assistant Director of the HSE's National Hospitals Office said the health service is 'failing miserably' to meet assessment times for breast cancer diagnosis. Case after case that comes to light highlights the lack of accountability of the HSE in terms of providing timely information and reporting on issues of patient safety. Many find the HSE unresponsive and unhelpful when there is a worry or indeed proof of misdiagnosis. This results in patients going public with their stories in order to find out what actually happened, to secure independent scrutiny, to get the truth.

In response to the Neary case and on the basis of advice from senior departmental officials, Mary Harney set up a patient safety commission in January 2007. Its remit was to develop clear and practical recommendations which would ensure the safety of patients and the delivery of high-quality health and personal social services. The commission published its report – 'Building a Culture of Patient Safety' in August 2008.[35] The report is a damning indictment of the absence of standards and regulation of healthcare in Ireland. In essence, in Ireland in 2008, anyone can open any type of healthcare facility and have little to worry about in terms of meeting standards or ever being inspected. The commission recommended a very different scenario where all public and private healthcare providers would be licensed.

The report highlighted that despite 'huge investment in healthcare services over recent years, the Irish system does not yet appear to have a framework in place to lesson the likelihood of errors occurring'. It found 'that patients safety was down the list of priorities on the agenda in the health services for a variety of reasons including the head in the sand mentality'. It was critical of the absence of a 'universal system that collects and collates adverse event data from all elements of the health sector'. Adverse events are those that harm the patients. No data is collected in Ireland on numbers and impact of adverse events. International research shows that between four and 16 per cent of all hospital patients will experience adverse events. In the United States of America, it is estimated that there are 98,000 deaths per annum as a result of adverse events and that ten per cent of all healthcare is taken up with dealing with the impacts of adverse events. If these figures are extrapolated for Ireland, it is estimated that between 800 and 4,000 people die each year in Ireland because of adverse events which occur in the healthcare setting. Reducing the numbers of adverse events and learning from those that do occur can save lives and money. In 2008, adverse events cost €60 million. Minister Harney estimates that this will go up to €300 million very soon.

The report was critical of poor leadership and organisational arrangements in the health system that act as systematic obstacles for patient safety. Under the new system, any type of health and social care provider would have to apply to HIQA for a licence and chief executives of healthcare would be formally responsible for patients' safety and held accountable for the same. The report proposes a detailed range of actions including 'compulsory reporting of adverse events; protection for those who blow the whistle; mandatory clinical audit; the sharing of information to ensure accurate information on employees before hiring them; greater patient involvement in the delivery of healthcare and patient safety'. All hospitals, GPs and community services would be included.

Acting on the recommendations in the patient safety report requires legislation. The timeframe set out in the report says that work should begin 'on this Bill immediately with a view to its publication in late 2009 at the latest, with passage through the Oireachtas in early 2010'.[36] The chances of that happening are slim, even if it does happen, then all healthcare institutions have to be licensed, standards set and monitored. Speaking on the timeframe for implementation of the patient safety report in February 2009, Minister Harney said that it would be 2011/12 before all healthcare facilities, public and private would be licensed. Also problematic at the moment is that private healthcare providers do not come under the remit of HIQA. This will have to change in order for them to be licensed by HIQA. This too will require legislative change. All this takes time. And of course, the old chestnut, making these solid recommendations a reality will also require substantial funding. Questioned about this matter on the day of the report's publication, the minister said 'patient safety will be a priority in the allocation of resources'.[37] Given the track record of unimplemented government policy, only time can tell whether this most vital report can or will be acted upon.

Hospital care in Ireland

This chapter has focused on one of the thorniest issue of all in Irish health politics, the location of hospitals and specialities across the country. It has done so through the lenses of Hanly, using the northeast and cancer care as case studies. Some other issues related to hospitals have been dealt with in Chapters 4 and 6. Of course, there are many, many more aspects to hospital care – their provision, the experience of patients, the places where people are cured and go home safely, often grateful for the good care they received but for others there is the virtual absence of care for some of the people who need it most. A few obvious areas that have not been considered here are given below.

Diseases of the circulatory system, such as heart disease, strokes and other circulatory diseases, are the main cause of death in Ireland making up over one-third of all deaths, yet we fall well behind our European neighbours in terms of quality of care in this area. A European survey of heart healthcare found that Ireland ranked sixteenth out of 26 countries. The best cardiovascular care was to be found in Luxembourg, France and Norway. Ireland scored particularly poorly in terms of prevention of heart disease and had the lowest numbers of cardiac consultants.[3839]

Ireland also fairs particularly badly in terms of stroke prevention and care. Each year 10,000 people suffer strokes, while it is estimated that there are 30,000 stroke survivors. Yet just one per cent of those who could benefit from clot busting therapy were assessed for it, while there is a near complete absence of specialised stroke units. Specialised stroke units could save up to 500 lives each year and would greatly enhance the quality of life and recovery of those who do experience strokes. The dearth of occupational and speech therapy also has a significant impact on stroke patients. A major audit of stroke services carried out by the Irish Heart Foundation found that the quality of care stroke sufferers receives is determined by chance, location and haphazard circumstances. Just one of 37 hospitals included in the study had a dedicated stoke unit. It found these matters are made worse by the lack of funding and the staff ceiling in place across the HSE.[40]

There are also a range of diseases that people live with that have very poor quality care in the Irish health services. The poor provision of care for cystic fibrosis patients is one which has hit the media spotlight in recent years, again due to the brave speaking out of sufferers like Orla Tinsley.

And there are tens of thousands of people with hidden diseases and chronic diseases whom the Irish health and social care service let down day-in, day-out. The exceptionally poor provision of services for people with mental illness is one of particular shame and one that is dealt with in Chapter 8. Each of these areas, among others, requires attention and a chapter of their own. The ones that I have focused on were chosen as being illustrative of a bigger picture.

It must also be said that, each day, hundreds of thousands of patients receive good-quality public health services from tens of thousands of public health staff.

However, without standards in place, without the monitoring, auditing, planning and delivering of care, without adequate funding and courageous leadership and management, as detailed in so many reports produced by the Department of Health and HSE, there is no way Irish patients can be guaranteed the best possible care, the 'world-class health' system, they are told so often that they deserve.

What is clear is that, in 2009, in so many areas of hospital care in Ireland, politicians and policy-makers have failed patients. They have failed to deliver patient safety. They have failed to invest sufficiently to provide quality, accessible hospital care to all on the basis of need. They have failed to take the courageous steps necessary to deliver specialist centres of care supported by good quality primary, community and continuing care. They have failed to fill in the different parts of the jigsaw that include promoting public health, getting communities on side and delivering top-class transport to healthcare facilities. The most fundamental of all their mistakes is the failure to win back the confidence of the patients and the communities they are there to serve.

There are some seeds of hope evident in February 2009 in terms of cancer services. Under the masterful leadership of Professor Tom Keane, combined with the political clout and support of Minister Mary Harney, cancer services in Ireland are being transformed. Just two years previously cancer care was carried out in 30 hospitals. By the end of 2009, it will be orchestrated under the supervision of eight specialist centres. Significant progress has been made in terms of breast cancer and the plan is to apply that model to other cancer areas such as prostrate, colon and lung where considerable progress is required.

Chapter 6

The drive to privatise

'Co-located hospitals are the best way to ensure equity of access,' said Mary Harney, as Minister for Health speaking at a debate in Dublin on 8 April 2008. The debate, organised by the St Vincent de Paul Society in Trinity College, had the motion that 'this house believes the Irish health system fails the disadvantaged'.

It was a rare occasion. Mary Harney does not usually come face to face with her most vocal opponents in a public environment. She rarely mixes with hostile audiences or when she does the events are orchestrated – she comes, she talks, she opens, she launches, she listens and leaves, quickly. Just like the way she will not give interviews to journalists, she does not stay to hear her opponents. She does not have to, she is the minister after all.

All her media as Minister for Health is schemed. All her public appearances managed. She takes detailed questions at press conferences, of which she has quite a few. She also does 'door steps' (the media term given to ad hoc questions being put to politicians before or after they appear at a public or political events) and speaks confidently on the hoof, at every health 'crisis'.

She is an impressive orator with a huge command of facts and figures about health and the health services. In the Dáil and at press briefings, she speaks without notes or a pre-written speech, a very rare characteristic for any politician in Ireland these days. She is better than most at speaking in public and handling difficult questions. She was an award winning orator in her college days and has decades of practice from political life.

But despite repeated requests, she will not sit down with this author regardless of her promise of an interview. I attended as many health-related press conferences as possible in the run-up to the 2007 general election. Each occasion was used as an opportunity to ask Mary Harney about her broken promises on health, to challenge her drive to privatise healthcare, to question her inconsistent claims of progress made in healthcare provision. At the final press conference before the May election, when I put it to Mary Harney that this was her last as Minister for Health, she suggested that we meet for lunch in the autumn when she was back in the department.

Despite losing most of her party and electoral support in the 2007 general election, and therefore her strongest hand at the cabinet table, Harney was reappointed to the health ministry. The word put out was that no Fianna Fáiler wanted the job, that it suited Bertie Ahern to leave her in Health. And then it suited Brian Cowen in his cabinet reshuffle in May 2008, to hold off removing her so that when he needed a head to roll, Harney would be removed after the local and European elections in 2009.

So in September 2007 on the request of the minister, we met for an 'off-the-record' lunch, with the promise from the minister of a one-to-one interview within three weeks. Despite uncountable numbers of requests, the interview never materialised.

But Mary Harney did make that atypical appearance at a public event with some of her most vocal opponents in Trinity in April 2008. It was, after all, her alma mater. She had been a member of the St Vincent de Paul Society when in college there. As she said in her opening remarks, she 'passionately believes in a health service that delivers on the basis of medical need'.[1]

The hall was packed. Many were articulate young members

of the St Vincent de Paul Society, some Trinity students, a good proportion were medical students with a concern for the disadvantaged. Others present were members of the public interested in the health services who were taking this chance to hear the minister on one of the most intransigent, divisive issues in Irish society.

Mary Harney was speaking against the motion and provided a robust attempt to defend the Irish health system and her belief that huge progress has been made during her time in the Department of Health. She defended her plan to co-locate private hospitals on the grounds of public hospitals, alongside a litany of examples of the progress made in the Irish health system.

To give her credit, Mary Harney was by far the strongest member of a poor debating side. There was a young member of the colleges' Progressive Democrats who was out of his depth. Sean Barrett, an economics lecturer in Trinity whose main premise was that the health system has failed everyone, not just the disadvantaged. And Frank Mills, a social inclusion manager in the HSE who outlined the health services provided to the most excluded groups, including drug users, the homeless, Travellers, refugees and asylum seekers. They were each defending the indefensible.

Speaking in favour of the motion were Orla Hardiman, from Doctors Alliance, Fergus O'Farrell from the Adelaide and Meath Hospital Society, Audry Deane from the St Vincent de Paul, and John Crown, oncologist and outspoken critic of the health service.

Each of the proponents of the motion was an experienced, well versed critic of the health system. Orla Hardiman told the students they should be angry, they had a right to be angry with the system we have. Fergus O'Farrell made the case for a one-tiered social health insurance that would meet the needs of the most disadvantaged. Audry Deane gave examples from letters received by the St Vincent de Paul of the HSE looking for money from them towards particular health service developments, i.e. the state-run HSE looking to a charity providing care for the poorest to fund services, an extraordinary request in an Ireland of plenty.

And as usual, John Crown made a tour de force speech against the two-tier system of Irish health, equating the public–private mix with the pass laws in South Africa. He railed against waiting lists for colonoscopies, the fact that the truth about the Irish health services is confounded by spin from the HSE and the Minister for Health, referring to the HSE as 'Bureaucrasic Park'. He challenged those present to think about why no other country had institutionalised inequality and encouraged those present to object to it.

Unfortunately, the minister did not stay for most of the speakers. Neither did she stay to hear from the floor, story after story of complaint about the health system, some people with personal stories, others with more principled positions on the unequal system of care in Ireland. It would have been interesting to see and hear how the minister would have responded to the anger, the hurt and ideology that emanated from the dining hall of the university where she was once an idealistic student.

The motion was overwhelmingly defeated.

During the debate, Mary Harney made reference to the Kerry saying that 'If I was choosing where to start from, I would not start from here.' Mary Harney is right, we cannot choose where we are starting from in Ireland in 2008. The public–private mix is fundamental to healthcare provision, a position propagated by every government since the foundation of the state. Yet, we do have a choice about the type of system we develop from here on in. And the choices being made in the first ten years of the twenty-first century are detrimental to the chances of a quality health system, provided equitably on the basis of need, in particular the choices made and supported under McCreevy's reign in Finance and Harney's tenure in Health.

Private healthcare is neither new nor unique to Ireland. As detailed in Chapter 2 there has always been a public–private mix in Irish healthcare. But what has happened over the past ten years is a new development of this 'mix', with government actively encouraging the entry of for-profit healthcare into the market.

Up to the 1980s, the 'private' part of the healthcare mix was predominantly provided by the not-for-profit voluntary sector. Traditionally, these were religious orders, more recently other voluntary providers have entered the not-for-profit healthcare sector.

However, since the 1990s, there has been a proliferation of for-profit private care providers. This has increased significantly since 2001 with incentives in place to build and develop private nursing homes and hospitals. The announcement in July 2005 to 'co-locate' private hospitals on the grounds of public hospitals firmly institutionalised for-profit care into the public health system.

So why is it that there is increased dependency on for-profit care in Ireland? Is this the best way to provide care? Why is it so encouraged by government? Are we building too much capacity in the private health sector while neglecting the development of the public health sector? And are there sufficient checks and balances in place for private healthcare providers in Ireland?

Health policy and privatisation

In the health strategy 'Quality and Fairness – A Health System for You', it clearly states the situation in relation to the public–private mix.

> The private sector makes an important contribution to service needs which must be harnessed to best effect for patients. One of the key concerns of the Health Strategy is to promote fair access to services, based on objectively assessed need, rather than on any other factor such as whether the patient is attending on a public or private basis.
>
> This is of particular concern in the area of acute hospital services. The current mix of public and private beds in the public hospital system is intended to ensure that the public and private sectors can share resources, clinical knowledge, skills and technology. This mix raises serious challenges, which must be addressed in the context of equity of access for public patients.[2]

As detailed in Chapter 1, 8 years after the publication of the strategy, this inequitable mix has not been addressed. The way health services are funded, delivered and structured in 2009, firmly privileges private patients over public patients in access to diagnosis and treatment in the hospital system.

The same health strategy specified 'improved access for public patients' in the same paragraph as 'increasing capacity through further investment' and 'working in closer partnership with the private hospital sector' as key elements of the framework to 'reform the acute hospital system'. The inherent contradictions acknowledged in the strategy were neither recognised nor addressed. Meanwhile, changes in the Finance Act allowed for tax breaks in the private hospital sector. In the 2001 Finance Act, Charlie McCreevy introduced measures that allowed tax relief for hospitals run as charitable foundations, a move lobbied for by a founder of the Blackrock Clinic, Jimmy Sheehan. Interestingly, it was Sheehan who objected to moves by McCreevy the following year to allow for-profit hospitals also to be eligible for tax breaks.[3]

The Irish Independent Hospitals Association successfully lobbied the Department of Health for for-profit hospitals and nursing homes to be included in 2002 Finance Act thereby making private for-profit hospital development eligible for tax breaks. These changes introduced in the 2001 and 2002 Finance Acts have had most impact on changing the landscape of hospital care in Ireland. Interestingly, there was no mention of such development in the health strategy published 12 months earlier. Pre-2002, there was a handful of for-profit hospitals in Ireland. Within months of the 2002 tax breaks, there were eight groups looking to build for-profit hospitals.[4]

Documents obtained by Maev-Ann Wren at the time show that there were objections to the generous tax breaks being given to for-profit developers by Department of Health and that even elements in the Department of Finance objected.[5]

The Department of Health objected on the grounds that the tax relief was contrary to government commitments to end public subsidy of the private health sector. They also warned that they could drive up the cost of health insurance premiums and that the relief would go to small hospitals, when international trends and government commissioned reports, such as the Hanly Report were recommending fewer, larger specialised hospitals catering for bigger populations.

The Department of Finance was wary of the proposed tax relief as it looked expensive and there was not much on offer to public patients. Under the Finance Act, public patients would have to pay 90 per cent of the private cost. So, if the Department of Health and the Department of Finance were warning against such changes, why did they come about?

Ultimately, it is the Minister for Finance who makes such decisions and clearly, McCreevy was behind the tax breaks for private hospitals. The changes introduced by the 2001 and

2002 Finance acts were effective, they led to a proliferation of building of hospitals, clinics and health parks from 2002. The tax breaks to the private sector fitted with McCreevy's neo-liberal ideology, that the private sector could solve the ills of what he perceived as an expensive and dysfunctional public health service. By the end of 2008, there were over 19 private hospitals, clinics and health parks up and running with ten more in the pipeline.

Some light may be thrown on the absence of planning in relation to private sector development of hospitals and health clinics and the inability to overcome the inherent contradictions outlined in the strategy by Michael Kelly's reflections on the health strategy development. Kelly was the secretary general in the Department of Health at the time and the central person who drove the development of the strategy.

Writing in 2007, he stated, 'In my experience, deep down, every official of the Department of Health stands first and foremost for a better deal for people who depend on the public health system and for securing good value for the taxpayers investment. The department corporately tended to be much less concerned about the interests of private deliverers of services or the users of such services. This was based on the belief that parties or private arrangements had the motivation either of private profit or preferential access to services and were generally well equipped to look after their own interests.'[6]

This helps explain, to a certain extent, the Department of Health's large emphasis on building up the public health system within the health strategy and the absence of planning and strategy in relation to the private health sector.

In this vein, the 2001 strategy committed to an additional 3,000 hospital beds, of which it was planned that 2,800 beds would be inpatient.[7] In particular, the strategy stated '650 of the extra beds will be provided by the end of 2002, of which 450 will be in the public sector, thus providing extra capacity for the treatment of public patients on waiting lists. The private hospital sector will be contracted to provide 200 beds, all for treatment of public patients on waiting lists'.

So in 2001, it was envisaged that a limited number of the additional 3,000 extra beds to be added to the Irish system would be in the private sector. The rest would be added within the public sector, a very different scenario to what actually emerged less than four years later under the leadership of Mary Harney.

Progress was slow on all the commitments in the health strategy. No progress report has been published since the establishment of the HSE in 2005 and many of the commitments remain outstanding. As detailed in Chapter 3, a lot of the energy of the senior managers in the Department of Health and the health boards went into the planning and setting up the HSE. So while the Department of Health and the health boards were working on 'reforming' the health system between 2003 and 2005, developers were busy planning their expansion into privately run, for-profit healthcare in Ireland. The Irish health services were open for business. And business was happy to get involved.

Radiotherapy services

Radiotherapy facilities are a good example of how the private sector was left out of health planning. In 2000, the Department of Health and Children set up an expert working group on the development of radiotherapy services. Its recommendations were published in October 2003 and adopted by government. Amidst widespread criticisms over the absence of radiotherapy facilities in the southeast, mid west and northwest, the government agreed to local demands to have units in Limerick and Waterford. A progress report in 2006 said the timeline for completion of all units by 2011 could not be met. In January

2007, Minister Mary Harney insisted the network would be delivered on time. In September 2007, when Tom Keane was appointed cancer chief, the plan was restructured so that phase one will be completed by 2010, and phase two by 2015.

Best practice says there should be five linear accelerations (the machines that carry out radiotherapy) per one million of population, that means Ireland needs 20. However, by 2008, the country already has 25 machines, 12 of which are in the private sector. If the plan to build up supplies in the public sector goes ahead, by 2015 there will be 34 such machines, nearly double what is required. The cost of bringing the capacity up to the required level for the public system to cater for the entire population is €500 million. What is happening as a direct result of different government policies – one promoting development in the private sector, another slowly developing the public sector – is the over provision of radiotherapy facilities.

Put simply what happened was that the elements of the public health strategy which required investment were sidelined, while McCreevy and then Harney's leadership fuelled the drive to privatise the health system. It was not planned, nor publicised. But it happened silently and successfully.

The drive to 'co-locate'

Announcing the launch of the co-location project on 14 July 2005, Minister for Health (and then Tánaiste) Mary Harney said:

> I wish to announce a strategic reform initiative for our health services. The government has identified the need for new public beds in our hospitals. We are already investing substantial amounts in providing new beds. By now encouraging new private hospitals

> to take a substantial number of private and semi-private beds out of our public hospitals, we will create new beds for public patients in the fastest and most cost-effective way in the next five years ...
>
> The policy is to allow up to 1,000 private beds to be moved from within the public hospital system over the next five years. This is an achievable and prudent target.
>
> This initiative today will improve access for public patients, while providing insured patients with purpose-built, new hospital facilities.
>
> This policy sets out clearly a very important aspect of the configuration of our hospitals for the future. It is a key part of the context for a new consultants' contract.
>
> This is a practical strategy aimed at achieving a fast response and a quick impact.
>
> It will pull together in a concerted and focused way the different strands of government policy in relation to the Health Strategy commitments, tax breaks under the Finance acts, private insurance and economic charging. It will ensure greater capacity for public patients and, at the same time, a more vibrant and innovative role for the private sector.
>
> It makes health policy sense and it makes economic sense. All patients will benefit.[8]

Nearly four years after the announcement, it looks very unlikely that any co-located bed would be added to the system within the five-year timeframe announced.

While it has been government policy since 1999 that the full economic cost of private beds in public hospitals should be paid by insurance companies or private patients, by 2009, this is still not the case. Private patients' care in public hospitals is still subsidised by state money. While the costs of consultant-provided care and accommodation are charged to the patient or their insurer, other costs, such as surgical theatre facilities, nursing and other allied health professional costs, are absorbed by the public system. Before the increased charges introduced in October 2008, it was estimated that 80 per cent of the private care in public hospitals was subsidised by public money.

The plan for the co-located beds is that the full economic cost will be charged, but this is also the plan for all other private beds, including those in public hospitals. How the full cost will be achieved has never been laid out by the government or the HSE and has never been achieved in previous efforts to do so.

The rationale for co-location is that the new 1,000 co-located beds in the private hospitals, built on the grounds of public hospitals, will free up 1,000 public beds currently used by private patients in the public hospital system. In the words of the HSE website, this would 'enable private patients to "migrate" from public hospitals to private facilities on the same site thus freeing up significant capacity for public patients ... This is considered to be a practical and relatively inexpensive method of providing significant additional capacity for public patients'.[9]

The idea for the co-located hospitals came from a group of consultants in a regional hospital, who suggested to Mary Harney that they could free up 70 beds used by private patients if a private facility was built in an adjoining building. There, the same consultants could care for the private patients without occupying the public hospital beds. The same doctors would provide care for both the public and the private patients.

At the time of announcement of co-location, there were 2,500 beds used for private care in public hospitals. Mary Harney's logic is simple – let the private sector build and provide 1,000 extra beds. They will carry the burden of the cost. The co-located facility leases the land from the HSE at a higher than market value. The initial claim was that the 1,000 beds would come on stream quicker than if they were built by the public sector, as the public sector take a notoriously long time to build hospitals. The example of the building of Tallaght Hospital is cited again and again by the minister, HSE officials and private sector developments. It took 18 years to build.

The plan will ensure the full cost of the private beds in the new co-located hospitals will be paid by the insurer or the patient at no cost to the state. The public sector can buy private care in the private sector for public patients who have been waiting too long. And 1,000 beds will be freed up in the public sector. So what's the problem?

The 1,000 co-located beds in co-located private hospitals may not free up 1,000 beds in the public hospital system on a simple one-for-one basis. Over 65 per cent of admissions to public hospitals come through emergency departments. Usually, they are very sick people, often older people, needing expensive, maybe long-term hospital care, before they can return to be cared for at home or in the community.

Traditionally, nationally and internationally, private for-profit hospitals do not have emergency departments. They take patients on a planned basis, usually for elective surgery. Often this surgery is of an important but not an urgent nature. For example cataract and hip replacement surgery is often carried out in Ireland's private hospitals. Increasingly, other more complex surgery and treatments such as cancer treatment and heart surgery are also carried out. However, the care of people who have had a stroke, or people with psychiatric conditions, or anyone who has been in a serious road traffic crash does not usually occur in the private hospitals. This sort of treatment is often much more expensive and requires more long-term, complicated care.

In the health policy literature, selecting younger, more profitable patients for treatment is known as 'cherry picking', whereby for-profit providers 'pick' the less expensive, more profitable 'cherries' as their patients and leave the more expensive, less profitable healthcare to the public or voluntary providers. This is what currently happens in the Irish health system and in most health systems across the globe. For example, a patient who has the most comprehensive type of health insurance may receive medical treatment in one of the for-profit hospitals where the insurance company covers the full cost of her/his care. However, if that same patient becomes urgently ill, it is most likely that she/he will end up in the care of the emergency department at the nearest major public hospital.

Already some hospitals, like the Mater Private and St Vincent's Private are 'co-located' alongside the public hospital. Both the Mater and St Vincent's private hospitals were set up by the religious orders that founded them and were operated on a not-for-profit basis, with money earned being reinvested in other projects operated by the religious orders in charge.

In 2000, the ownership of the Mater Private was transferred from the Sisters of Mercy to a Board of Directors who now run it and other private hospital developments in Dublin and Limerick under the remit of Mater Private Healthcare. Since 2000, it has been independently owned and run on a for-profit basis. When queried by the author about its profit status, the response was 'the Mater Private is not a not-for-profit organisation'. Yet, they declined to say they were for-profit.

The Sisters of Charity set up St Vincent's Private Hospital in 1974. The hospital is now run by St Vincent's Healthcare Group Limited which includes St Vincent's University Hospital (a public voluntary hospital) and St Michael's Hospital in Dún Laoghaire, County Dublin.

All unplanned admissions to the 'co-located' hospitals currently in operation enter through the emergency department in the public hospital. While some of the privately insured patients move on into the private hospital, many privately insured patients do not.

They do not if they are very sick. For example, if you have brain injury or a stroke, the chances are you will be dealt with in the public hospital system. Also if you are dying in a public hospital with private health insurance, the chances are that the private hospitals will just not accept you. The public system carries the disproportionate burden of their care.

However, information received under a Freedom of Information request states that 'the specific minimal requirements the co-located hospitals have confirmed that they will provide includes; the ability to admit private patients direct from public hospital emergency departments, primary care centres and GPs on a 24/7 basis; capacity to treat all patients currently catered for in the public hospitals; R&D programmes; Joint Clinical Governance between public hospital and the co-located facility; Performance Management requirements and documented service level agreements; shared information and record management'. [10]

This would indicate that the new co-located facilities will have to take patients on a one-for-one basis, i.e. that no patient can be too sick to go to a co-located hospital.

However, this is contradictory to the actual reality of what type of care private for-profit hospitals usually provide in Ireland and abroad and the opinion of HSE CEO, Brendan Drumm. Speaking on *Morning Ireland* on 13 April 2007, Drumm said, 'I don't think that anybody including the minister would claim that all healthcare for paying patients can be provided within the private sector ... The private health sector provides mainly elective procedures in a controlled manner without any accident and emergency access and that ... the complexity of care that has to be provided in the public health services way outstrips what can or is provided in the health sector ... For those of us who end up with very severe complicated illnesses, the only service that will provide some of those supports is the public health service and you will end up coming to us for treatment.'[11]

There is little truth in the idea that the private sector is able to build large-scale developments more quickly than the public sector. The private sector cannot circumnavigate any of the required planning or public-tendering processes that the public sector must adhere to.

The last major hospital to be built in Ireland was Tallaght Hospital and it took nearly two decades to build. In contrast, private sector hospitals like the Beacon, the Hermitage in Dublin and the Galway Clinic were built in relatively short space of time, both completed in just under three years. However, this is not a fair comparison of the time it took to actually build these hospitals. There were a large number of delays in Tallaght that went beyond the control of developers. It was the amalgamation of three hospitals which took years to achieve agreement on. Also, although agreed and sanctioned, it took decades for funding to be secured and then new plans had to be made to adjust to the growing population and changes in planning laws.

Other public sector developments like the building of new emergency departments in St Vincent's or the Maternity Unit in Cork were built within a reasonable timeframe, when the funding and political will was there to make them happen. Also, there are examples in Ireland of other major infrastructure developments being fast tracked to prevent the long delays of public sector developments in the past. There is no reason why government should not decide that this would be the case for hospital development, if they prioritised the development of public hospital infrastructure. Surely building hospitals in a reasonable timeframe is as key to our future as road and transport infrastructure developments?

The most fundamental difficulty with the co-located beds is

that their existence firmly institutionalises for-profit hospital care into the healthcare system in Ireland. Forty years of the public and private mix in healthcare has failed to ensure equity of access for public patients. Locking in for-profit care into the public health system will make the aim of equitable healthcare on the basis of need even more distant.

The detail of how patients will be managed clinically in a co-located scenario is not yet clear. The proposal is that all emergency patients are admitted to the public hospital emergency department. The co-located private facility must be able to take the patients within two hours. Patients who have insurance will go to the new shiny, high tech private facility while public patients or those with insurance that does not cover co-located facilities will remain in the over burdened, under resourced public hospital. At least in 2009, all patients in a public hospital both public and private are treated in the same facility. Co-location exacerbates the two-tier nature of hospital care.

Mary Harney insists that a common waiting list for all patients, public and private will ensure equity. However, as long as the incentives remain in place, so that consultants are paid a fee for each private patient and a salary for a public patient, then private patients will continue to be privileged over public patients. Also, there are ways around it as outlined in Chapter 4. Patients can still get an outpatient appointment for a diagnosis in a for-profit hospital which is not co-located and does not have a common waiting list and then opt for treatment in the co-located hospital, thus skipping the queue. Also the consultants' contract has no mention of a common waiting list for treatment.

Much of the detail of the new consultants' contract is about monitoring consultants who work in both the public and the co-located hospitals. According to consultants involved in the contract negotiations, this is to ensure that there are sufficient numbers and incentives in place for consultants to staff the co-located hospitals. Also co-located hospitals will hire some staff who will work in the co-located private facility only.

There are obvious dilemmas to being a consultant in both the public and the co-located private hospital. If a consultant has a patient in the public hospital and has the option of treating him or her in the co-located hospital, there is an incentive for the doctor to treat the patient in the co-located hospital. Not only will the consultant benefit individually, as he/she will be paid a fee for the service provided, but the private hospital in which he/she may have shares will also profit from the patient's treatment. If the patient is treated in the public hospital, the consultant gets no additional payment, only his generous public salary for working in the public hospital.

The cost of co-location

One of the key selling points of co-location is that it is the cheapest way to provide 1,000 new beds. However, the co-located beds may not be the cheaper option for the state and the citizens as advocated by their main sponsor, Mary Harney.

Analysis carried out by Dale Tussing and Maev-Ann Wren shows that for every €100 million invested by the private health sector, €40 million is paid for by the state through tax relief for the investors. Writing on this in 2005, Tussing and Wren asked, 'So is this a good way of getting value for money for state investment? Absolutely not, the government has paid €39.4 million for a €22 million investment in a private, for-profit institution, in which it has acquired no stake or control ... It would have been much cheaper to for the government to have grant aided the private hospital for €22 million. It would have been a better use of state funds to invest in a public hospital, an institution that the state controls and to which the government would ensure citizens gain equal access on the basis of need ...

The government could borrow the money more cheaply on the money markets than by this arrangement.'[12]

Analysis from the United Kingdom on the Private Finance Initiative, which has been used as a way of incentivising the private sector to build hospitals and schools for the public sector, shows that they work out as more expensive, than if they had been built by the public sector.[13]

There is huge disagreement about how much the co-location plan will cost and who will pay for it. Tussing and Wren in their 2005 analysis for the Irish Congress of Trade Unions estimated it would cost the Irish exchequer €400 to €500 million.[14]

Whereas Michael Cullen, Chief Executive of the Beacon Medical Group which won the tender for three of the first six planned co-located hospitals, says 'the state will benefit to the tune of up to €500 million for each completed facility of which there are eight planned ... this represents a net gain of approximately €4 billion'.[15]

Initially, there was controversy and lack of clarity as to how the private investor would gain access or ownership to the land of the public hospital, with huge concern that the state would be 'giving away' such valuable land. This was especially the case in 2005 when the announcement about co-location was made and when land prices in Ireland were at a premium. However, it has since been clarified by the minister and the HSE that the land will be leased to the investors for a 65-year period for a higher than market value of the land.

This €4 billion figure estimated by Cullen is on the basis of the lifetime leases of the eight co-located hospitals. He also counts taxes generated by the people employed in the proposed co-located hospitals as part of his figure.

Cullen produced these findings in response to figures produced by Eamon Gilmore, leader of the Labour Party in May 2008.

Gilmore based his results on a briefing document given to

him by Taoiseach Brain Cowen. The briefing document stated that a policy directive issued to the HSE in July 2005, 'required it [the HSE] to undertake a rigorous value for money assessment of co-location proposals to take account of the value of the public site and the cost of tax foregone. The HSE has to satisfy itself that all co-location proposals represent better value for money than building, commissioning and operating beds in the traditional way. The National Development Finance Agency (NDFA) has confirmed that the tenders received by the HSE provide value for money ...'[16]

The briefing note also says that the six co-located hospitals which had the green light by May 2008, would lose 'private health insurance income to the hospitals from private health insurers, estimated at €80 million ... The loss of income will be mitigated, in part, through income from the lease of the land and a potential share of profits from the co-loated facility'.

This briefing document backed up the findings from Tussing and Wren that the cost of tax relief to investors for each €100 million invested in capital expenditure would amount to €41 million over seven years.

Obviously, Michael Cullen, the chief executive and co-founder of Beacon Medical Group and Eamon Gilmore fundamentally disagree, with Gilmore claiming the state would lose and Cullen firmly believing the state will benefit both financially and in getting extra hospital beds.

Cullen said Gilmore's claims were 'bizarre and naïve' yet, he also admitted that the Beacon Group hoped 'to make a lot of money' from the co-located hospitals, although it had to borrow €800 million to build the three hospitals. Cullen admitted that the revenue going to the state would be accrued over 65 years, the length of the lease. A Parliamentary Question response issued in July 2008, stated that the co-located plan was 'researched and analysed under the public sector benchmark, it proved it would deliver terrific value for money for the taxpayer'.[17] The Labour Party are calling for an independent cost-benefit analysis of the co-located project. The HSE said, 'a detailed cost-benefit analysis has been carried out on each site and reviewed by the NDFA, on behalf of the state, and in each case value for money has been demonstrated'.[18]

A document presented to cabinet obtained under Freedom of Information in relation to co-location said: 'It will be necessary for the HSE to demonstrate to the department that it has obtained optimum return for the taxpayer in respect of the lease of sites in question and have full transparency. Under the agreement with the private hospital, the private hospital must pay an annual sum to the public partner. The public hospital may use this money to pay for services from the private hospital but is not obliged to do so. Accordingly the provision of services does not form part of the transaction. It is difficult to predict what charges might be levied in the new co-located private hospitals. They could amount to €1,000 per bed per night or €310 million a year based on 85 per cent occupancy. In 2006, eight public hospitals charged €96 million for private and semi-private beds. In this regard, the loss of income from private health insurance to the HSE will have to be made good on an ongoing basis from 2010 when the co-located hospitals will be commissioned.[19]'

In response to Gilmore's comments, Mary Harney issued a statement saying: 'We have always set out that the co-location policy includes costs to the state, in terms of capital allowances and the removal of bed charges for private patients in public hospitals. We have also set out from the start that the benefits greatly outweigh the costs.'[20]

Speaking in the Dáil in June 2008, in response to questions from Labour spokesperson on health Jan O'Sullivan, Mary Harney said, 'in the case of the six hospitals, we are talking about 600 beds. These 600 beds will be provided for €80 million in addition to 300 day beds that are used for private patients, so we will get 600 inpatient beds and 300 day beds for €80 million'.[21]

The numbers and figures stated by Mary Harney in the Dáil just do not add up. The six hospitals will have more than 600 inpatient beds and will cost more than €80 million to the exchequer.

Exactly, how much the co-located hospitals will cost and to whose benefit remains unknown because all of the financial details agreed between the hospital developers and the HSE are considered 'commercially sensitive' and therefore have not been released publicly, even under numerous Freedom of Information requests made by this author.

Without access to such information, clarity on the numbers of beds and types of service provided, there are too many variables to be certain whether the 'co-located' scheme will prove a worthwhile investment for the public or the investors.

The co-location project is an example of a policy and ideological divide between the minister and the HSE. Mary Harney believes that the private sector can solve the shortfalls of the public hospital system. Some close to the scheme claim that many senior HSE personnel do not believe in for-profit care, that the HSE put so many stipulations in place, that the co-located hospitals could never be viable. In spring 2009, their providence is not known, but one thing is for certain: not one of the additional 1,000 co-located beds promised for mid 2010 will be in place.

Who's who in the co-located, for-profit hospital market

Nearly two years after their announcement, on 19 April 2007, the HSE board approved the Invitation to Tender documents for the co-location projects in six hospitals; Waterford Regional Hospital; Sligo General Hospital; Limerick Regional Hospital;

St James's Hospital, Dublin; Beaumont Hospital, Dublin and Cork University Hospital.

Connolly Hospital in Blanchardstown, Dublin was subsequently agreed and Tallaght Hospital, remained in 'continued competitive dialogue' with the HSE.[22]

The Beacon Medical Group won the bids for the co-located hospitals in Cork, Limerick and Beaumont. Beacon is also looking at building hospitals in Northern Ireland and the Middle East.

The Beacon Medical Group is a classic example of who is entering the private healthcare market in Ireland. Its board of directors in 2008 was made up of developer Paddy Shovlin, financier John Delaney, its CEO and co-founder, a UCD business graduate, Michael Cullen, Dr Mark Redmond, a US-trained Irish cardiothoracic surgeon. Redmond returned to Ireland in 2000 and worked as a consultant cardiothoracic surgeon at Our Lady's Children's Hospital, Crumlin and the Mater. Also as directors were ex-health board and Our Lady's Children's Hospital CEO, Michael Lyons, and Finbar Flood former MD of Guinness and Chairman of Labour Court. It is a gallery of the 'great and the good' of Celtic Tiger Ireland – developers, financiers, medics, public servants – all coming together to drive the private healthcare market in this country.

The operation of the Beacon Hospital in Sandyford and the Whitfield Hospital was taken over by American group, University of Pittsburg Medical Centre (UPMC) in January 2008. It is planned that UPMC will also run the co-located hospitals for the Beacon Medical Group.

The Mount Carmel Medical Group was backed by developer Jerry Conlan. It got the deal for the co-located hospital in Sligo and Connolly Hospital in Blanchardstown. The Mount Carmel Medical Group runs three other private hospitals – the Mount Carmel in Dublin, Aut Even in Kilkenny and St Joseph's in Sligo.

The Bon Secours Hospital Group, which already had private hospitals in Cork, Dublin, Tralee and Galway, won the bid for the co-located hospital in Waterford. Bon Secours is different to the other groups involved in co-location as it operates as a not-for-profit organisation, according to its CEO 'reinvesting its return in maintaining and developing their facilities'.

The Synchrony Consortium got the go-ahead for the co-located hospital in St James's in late 2008.

Both the Beacon Medical Group and the Synchrony Consortium are in the running for the co-located hospital in Tallaght Hospital.

The devil is in the detail of 'co-location'

There is no detail on the HSE website about what stage the co-located projects have reached. In fact, the HSE's Service Plan for 2009, stated that the co-located plans will progress 'subject to satisfactory banking arrangement'.

On 1 July 2008, in response to a Dáil question from the Fine Gael health spokesperson in relation to what stage the co-located hospitals were at, Tom Finn, of the National Hospitals Office in the HSE, gave the following response.

> Project agreements have been signed for the Limerick, Cork and Beaumont sites. Planning permission has been granted for these sites by the local authorities and is now subject to Bord Pleanála appeal. Preferred bidders have been identified for St James's, Sligo and Waterford hospitals and project agreement will be signed in the near future. Connolly is at preferred bidder stage and is likely to be presented to the Board of the HSE at its September meeting for ratification. The cost of the facilities cannot be disclosed at this stage due to its commercial sensitivity.[23]

In response to how many beds will be delivered, the following response was given:

> The size of each co-located hospital will depend on the current level of private work at each site. The approximate bed sizes are as follows:
>
> | | |
> |---|---|
> | 1. Waterford Regional Hospital | 132 |
> | 2. Cork University Hospital | 150 |
> | 3. Limerick Regional Hospital | 160 |
> | 4. Sligo General Hospital | 100 |
> | 5. Beaumont Hospital | 170 |
> | 6. Connolly Hospital | 75 |
> | 7. St James's Hospital | 170 |
> | 8. AMNCH Tallaght | 150. '[24] |

This total adds up to 1,107, over 100 more than the initial figure promised.

As detailed in Chapter 4, there are differences of opinion about how many hospital beds are already in the healthcare system, although exactly how many beds are needed and, vitally, where these beds should be located is equally contentious.

The PA Consulting Report, commissioned by the HSE and published in January 2008, on the required numbers of hospital beds in the future said that 900 fewer private beds will be required by 2020 under the 'preferred health system'.[25] They explained this reduced need would come about as a result of the already planned increased capacity in the public sector, shorter lengths of stay in hospitals, increased day activity and the transfer of more patient activity to community services. The 'preferred health system' is HSE chief Brendan Drumm's preferred model as it shifts the emphasis of care from the hospital to care in the community.

According to the Acute Bed Capacity Review, in 2007, there

were 4,257 private hospital beds in Ireland, 3,779 of these were inpatient beds and 2,461 of the private inpatient beds were in the public hospital system. PA Consulting predicted by 2020, 2,415 private inpatient beds and 965 day beds/places would be required, in effect a total of 900 fewer private beds.

The report also gave figures from the National Hospitals Office in the HSE and the VHI as to the number of planned additional beds to come on stream between 2007 and 2011. This states that there will be a total of 428 public beds and 770 private beds, noting that 'the co-location project will therefore deliver more than the required additional 611 public patient beds and therefore no further beds are required'.[26]

On the basis of figures in the HSE report, there are currently 3,779 private beds, with 770 planned (as of 2007) and another 1,107 (according to the NHO in June 2008) to come about as a result of co-location. If all these beds happen, under the preferred health system detailed in the report, there will be over 2,200 unrequired private beds in the system.

At the launch of the PA Consulting Report, the HSE said that it would rely on the '600 private beds in co-located hospitals' due to come on stream in years ahead. Speaking at its launch, Brendan Drumm said that private hospitals would play a role, if and when public and voluntary hospitals failed to meet HSE targets set for the timely treatment of patients. 'If patients cannot be seen in a voluntary or HSE hospital within the targeted time of 12 hours from being admitted to A&E. I think the HSE could use the facilities of a private hospital and charge back those services to the public hospital's budget'.[27]

As can be gleaned from all the information above, the reality of how many beds there will be, where they will be located, who will pay and who will benefit most from co-located hospitals is not yet known. What is also apparent is the uncertainty and confusion within which this policy development is taking place and a continued vagueness that it will actually take place.

Ireland was particularly hard hit by the decline of financial capitalism witnessed globally in late 2008 and early 2009. The viability of co-location was no longer certain. Speaking in early January 2009, chief economist and commentator for Friends First, Jim Power said the co-location plan no longer stood up to scrutiny due to the shortage of bank credit for developers. In spring 2008, rumour abounded in the health sector, that the government was going to underwrite the co-location scheme. In response to this, Minister Harney and HSE personnel came out denying that this would happen in any circumstances. It seems hard to see how the banks will give credit to the co-located hospitals in the economic and banking chaos of 2009.

Private hospitals

Since the 1990s, there has been a significant increase in the numbers of private hospitals in Ireland. In 1988, there were two, in 2008, there were 18 private hospitals in operation and at least eight more in planning or development stage.

There are two different groups of private hospitals. The first, as referred to above like St Vincent's is where religious groups have handed over running of their the private hospital to a not-for-profit group. These include the four Bon Secours hospitals in Dublin, Cork, Galway and Tralee.

Others are hospitals which changed their ethos. For example, Barrington's in Limerick was closed as a public hospital in 1988 during the country's health cutbacks and reopened in 1989 as a private medical centre and as a private for-profit hospital in 1994.

The for-profit group of hospitals has really only blossomed since the 1990s and in particular in the first ten years of the twentieth century after tax breaks were introduced.

These include groups like the Mount Carmel which runs the Mount Carmel in Dublin, the Aut Even in Kilkenny and St Joseph's in Sligo.

The term 'independent' is used as a term the for-profit sector. It has it origins in the United Sates of America where the for-profit sector is part and parcel of their even more unequal system of care. So who makes up the so-called 'independent', namely the for-profit sector in Ireland?

The people who are investing in the private healthcare market in Ireland in the first decade of the twenty-first century are those who have made substantial wealth in property, aviation, horse racing, development and private equity.

Well-known, beef baron Larry Goodman is involved in Irish private healthcare. Sean Quinn of Quinn Insurance and Healthcare entered the market in 2008. Developers Sean Mulryan, Paddy Shovlin and Jerry Conlan are in the market. So, too, are Des and Ulick MacEvaddy, known for their success in aviation. In 2007, the MacEvaddys announced that they would be opening a 'state of the art' primary care centre in Naas, County Kildare in 2008 with others in Sligo, Mayo and Westmeath in the pipeline. Seamus Fitzpatrick co-head of CapVest, a UK-based equity firm owns just over 50 per cent of the Mater Private. Paddy Kelly, one of the country's largest hotel owners, health entrepreneur Fergal Mulchrone and businessman Niall McFadden are all part of the Synchrony group that won the bid for St James's co-located hospital.

J.P. MacManus, John Magnier and Dermot Desmond have all been significant shareholders in the Barchester Healthcare Group since 2003. Barchester is the fourth largest nursing home operator in the UK and has 160 nursing homes and care villages there. In May 2008, they opened their first care village in Ireland in Trim, County Meath. The company plans to become the largest residential care provider on the island of Ireland, planning to build 20 more homes and villages in the next five years.

Also included in for-profit healthcare market are medical doctors, often consultants themselves who work in the for-profit hospital sector, ex-health service managers, e.g. in 2008 two ex-health board CEOs were involved in for-profit hospital development, even a professor of medicine is involved. The investors and developers of the new 'independent' sector in 2008 read like a who's who of Irish life.

Many of these investors are among our highest earners and they are attracted by the generous tax breaks. Some enter the private hospital market with one thought in mind – profit. Their logic is simple. The public system cannot cope. Over half the population has private health insurance. The population is ageing. Healthcare is not cyclical or open to ups and downs in the market like oil or equity shares or property. If anything, it is a guaranteed winner with increased demand from a growing population.

But investment in private healthcare is not a new phenomenon, although the surge in interest in it is relatively recent.

Prior to the 1980s, many of the religious orders that ran the voluntary hospitals opened private nursing homes beside their hospitals. These provided convalescent care to those who were not sick enough to be in hospital nor well enough to be at home, and crucially those who could afford to pay for such care. There were also private nursing homes where wealthier women went to give birth.

In 1984, Blackrock Clinic was the first private hospital to open in Ireland, initially with only day patients and then, in 1986, taking inpatients. In 1986, the Mater private also opened its doors on Dublin's northside. The religious orders who ran the for-profit nursing homes, used the money to provide other services in the community for those who could not afford to pay for care they needed – one could argue it was a modern day version of Robin Hood.

But Blackrock Clinic and the Mater private were new departures, although neither opened with a for-profit stake in mind, they were both to become for-profit hospitals seeking to provide care solely for those who could afford it. Jimmy Sheehan, an orthopaedic surgeon and high-profile advocate of private healthcare, founded the Blackrock Clinic. When it opened, Sheehan committed himself to working full-time in the clinic, an unusual move at the time, when most consultants worked their 33-hour week in the public hospital system and then practised privately with the rest of their time. His brother Joe Sheehan, cardiac surgeon, Maurice Nelligan and another medic, George Duffy, were also investors.

Over two decades later, Maurice Nelligan, who subsequently sold his shares in the Blackrock Clinic, is one of the most strident opponents of Harney's co-location project. In his weekly column in *The Irish Times* health supplement, he makes persistent attacks on Mary Harney as minister, the dysfunctional nature of the HSE and the mistake of privatising the healthcare system.

At the time of their establishment in the mid-1980s, then Minister for Health, Barry Desmond made sure that existing insurance premiums would not cover the new private hospitals which resulted in higher premiums and new insurance schemes to cover care in 'for-profit' hospitals.

The Blackrock Clinic Group expanded its remit in 2004 building the Galway Clinic which was the first private hospital to be purpose built in 20 years. Coincidently, it was also the first private hospital development to avail of the tax incentives put in place by the 2002 Finance Act. Fifty per cent of the Galway Clinic is controlled by Larry Goodman. Goodman also invested in the other hospitals started by Sheehan, the Blackrock Clinic and the Hermitage, which was opened in

Lucan, County Dublin, in 2006. When the Hermitage opened, its 39 consultants' suites were over subscribed and reportedly sold at €1 million each.[28]

Also in 2006, the Beacon in Sandyford, which was also purpose built, opened its doors.

In 2008, the Blackrock Group were planning to double the size of the capacity of the Blackrock Clinic.

Jimmy Sheenan founder of the Blackrock, Galway and Hermitage clinics has criticised the monopoly of the VHI in the Irish health insurance market which resulted in more limited use of the Galway Clinic than expected by private patients as only those covered by the more expensive insurance schemes could utilise it. Both Galway and Hermitage hoped to provide care for public patients through the National Treatment Purchase Fund but found that this was slower than they imagined in their first years of operation.

Apart from the eight planned co-located hospitals, there were a number of other private hospitals in the pipeline in 2008. Tom Kane, owner of five-star Adare Manor Hotel and Golf Resort in County Limerick, is building a private hospital on the grounds of Adare Manor. Also involved in the venture are Ed Walsh, ex-president of Limerick University, Prof Paul Finucane, Foundation Head of the University of Limerick Graduate Medical School and half a dozen other medical professionals. It is planned to be completed by 2011.

Another hospital is also being developed in Limerick City and is due to be open in December 2009. Local businessman Shay Sweeney of Blackberry Park Properties is the developer behind the scheme and, in 2008, did a deal with the Mount Carmel Medical Group who will run the hospital.

In Tullamore, the Wellwood Healthcare Park includes a private hospital. Tullamore-based developer John Flanagan Developments are building a 60-bed private hospital, a 30-bed convalescent home, a 70-bed nursing home and a 20-bed hospice. They are also building a large primary care clinic and childcare facility on the site. Denis Doherty, ex-CEO of the Midland Health Board and consultancy firm Health Partnership are advising Flanagan Developments on the healthcare aspects of the development. Phase one began in 2008. The private hospital is situated next to the public hospital and it hopes to provide care for public and private patients.

In November 2006, the Whitfield Clinic opened its doors. A 40-bed for-profit hospital built by Eurocare International.[29] Eurocare also runs the Carlow Clinic which does not provide inpatient care but has a range of medical services including diagnostics, day surgery, step down and nursing home care, eye laser treatment and physiotherapy.

In July 2008, building began on the Wyndale Hospital in Letterkenny, County Donegal. Pat Harvey, former chief executive of the North Western Health Board, Noel Daly and Deirdre Foley-Woods of the Health Partnership; business consultants Pat Gleeson and Terry Hannaway of Private Wealth Managers (PWM) are involved in the Letterkenny for-profit hospital. According to Gleeson, PWM clients have taken a substantial stake in the €75 million venture. Wyndale is using a different type of investment model in which investors are shareholders in the hospital and are not availing of tax breaks.

The who's who of private healthcare in Ireland is relevant because it shows how building hospitals and health clinics became a business venture in Ireland after the tax breaks introduced in the Finance acts in 2001 and 2002. It also shows that despite the best efforts to plan and develop hospital services in a more coherent manner in the first nine years of the twenty-first century, private hospital developments were springing up all over the country, unplanned, unmonitored and unregulated.

Privatising other health and hospital services

Since the 1980s, there has also been increased contracting out – i.e. privatising – of many aspects of healthcare. This includes cleaning, catering, security, and running and maintaining car parks. It also includes the contracting out of research and reviews to private consultancy firms which can determine the future of public health service provision.

Relatively new to the private care market is 'emergency departments'. However, what are advertised as 'emergency departments' in private hospitals and clinics are often only open Monday to Friday or Saturday from 8 a.m. to 6 p.m. The cost of a consultation in early 2009 was €120 and then a patient pays for every treatment given on top of that. Also, if someone is very sick or injured and needs admission, then all treatment as an inpatient is charged at full economic cost. However, people in critical conditions will be referred on to a public hospital 'emergency department' where everybody, no matter how sick is treated with little if any cost incurred on admission.

Private 'emergency departments' do not cater for children, pregnancy or psychiatric problems. In effect, private 'emergency departments' are more like 'injury clinics' where minor ailments can be dealt with for those who can afford to pay and may not want to wait in an ED of a major hospital. In September 2008, there were three private 'emergency departments' in Ireland, with many more promised in new health parks in development.

Other private developments in the health sector include the development of private urgent-care centres. Centric Health opened its first urgent-care centre in Dundrum at the end of 2005 in collaboration with VHI and, by early 2009, they had five centres up and running in Cork, Waterford, DCU and Swords in north County Dublin. In 2008, Centric merged with an international firm Global Diagnostics. The urgent-care centres deals with sprains or possible breaks, minor burns, cuts that may need a stitch, minor eye and ear conditions, sports injuries and general medical conditions.

Point of Care are another private healthcare company which opened a range of clinics around the country providing care for people with chronic conditions outside of the hospital setting since 2007. They provide nursing and specialist infusion services required for people with chronic conditions like rheumatoid arthritis, Crohn's disease, psoriasis and osteoporosis.

In May 2008, USA company Quest Diagnostics was awarded the contract to analyse all smear tests under the cervical cancer screening programme introduced in September 2008 for all women between 25 and 60 years of age. Consultants and pathologists working in the state hospital and laboratories were critical of the move wondering why such a big contract was out-sourced outside Ireland. In particular, concern was cited over smears sent to the USA in 2007, where there was a lower standard of testing than in Ireland, which resulted in some tests only being reviewed once not twice as is the practice in Ireland.

Quest Diagnostics paid out $40 million in settlements to the US government authorities in 1998, 2001 and 2004 for fraud and over-charging. Tony O'Brien head of the National Cancer Screening Service said that the new service provided by Quest would be as efficient and safe as Irish laboratories, while Mary Harney said that the tender from Quest was less than one-third of the cost of any submitted by an Irish laboratory, its services were quality assured and would be back in ten days.[30] She said they were aware of the Quest's fraud payouts but still thought it appropriate to award Quest the tender.[31]

Within a month of Quest winning the contract for 300,000 smears tests per year, a pathology conference in Dublin was told that recommendations of an as yet unpublished report carried out by a private consultancy firm in 2007, were endorsed by the HSE board and that cabinet had been briefed on its content. Although the report remains unpublished in January 2009, the report recommended that the services existing in over 40 hospital laboratories should be rationalised, that significant savings could be made by the HSE on its current bill for €328 million per annum on pathology laboratory services, new facilities should be based in eight to 14 acute regional hospitals and that the private sector could provide the proposed facilities.[32]

While, the National Treatment Purchase Fund and the co-location projects are the two most obvious manifestations of the privatising of Irish healthcare, the above snapshot of increased for-profit provision in Irish healthcare shows its permeation in Irish health services is insidious and widespread.

The cost of privatising healthcare

Ireland is not alone in its effort to privatise healthcare. Across the developed and developing world, governments are turning to the private sector to provide and pay for care. So what does the international literature on this tell us?

In 1997, when the Labour government came to power in England, they promised to 'restore the NHS as a public service working co-operatively for patients, not in a commercial business driven by competition'.

By 2008, there were 90 NHS Foundation hospitals which operated outside of direct government control. Since 1997, the Private Finance Initiative has been used to sell and liquidate hundreds of NHS hospitals and clinics. The new PFI hospitals are leased back from the private sector under 30 and 60 year leases.[33]

Extensive research shows that markets (i.e. private healthcare) 'introduces news costs that do not occur in integrated public services; billing, invoicing, marketing and profits. All these divert resources away from the service, creating enormous inefficiency'.[34] Pollock estimates that market-related costs now account for between 6 per cent and 14 per cent of the NHS budget.[35]

Research emerging from Scotland through Freedom of Information requests found that due to the high costs of financing PFI debts and the huge profit garnered by the private sector, the taxpayer gets one PFI hospital for what three public hospitals would have cost.[36]

Another major finding from research on the private sector in healthcare in England is that huge amounts of money are being invested in it by government without any 'meaningful data on beds, staffing, performance, quality of care or value for money'.[37]

Meta-analysis carried out in North America has shown that private for-profit ownership of hospitals, in comparison with private not-for-profit ownership, results in a higher risk of death for patients.[38] This study shows that mortality is two per cent higher in for-profit hospitals. It involved 15 observational studies, involving more than 26,000 hospitals and 38 million patients. Subsequent research has found that for-profit hospitals are more expensive, i.e. that care costs more in for-profit hospitals, also that they hire fewer nurses and more managers.[39]

An economic analysis of data for every urban acute American hospital between 1988 and 2000 found that for-profit hospitals are most likely to offer relatively profitable medical services, while government hospitals are most likely to offer relatively unprofitable services.[40] Other research into dialysis treatment, shows that mortality is eight per cent higher in for-profit units than in not-for profit units. If all the patients who died in for-profit dialysis units were treated in not-for-profit units, there would have been 2,500 fewer deaths in the US for each year studied.[41]

It is no coincidence that in the United States of America where private healthcare is predominant, the government spends 15 per cent of its GDP on healthcare, yet over 46 million Americans, or 16 per cent of the population, were without health insurance in 2005, the latest government data available.

Non-regulation of private health and social care

While Irish government policy has resulted in a huge increase in the provision of private health and social care, government has been much slower to regulate the standard of the care provided. Indeed, in Ireland, we have been very slow to monitor standards and quality across the health system, this was particularly true of the private sector.

It took two major scandals to bring the lack of standards and monitoring of private care to the public's attention.

The first was the exposure of abuse and neglect of older people resident in Leas Cross a private nursing home in north County Dublin, by RTÉ's *Primetime Investigates* programme. Undercover cameras showed the older people were being unnecessarily restrained and abused, and that the standard of care was well below what was acceptable. So how did this situation come about?

In the early years of the twenty-first century when the 'crisis' in A&E was hitting the headlines, there was a push to move older people out of hospitals, but because of the shortage of long-term, publicly funded, nursing home beds in the community, the health boards began paying the private sector to look after older people. Also the changes introduced in the 2001 and 2002 Finance acts incentivised the building and development of private nursing homes with the numbers of beds in the private sector doubling, while the numbers in the public sector stood still.

It was cheaper for the government to give tax breaks to the developers, pay less than the adequate rate to private providers and not monitor the standards of care in those homes. Since the

Leas Cross scandal, the HSE inspects all nursing homes which are run privately, but still does not inspect its own publicly run homes. In the aftermath of the Leas Cross scandal, Mary Harney promised that by summer 2007, all nursing homes would be independently inspected. The Health Information and Quality Authority set up in May 2007 has the responsibility for doing this. In August 2007, draft National Quality Standards were published, followed by a public consultation process.

The standards were submitted to the Department of Health and Children who are in the process of developing new regulations. When the regulations are in place, the Social Services Inspectorate of HIQA will register and inspect all residential care settings, public, private and voluntary.[42] In February 2009, Mary Harney said that by July 2009, all nursing homes both public and private would be independently inspected by HIQA.

The absence of standards in the private hospital system was brought to light by breast cancer misdiagnosis in Barrington's Hospital in Limerick. Barrington's is now principally a day care hospital which carries out large amount of work for the National Treatment Purchase Fund. The review of Barrington's which was carried out in the aftermath of the misdiagnosis found evidence of inappropriate clinical care to more than half of the 285 women whose records were reviewed. The review was critical of patients not being x-rayed before surgical biopsy and the unnecessary removal of some lumps. Although HIQA's remit is specific to ensure quality and standards of treatment and care in Irish hospitals, private hospitals do not come under their remit.

Conclusion

In conclusion, there has been a surge in activity in private hospital care in Ireland in the first decade of the twenty-first century. It was unplanned, although incentivised. It is unclear who will benefit financially, although it is unlikely so many developers and financiers would have entered the market if it was not going to prove profitable for them. However, it does seem there are too many places in private hospitals as a result of incentives to develop them. Private hospital care remains unmonitored and unregulated, despite calls from private hospitals that they too want to be included under the remit of HIQA.

Mary Harney, as the minister who introduced the 'co-location' scheme and the private hospitals providers who won the contracts for the co-located hospitals, are adamant that the co-located hospitals will provide all the service of the public hospital and that their existence will not increase unfairness, inequity and the two-tier divide.

But many others disagree. The Doctors Alliance was formed in 2006 specifically to protect the public hospital system. Other medics such as ex-IMO presidents Paula Gilvarry and Christine O'Malley advocate an end to co-location and privatisation of healthcare. At regular intervals, consultants and medics working in the hospital system have debates on the letters page of *The Irish Times* on the pros and cons of the privatisation of healthcare.

An analysis of letters in 2008, shows a strong majority against private healthcare. Even heads of private hospitals disagree with the minister and other private hospital CEOs. Fergus Clancy, CEO of the Mater Private, said in an interview in the *Sunday Business Post* in November 2007, that the beds in co-located private hospitals will not free up beds in the public hospital on a one-for-one basis as 'the number of patients switching from the public hospital to the co-located private hospital won't be as high as expected'.[43] Why?

'The reality is that with changes in the insurance market, not everyone who turns up at the door is equal. Some will have a cheap and cheerful product and may be told they will have to contribute to the cost of their care. Those people may decide to stay put in the public hospital and they are constitutionally entitled to exercise that option.'[44]

Clancy does not believe that co-location will result in a mass exodus of the best doctors from the public system into the private but he believes 'the new [consultants'] contract will herald the gradual deterioration of the public sector'. He has spoken out against the new consultants' contract, believing it will lead to a greater divide between public and private hospitals. He thinks that, when it is in place, he will be able to attract more qualified consultants than the public system and admits that 'if I take my commercial hat off, this is not the way to go'.[45]

The more the co-located project is investigated, the more confusion there is. For example, co-located hospitals will not have emergency departments, according to the minister and the HSE, yet they may take referrals from EDs if the public or voluntary hospital does not meet its target for admission, according to Brendan Drumm. How will a patient be admitted through the public emergency department and accommodated in the private hospital if the public hospital does not meet its target? Does this make sense? Does it have equity at its core? Does it ensure equity of access to hospital care on the basis of need?

What about beds? Are we building more hospital beds than we will ever need? And are these predominantly in the private hospital sector? Will the state just end up buying back these beds at a multiple of the actual cost to the public purse?

What about profit? Who will benefit? Why is the government committed to such a scheme if it is not economically beneficial to the state and most fundamentally of all to its citizens? Yet why on earth would any private investor be investing in co-located hospitals if there were not substantial profits to be made?

What about equity? Does co-location not enshrine an unequal provision of care in Irish hospitals with private patients being treated in one, more luxurious, better resourced hospital and the public patients treated in the neighbouring, under-resourced, already over-pressurised public hospitals? Will it result in an American-style system where the better trained, more ambitious doctors work in the private system, who will provide care for the better off in society and leave the public system to care for the rest? Will the co-location project actually happen? In early 2009, these questions remain unanswered.

What is clear is that private for-profit care has been firmly incorporated in to Irish health through McCreevy's changes to the Finance Act in 2001 and 2002 and copper-fastened during Mary Harney's tenure in health from 2004 onwards. It is a product of the neo-liberal philosophy promulgated by the PDs but happily adopted by Fianna Fáil during their time in office since 1997.

Given the collapse of financial capitalism in 2009, it will be interesting to see what happens in the private for-profit healthcare market. Will it increasingly fill the profitable cracks of a crippled public health system? Or will it be regarded with scepticism that the free markets deserve in 2009, leaving the way for a more effective, high quality public health system?

Chapter 7

Public health – the missing link in Irish health policy

The importance and value of the health of the Irish people has never really permeated the public or political psyche. Unlike in Britain or continental Europe where public health was a driver of many key public policy developments, policies which support people's health and well being have always remained far down the political agenda in Ireland. Michéal Martin's smoking ban was a complete exception to the rule and it is a perfect exemplar of how a single policy change can protect health and change behaviour. Footage of party political Ard Fheiseanna as recently as the 1980s, show tables of men sitting in front of full ashtrays with cigarettes hanging from their mouths. Now, in the majority of Irish households, it is unacceptable to have a cigarette indoors. So how do the Irish fare in terms of health (not sickness) status and how is it that we are global leaders on the smoking ban yet laggards when it comes to our public health infrastructure and public health policies?

Life expectancy

Life expectancy – how many years you can expect to live at birth – is one of the main indicators used to compare health and progress across the world's nations. Irish people born in the first decade of the twenty-first century can expect to live at least 30 years more than their ancestors born 100 years earlier.

In 1900, average life expectancy in Ireland was 48 years. In 2009, it is over 79 years.

In 2006, life expectancy at birth was 81.6 years for Irish women and 76.8 years for men[1]. The age advantage for women is consistent globally, with women usually living longer than men, although the reason for longer women's lives is not understood.

Increased life expectancy over the past 100 years has come about because of a combination of factors, including economic prosperity, improved housing, sanitation and nutrition, combined with better medical care. One of the most important factors influencing our longer lives is the dramatic decrease in infant mortality rates. Enhanced standards of living, and, in particular, better sanitation and housing have resulted in a decrease of infectious diseases. The major killers today are cancer and heart disease.

For most of the twentieth century, populations lived longer across the globe. However, in the last two decades of the twentieth century, some developing world countries saw a reversal of progress made with many countries experiencing a deterioration in life expectancy, mainly due to the prevalence of HIV/AIDS and associated diseases like tuberculosis and malaria. At the time of writing in 2008, Zimbabwe had the lowest life expectancy in the world with women born there expected to live to just 34 years and men 37 years. Iraq and Afghanistan also fare particularly badly, both seeing a significant drop in their life expectancy figures since 1990, with life expectancy for men in Afghanistan at 42 and in Iraq at 48 in 2008.[2]

Yet, despite Ireland's record economic development in the past decade, Ireland still lags behind many of our European neighbours in terms of life expectancy. Of 33 European countries assessed in Eurostat statistics for the most recent year available (2006), Irish female life expectancy is ranked at number 16, while Irish male life expectancy was twelfth from the top.[3] Globally, Ireland ranks twenty-ninth in life expectancy, although we were the tenth richest country in world when assessed by income per head in 2008.

Diseases of the circulatory system, such as heart disease, strokes and other circulatory diseases, are the main cause of death in Ireland making up just over one-third (36 per cent) of all deaths. Cancer is the second major cause of death, responsible for 28 per cent of deaths, while injuries and poisonings including suicide and road traffic collisions account for five per cent of deaths. Young men are most likely to die from suicide and road traffic deaths. Between 1997 and 2008, road traffic deaths declined by 40 per cent, going down from 447 to 279 per annum.

Suicide levels which saw significant increases in the 1980s and 1990s levelled off in the first five years of the twenty-first century, overtaking road traffic fatalities as the major cause of deaths for young males aged between 15 and 24 years of age. Between 1997 and 2006, there was a 14.5 per cent decrease in suicides in Ireland. In 2006, there were 409 suicide deaths. The increase in suicide numbers in the 1980s and 1990s is attributed to more accurate reporting, an agreed definition of suicide and less stigma being associated with suicide deaths.

Ireland's population

Ireland has a healthier population today than at any other time in its history, and, like most developed countries, the Irish population is also growing older. From the Great Famine in the 1840s, Ireland's population declined. This decline continued right up to the 1960s, with low birth rates and high levels of emigration. In 1841, the population of the area of what is now the Republic of Ireland was 6.5 million. It had dropped to three million by the 1920s and reached an all-time low in 1961, with a population of 2.8 million.[3] Since the 1960s, Ireland's population has grown consistently apart from a slight decline witnessed in the late 1980s.

The numbers of births, deaths and levels of inward and outward migration determine population. There was a high percentage increase in our population between 1997 and 2006, with an unprecedented increase of 15.7 per cent during this decade. This is mostly due to a dramatic decrease in emigration, significant increases in inward migration, alongside more births and fewer deaths. In 2007 and 2008, there were approximately 40,000 more births than deaths in Ireland, which is an exceptionally high natural increase in the population. In 2007, there were over 70,000 births registered, in 2008, over 73,000, way above even the most optimistic of population projections.

Ireland, like all other developed countries, has experienced a decline in fertility rates, though rates here are still above the EU average (a rate of 1.9 births per 1,000 births compared to an EU average of 1.45 births per 1,000 births in 2005). In 2005, Ireland had the second highest fertility rates of 27 European countries. With advances in medicine, people are living longer. However, we are still behind the European trend, in 2006, 450,000 people (11 per cent of the Irish population) were aged 65 and over. By 2016, this will be over 600,000 people and by 2036, the figure will be well over one million.[4] In 2006, 17 per cent of the European population was over 65 years of age. As Ireland is behind its European neighbours in the ageing trend, there is time to plan for the healthcare needs of the older population, which will double over the next 30 years.

Health status

Despite the poorer health status and lower life expectancy of Irish people when compared with many other European countries, Irish men and women both assess their health as good or very good, when asked in surveys.

Ireland comes out top of the league of countries that participate in this self-perception survey (EU SILC) with 85 per cent of the population rating themselves as in 'good' or 'very good' health.[5] However, the same survey also shows high levels of chronic illness and limited activity strongly related to ageing, somewhat contrary to people's perceived health status. Irish participants have a tendency to rate themselves high or perhaps to overrate themselves on other perception surveys, e.g. Irish people also rate amongst the highest on happiness and quality of life surveys.

The same survey in 2005, found that 22 per cent of all males and 25 per cent of all females in Ireland were living with a chronic illness or condition, while 18 per cent of men said their activities were limited due to health problems, the corresponding figure for women is 21 per cent.[6] So while Irish women live on average five years longer than men, they carry a disproportionate burden of ill health throughout their lives.

In terms of lifestyle behaviours, Irish people are more aware of the impact of lifestyle behaviours on their health, with people making substantial efforts to change their health behaviour. Breastfeeding which is known to have positive health impacts for both mother and child increased from a rate of 32 per cent in 2002, to 42 per cent in 2007 but still remains low compared with other continental European countries.[7] The number of people participating in moderate and/or strenuous exercise three or more times per week was up slightly from 38 per cent in 1998 to 41 per cent in 2007. The percentage of people eating four or more servings of fruit and vegetables per day has increased from 56 per cent in 1998 to 77 per cent in 2007. However, there are fewer people eating the recommended daily servings of cereals, breads, potatoes, milk, cheese and yoghurt products.

The numbers of people overweight has increased from 31 per cent in 1998 to 36 per cent in 2007, while the numbers of those who are clinically obese is also up slightly. In 1998, 11 per cent of SLAN respondents assessed themselves as clinically obese, while in 2007 it was 14 per cent. However, a subset of the survey respondents who were independently measured for height and weight found that 25 per cent of them were clinically obese and 39 per cent of them were over-weight. This figure is in line with international trends.

Rates of smoking decreased between 1998 and 2002 from 33 per cent to 27 per cent of the population, however figures went up to 29 per cent in 2007. In 2005, almost one in four of the population over 16 smoked, with smoking being most common among lone-parent households (54 per cent), the unemployed (49 per cent) and the ill or disabled (38 per cent).[8] The average number of alcoholic drinks consumed per week has dropped from eleven in 1998 to seven in 2007, while the percentage consuming six or more drinks per week decreased from 45 per cent in 2002 to 28 per cent in 2007. However, Irish people's consumption of alcohol is well above the European average, with Ireland consuming over ten litres of alcohol per person, per year, compared to the EU average of nine litres in 2005.[9]

While health-related behaviour is an important factor in influencing health, most of the determining factors are outside individuals' control.

Influencing health

Information and explanations on what causes good and bad health and what can be done to improve health is relatively underdeveloped in Ireland. However, there is a large body of international evidence on what determines people's health status.

The seminal work in England in the 1980s, in the form of

the Black Report, showed that there is an inherent link between social class, status and health.

Other work in Europe and from further a field has shown a range of factors that influence health, including: poverty, inequality and levels of income; living and working conditions; education and work opportunities; housing and environmental circumstances; access to clean water and sanitation; healthcare provision; food and nutrition; social networks and support; and individual factors, such as lifestyle, age, gender and hereditary factors.

So what determines individuals' health status is frequently the broader world in which they live, over which they may have little control. And while there is a good understanding that these factors influence health, the exact causal pathways showing how and when they actually do has yet to be determined, particularly in an Irish context.

There is also an increasing body of knowledge showing that early life and parental socio-economic position is particularly influential on health experience in later life, and with this has come an interest in health across the life course. Ireland's improved health status over the past 100 years, evident in longer lives and fewer infant deaths, can be partly explained by higher standards of living, better living conditions and sanitation, and access to improved medical care. However, significant inequalities exist between different sections of the population and between Ireland and our European neighbours.

Inequalities in health status

Inequality in death

The most glaring inequalities that exist in Ireland are the unhealthy lives and early deaths experienced by poorer people. In Ireland, as across the world, poorer people get sick more often and die younger.

In 2000, the Institute of Public Health in Ireland published an influential report on health inequalities on the island of Ireland. This assessed the mortality rates for different social groups across the island of Ireland over a ten-year period from 1989 to 1998. The key finding of the mortality report was that 5,400 people die prematurely every year on the island of Ireland due to inequality and poverty. The research found that the mortality rate in the lowest occupational class is 100–200 per cent higher than the rate for highest occupational class, i.e. people in the lowest class are twice as likely to die prematurely than people from the highest class.[10]

For respiratory diseases the death rate was 200 per cent higher for those with the lowest incomes, for injuries and poisonings (which includes road deaths and suicides) the rate was 150 per cent higher, for circulatory diseases it was 120 per cent higher, while for cancer it was 100 per cent higher. While there have been improvements in rates of cancer diagnosis and survival for the whole population, people in lower socio-economic groups have higher rates of cancer and poorer cancer survival rates when compared to higher socio-economic groups. The mortality rate for road traffic deaths is 354 per cent higher in the lowest occupation groups than in the highest, while the comparative figures for homicide is 225 per cent.

This report also compared mortality rates on the island of Ireland with rates in the EU 15 and found that for the same period, the Irish rate was 21 per cent higher for females and nine per cent higher for males than their European neighbours. Irish cancer survival in 2008 is still 10 per cent below our European neighbours.

Poverty and health

In 2006, there were 720,774 people (17 per cent of the population) in Ireland living in relative income poverty.[11] Relative income poverty is defined as people living on 60 per cent of national median income. In 2006, 60 per cent of the median income was €202.49 per week for a single person. For a family with two adults and two children, it was €469.77 per week.[12]

Some groups of the population are particularly at risk of relative income poverty, these include those who are unemployed, ill or disabled, lone parents and children in households where the head of the household belongs to one of these categories.

Irish people are amongst the most at risk of poverty when compared to the 27 EU countries. Only in Spain, Greece, Poland and Lithuania were more people at risk of poverty than Ireland in 2006. Ireland was one per cent more at risk than the UK, six per cent more than Germany and ten per cent more than Sweden, which has the lowest risk of poverty in the EU.[13]

The rate of consistent poverty in 2006 (the most recent year for which data was available at the time of writing) was 6.5 per cent, representing 290,000 people, a reduction from 8.2 per cent in 2003. Consistent poverty is the official government measurement used which combines those with 60 per cent of average median income with a range of deprivation measures. The deprivation indicators include not having a warm winter coat, two strong pairs of shoes, a roast once a week, an adequately warm home, an evening out once a month.[14]

Those 'at risk of poverty' in Ireland declined from 21.9 per cent in 2001 to 17 per cent in 2006. However, the 'at risk of poverty' rate is still more than it was in 1994, when it was 15.6 per cent. There was a significant reduction in the 'at risk of poverty' level for older people from 20.1 per cent in 2005 in 13.6 per cent in 2006, mainly due to large increases in the state pension scheme. Lone parents continue to be a high-risk group. Results show that 27.3 per cent of lone-parent households were in consistent poverty in 2006, compared to 26.9 per cent in

2005. Income poverty persisted amongst lone parents with 39.6 per cent of them 'at risk of poverty' in 2006, compared to 40.7 per cent in 2005 and 49.3 per cent in 2003.

There was a slight decrease in the consistent poverty rate for children, from 10.2 per cent in 2005 to 9.8 per cent in 2006. The percentage of children 'at risk of poverty' fell by one per cent, from 21.2 per cent in 2005 to 20.2 per cent in 2006, leaving one in five children at risk of poverty. There was an increase in the 'at risk of poverty' rate for unemployed persons, from 40.6 per cent in 2005 to 44 per cent in 2006. The consistent poverty rate for this group slightly decreased from 23.7 per cent in 2005 to 22.0 per cent in 2006. In the 2006 survey of poverty and living standards, non-Irish nationals were experiencing a significantly higher 'at risk of poverty' rate at 23.5 per cent compared to Irish nationals at 16.6 per cent. Non-Irish nationals also experienced a higher consistent poverty rate at 8.5 per cent compared to Irish nationals at 6.4 per cent. For people who are at work, both the 'at risk of poverty' rate and the consistent poverty rate is further reduced.[15]

People with a chronic illness or health problems are significantly more at risk of poverty than their healthier counterparts. Over one-third of people at risk of poverty (38 per cent) and almost half (47 per cent) those in consistent poverty report having a chronic illness compared to a quarter (24 per cent) of the whole population.

People without limiting health problems were significantly less likely to be at risk of poverty or in consistent poverty than those who had limiting health problems. Also, the higher a person's income, the more likely they are to report their health status as good or very good while the converse was also true – people who reported their health as bad or very bad had an average income of €14,000 per annum. Almost 34 per cent of people who reported their health as bad or very bad were at risk of poverty and 17 per cent were in consistent poverty, figures significantly higher than the population as a whole.[16]

Inequality in mental health

People from economically deprived areas and those who live in poverty experience higher levels of mental ill health and have higher usage of mental health services than the population as a whole. There is a persistent link between poor mental health and indicators of social exclusion, such as low income, poor education and low social status.[17] In the national survey of lifestyle attitudes and behaviour (SLÁN), 19.5 per cent of women surveyed reported they had been told by their doctor that they had difficulties with anxiety and depression, compared to 13.4 per cent of men.[18] Research carried out for the mental health strategy 'A Vision for Change' found that 70 per cent of people with mental illness were dependent on welfare payments or had no income.[19]

In Ireland the highest rates of admission to psychiatric hospitals are those from unskilled occupational class, while common mental disorders are twice as frequent among the lowest income groups compared with the highest.[20] Research shows that the rate of hospitalisation for mental illness in the unskilled manual groups is six times higher than that for the highest professional group. Men in unskilled jobs are four times more likely to be admitted to hospital for schizophrenia than higher professional workers. The incidence of male suicide is higher among lower socio-economic groups as compared to higher groups.

International research shows that about half of all people who experience mental health problems are no longer affected by their illness after 18 months but those with lower socio-economic status, the long-term sick and the unemployed are more likely to be unwell after 18 months.[21]

Inequality in early life

Inequality in life starts in the womb. Infant mortality is another crude measure of the 'health' of a nation. The infant mortality rate represents the ratio of deaths of children under one year and the number of live births in a given year; the value is expressed per 1,000 live births. The progress made in medical care services is reflected in a decreasing infant mortality rate.

In 1900, there were 100 deaths per 1,000 births, in 2005 there were four deaths per 1,000 live births. Yet there are differences across social classes. There is also a higher rate of peri-natal mortality (children who die before six weeks old) in less well-off areas than those born in more advantaged areas.

Low birth weight is another good gauge of inequality and one that has been shown internationally to be a good indicator of life-long health. Women from unemployed socio-economic groups are more than twice as likely to have low birth weight babies than women from higher professional groups.[22] Children from disadvantaged areas are much more likely to have untreated dental problems and are more likely to have accidents in the home than those from better off families.

Groups who experience very severe health inequalities

Some groups in the population experience particularly extreme health inequalities. These include people who are poor and/or socially excluded. Often it is a combination of poverty, exclusion and discrimination which causes such acute inequality.

Travellers

Travellers are a nomadic Irish ethnic group. Irish Travellers are a people with a separate identity, culture and history, although they are as Irish as the majority population. Members of Traveller community live on average ten years less than settled people.

Travellers are younger than the population as a whole with two out of every five Travellers being aged less than 15 in 2006 compared with one in five for the whole population. Older Travellers (those aged 65 years and over) accounted for just 2.6 per cent of the total Traveller population compared with 11 per cent for the general population. Travellers have a higher birth rate and shorter life expectancy than the general population.[23]

Travellers' low income and poverty is compounded by poor quality accommodation. The First Progress Report of the Implementation of the Task Force on the Travelling Community (2001) concluded 'one in every four Traveller families are currently living without access to water, toilets and refuse collection. The accommodation provision has not kept pace with increasing demand over the past five years'. In 2004, there were 788 Traveller families living on the side of the road with no hot water, electricity or sanitation and another 323 families sharing very basic facilities, while 352 families were living in emergency or temporary facilities.[24] There is no evidence that accommodation for Travellers has improved significantly since 2001 or 2004.

The persistence and range of chronic and long-term illnesses amongst Travellers is directly related to living conditions and exclusion from service provision.[25] Rates of Sudden Infant Death among the Traveller community over a five-year period were 12 times the rate of the settled population. Travellers, particularly those living in unofficial roadside sites, are at least eight times more likely to live in overcrowded conditions with limited access to water, sanitation and electricity, than the settled population.

Refugees, asylum seekers and undocumented migrant workers

Ethnic minorities are more likely to experience poverty and health inequalities than the non-ethnic population. Recent analysis of EU SILC data shows that non-Irish nationals are twice as likely to be in consistent poverty as Irish nationals.[26] Low-paid and undocumented migrant workers, refugees and asylum seekers are most likely to experience poverty and social exclusion. This combined with discrimination and racism can result in multiple discrimination and hinder integration into society. In February 2007, there were over 7,000 refugees living in Ireland with 5,711 asylum seekers awaiting a decision on their status. Of these, 5,210 were living in 'direct provision'. Under the 'direct provision' scheme, asylum seekers are accommodated in shared hostel-type centres, on a full-board arrangement.

Research carried out on asylum seekers, especially those living in 'direct provision', has shown poor levels of health and higher levels of stress amongst them. When an asylum seeker arrives in Ireland, he or she is put up in a reception centre before being 'dispersed' to an accommodation centre, usually outside of Dublin. In these centres, asylum seekers have full board provided, including their meals, and are given €19.10 per week to live on, €9.60 for a child. They are not allowed to work. Asylum seekers can be left to live in accommodation centres for a long time. At the end of February 2006, nearly 2,000 asylum seekers had been living in centres for more than 18 months. Prolonged lengths of stay in such accommodation have a negative impact on overall well being. Denial of the right to work also further compounds poor mental health through boredom, isolation, loss of self-esteem and poverty.

It is estimated that between 10 per cent and 35 per cent of those seeking refuge in Europe have experienced torture.[27] It is accepted that asylum seekers and refugees may suffer a disproportionate burden of mental ill health. This may be exacerbated post arrival in a country.[28] This poor mental health is experienced by children as well as adults, especially children and young adults who have been separated from their parents.

Research carried out in the northwest on the impact of 'direct provision' policy in health, found residents living in accommodation centres experiencing food poverty.

Expectant mothers living in 'direct provision' have been found to be malnourished, children are underweight and babies experience poor health related to poor diet. Adults were found to be going hungry to provide for their children. The general lack of privacy in residential centres has a negative effect on the mental health of asylum-seekers, while the lack of appropriate space for children to do homework and play hinders the development of the child.[29]

Refugees have significantly more rights and entitlements than asylum seekers, yet small-scale research shows similar health experiences between the two groups. Many of the traumas of being an asylum seeker may have lasting impacts on refugees' health and well being. This combined with fraught family reunification processes can accentuate existing stresses in their lives.

It is unknown how many undocumented migrant workers are living in Ireland but their irregular migrant status means they are particularly vulnerable. In particular, they are victims of low pay, unregulated work, substandard and overcrowded living and working conditions. That undocumented migrants are not entitled to medical services, except in emergency situations, further increases their vulnerability.[30]

Prisoners

Prisoners, by the nature of their living conditions, have significantly poorer health status than the rest of the population. Often confined to their cells for up to 23 hours a day, their small, cramped environment without daylight and exercise, impacts on their health. The majority of prisoners are addicted to substances and the vast majority of them suffer from mental illness and distress.

A 1996 study in Mountjoy prison found that one in two prisoners had received psychiatric treatment. One-third of women reported they had attempted suicide. Subsequent research carried out with prisoners in 2003 found over 20 per cent had a mental illness of some kind, while the rate for women was 30 per cent. It also found that between 61 per cent and 79 per cent were alcohol or drug dependent and the majority of prisoners with a mental illness also had drug and alcohol problems.[31]

A national survey of male prisoners in the year 2000 across 13 prisons in the state found that prisoners had high levels of ill health, including chronic activity-limiting illness, anxiety, depression and poor mental health.[32] Those with poorer mental health had lower educational status, are more likely to smoke and to have taken drugs. The study confirmed lower socio-economic status, high levels of ill health and adverse lifestyles among prisoners. It also found that prisoners who are subjected to verbal abuse or to be serving time for a more serious offence had poorer health.[33]

Homeless people

A health profile of homeless people in 2005 found that 90 per cent of homeless people had health complaints. Given their lack of appropriate shelter and safety, this is hardly surprising. Almost half of those profiled reported having a psychiatric problem. The majority said they had problems with alcohol and drugs.

Research carried out by the Simon Community in Ireland found that 55 people who used their services in 2006 met 'an untimely death'. The average age of those who died was 42, compared to the national average of 78. A significant proportion of these would be sleeping rough and are most at risk in terms of poor health, safety and early death.

Homeless people have an unacceptably high risk for preventative diseases, progressive morbidity and premature death. Research shows that persons who are homeless experience much higher rates of Hepatitis-C, HIV, TB, poor nutrition and drug and alcohol addiction than the general population.

Drug users

Alcohol is the most damaging drug of choice amongst Irish people. It is estimated that between 1999 and 2002, over 14,000 people died prematurely from the five leading alcohol-related causes of deaths. Alcohol is a greater risk factor in the lives of younger people with one in four deaths of young men in Europe aged between 15 and 29 years being alcohol related, the majority of which result from intentional and unintentional injuries. For young men, alcohol contributes to nearly half of all deaths from motor accidents, over one-third from poisoning, drowning, murder and falls, and one-fifth of suicides. Alcohol is a factor in 46 per cent of male attempted suicides and 38 per cent of female suicides. Alcohol is involved in 40 per cent of road deaths each year.[34]

Irish adults consume more alcohol, have higher levels of binge drinking and experience more alcohol-related harm than other Europeans. It is estimated that the alcohol-related cost imposed on Irish society was €2.65 billion in 2003.[35]

Illegal drug use also causes significant harm in Ireland. It is estimated that there are 13,500 heroin users in Ireland of whom 9,000 are on methadone treatment.[36] Heroin users usually come from disadvantaged neighbourhoods, with high levels of poverty and low educational achievement.

Health across the life course

Since 2001, a Lifeways Cross-Generation Cohort Study has been in place. This is the first such study in Ireland and it traces people's health and social status over time. Internationally, cohort studies are central to informing policy to improve health and reduce social and economic inequalities. For example, in the USA, cohort studies that started in the 1970s showed the positive impact of early intervention programmes, such as Headstart, on the life-long chances of disadvantaged children and led to their extended provision, a model that was copied in the UK under the programme name Surestart.

The Lifeways study reinforces international findings and the Irish inequalities in mortality data stating, 'the work has established beyond reasonable doubt ... that health variations do exist in modern Ireland ...'.[37] It finds the eligibility for a medical card (the poorest 30 per cent of the population) in Ireland is the most consistent predictor of poor health status.

It also finds 'the graduated pattern seen in other countries is true to Ireland too, from richest to poorest. Nonetheless and especially in urbanised areas, pockets of real disadvantage can be seen, suggesting special policy efforts must be made to reach the most disadvantaged'.[38]

This research discusses the difficulty of understanding the direction of the influences but states that 'it is clear that social position influences health and well being'.

Lifeways which began with a group of expectant mothers found that 'there was a strong, significant educational gradient: mothers with the lowest education had the worst health'.[39] Medical card eligibility, household income, marital status and maternal parental education each independently predict self-rated health. Women who work outside the home, and older women reported best health, while younger women and lone parents had poorer health.[40]

The research found that 76 per cent of women took their recommended five fruit or vegetable a day but that this was strongly socially patterned, related positively to older mothers and levels of education. Those with medical cards were less likely to achieve recommended daily intakes of certain food groups. Less than half of those in the study had taken folic acid and, again, this was strongly socially patterned with higher income, older, more educated women most likely to be taking folic acid.[41]

Children from a socio-economically disadvantaged background were significantly more likely to have asthma. Higher maternal fruit and vegetable intake and oily fish consumption are associated with reducing the risk of children developing asthma, while those mothers who had a high spreadable-fat intake were more likely to have children with a higher risk of asthma.[42]

Other analyses carried out by the UCD research programme have found that Irish people rated themselves highest in Europe in the self-rated health status measurement in 2002 and 2005. Further analysis of this data showed that there is a marked social gradient in self-rated health with statistical significant associations between self-reported health and social and labour market factors at individual level, i.e. those who reported better health were from higher socio-economic groups.[43] They also used the European Social Survey to determine the relationship between physical and psychological health, perceptions of the health service and voter turnout. This found that individuals who rated their health poorly were significantly less likely to vote in a general election. And dissatisfaction with the health service is also associated with a lower probability of voting. However, these effects interacted and those with poor health who were also dissatisfied with the health service were more likely to vote.

It found psychological well being had no effect on voter turnout. The research concludes that poor health is linked to low political participation and suggests that the perceived cost of voting for the unhealthy outweighs the perceived benefits of voting. The study shows that poor health leads to lower voter turnout, which suggests the interests of the unhealthy are less likely to be represented in government and that unhealthy non-voters are an untapped source of electoral support.[44]

Disadvantaged geographical communities

Some parts of the country experience much higher poverty rates and poorer health status than others. The highest poverty concentration can be identified by housing status. People living in local authority and private rented accommodation represent 60 per cent of all households experiencing poverty and deprivation, even though they are just 17 per cent of the population.[45] Some areas, predominantly urban areas, have particularly acute poverty clusters. Although, small area-based research is relatively underdeveloped in Ireland, there has been an increasing interest into looking at the health inequalities experienced by such local communities.

Fettercairn is a small housing area in West Tallaght, County Dublin. It was built in the 1980s, has 840 households, a population of 6,488 people the vast majority of whom live in local authority houses. It is an area occupied by low income families with a large population of young people, lone parents, Travellers and members of ethnic minority groups. It has no GP or health centre. It has very high proportion of adults who left school before the age of fifteen.

Research carried out in the wider Tallaght area by Trinity College researchers in 2001 found high levels of stress, smoking and chronic illness, with 40 per cent of household members smoking, 35 per cent consulting their GP about stress, 19 per cent being prescribed medication because of stress and with 54 per cent of pregnancies being unplanned.[46]

In 2006, the Fettercairn Community Health Project carried out a Participatory Rapid Appraisal to assess the health needs of the community. This found that residents of all ages experienced stress because of their low income, the dirty and dusty environment (they live next to a quarry), the boarded up houses in the area, the fragmented and isolated community in which they live and the lack of basic health services in the community. Some of the residents turned to alcohol and drugs to alleviate the stress they live with on a day-to-day basis. Young people from the area expressed concern over the high levels of drug abuse, early school leaving and the absence of jobs for people from the local area. The older people are lonely and isolated, and find the inaccessibility of shops and public services contributes to their poor quality of life. There is a high level of anti-social behaviour in the community, with many burned out and shuttered up vacant houses, and a lot of litter.

Residents feel the dust in the area from the local quarry may be a contributing factor to high levels of chest and breathing problems experienced by residents. This results in frequent visits to the GP which are costly for those who do not have medical cards. The estate is poorly managed and maintained and inadequately serviced by public transport. There is little faith in the Gardaí because of the length of time they take to respond and the failure to follow up or address issues of local concern. Residents have a vision of a healthy and safe community, with clean streets, well-maintained houses and gardens, and the absence of crime and anti-social behaviour. The community's priority is to secure an effective primary care team for the area, preferably in a local health centre.[47]

At the launch of the Fettercairn Report in September 2007, the local HSE manager made it clear that there would not be a primary care centre in Fettercairn and that, for years, they had failed to attract a GP to the area and were unlikely to do so in the future.

The experience of Fettercairn is not unique. There are many urban communities in Ireland in most of the larger cities and towns that experience similar or greater inequalities to those found in West Tallaght. Some rural areas also experience high levels of deprivation and health inequalities, although the causes of the inequalities may differ.

Fuel poverty

The island of Ireland has one of the highest rates of excess winter mortality in Europe with an estimated 2,800 excess deaths on the island over winter months.[48] There are strong links between low income, unemployment and fuel poverty – and fuel poverty is known to have direct and indirect impacts on health. Fuel poverty is highest among lone parents and older people. Certain households, like those with young children and people with a disability and/or a life-long illness are more vulnerable to fuel poverty.

Increases in fuel prices like those experienced in Ireland in 2007 and 2008 have resulted in more households finding themselves in fuel poverty, which means living in cold, damp houses that are not efficient at processing and keeping in the heat. Fuel poverty is defined as households who spend more than ten per cent of their income on energy in order to keep an acceptable level of heat in their home.

The risk of fuel poverty rises when incomes falls below €30,000 per annum. In the twelve months up to May 2008, the cost of home heating oil went up in Ireland by 47 per cent. By early 2009 fuel prices were beginning to decline. Fuel allowance did not change in Budget 2008, although it was extended by one week which in effect gave those eligible for it an extra 60 cents per week for the thirty weeks covered by the allowance. Fuel allowance only covers 24 per cent of a pensioner's fuel bill, thus fuel increases impact most on people on low income who are most likely to fall victim to excess winter mortality.

Psycho-social health

There is a growing body of knowledge about the imapct of 'psycho-social' factors on health. Stress, anxiety, low self-esteem, lack of control over occurrences in a person's day-to-day activity and insecurity all contribute to someone's psycho-social health.

People who are poor have more stresses in their life associated with trying to make ends meet on a low income. Social exclusion and low levels of social support also significantly impact on psycho-social factors. Psychological stress has negative consequences on both physical and psychological health. While the body can cope with short periods of stress, if it is experienced over protracted periods of time, it will impact on a person's physical health. International research shows that there is a social gradient in health, the higher a person is up the hierarchy of society, the better their health.[49]

The degree of isolation that a person experiences, the organisation of work and sense of control over their life affect the likelihood of developing and dying from chronic diseases, such as diabetes and cardiovascular disease.

Irish research has found that people living in poverty report higher levels of mental illness and stress; higher levels of 'fatalism' and lack of control over their circumstances, and lower levels of satisfaction with life than those who were better off.[50]

Rich and poor in Ireland

Ireland's immense economic growth since the late 1990s was also accompanied by escalating inequalities between rich and poor. And while many people benefited from our economic success, those who were left behind by it are now further behind. In 2008, over one million people in Ireland earned less than the average industrial wage. Figures from the Revenue Commissioners show that 1,038,700 PAYE workers earn less than €29,999.[51] About 136,000 workers earn more than

€80,000, and 25,000 earn more than €100,000. In 2006, there were 1.5 million workers earning less than the pay increase of €38,000 awarded to then Taoiseach Bertie Ahern.

Bank of Ireland's Wealth of the Nation report in July 2007 found that there were 33,000 millionaires in Ireland.[52] This report also found that the asset base, excluding residential property, of the top one per cent of the population was €86 billion. It found that one per cent of the population held 20 per cent of the country's wealth, the top two per cent held 30 per cent of the wealth, while the top five per cent had 40 per cent of the wealth. That means that 95 per cent of the population had 60 per cent of the wealth. If housing value was left out, the top one per cent held over 34 per cent of the wealth.

Other research carried out in 2008 found that 450 Irish people are each worth more than €10 million when their assets, apart from their family home, are taken into account. The 450 people collectively worth more than €67 billion were categorised as the 'new super rich'. It also estimates that the 100 richest people in Ireland are worth more than €100 million each. Just one per cent of this wealth was inherited, which is contrary to the global trend where 18 per cent of the super rich inherit their money. In Ireland, most of the super rich are self-made.[53] Of course, these figures pre-dated the market crash of 2008/9 but are demonstrable of the significant wealth gained during the Celtic Tiger years.

Poverty figures show there were 290,000 living in consistent poverty and 700,000 were living on less than 60 per cent the average income in 2005. There have been some measures to improve the living standards of the poorest in Ireland during the years of the Celtic Tiger through the introduction of the minimum wage and increased social welfare rates. However, neither social welfare rates nor the minimum wage kept apace with inflation or the income of higher earners.

Upon taking up office as the new Taoiseach of Ireland in

May 2008, Brian Cowen promised to care for those living on the margins of society. In a speech during his homecoming rally in Birr, County Offaly, Cowen said, 'If social inclusion was to be achieved then people would have to cherish community and reduce the tendency to self-interest and individualism'.[54]

Governments repeatedly and proudly remind the populous that Ireland is a low-tax regime and promise not to raise taxes. Even the Labour Party in the run-up to the 2007 general election proposed lowering taxes. Ireland's tax take is the lowest of all EU members, taking in just 29 per cent of GDP. In Britain, it is 35 per cent, the EU norm is 40 per cent. Yet, in 2005, the Department of Finance warned that tax breaks on property and other tax shelters were costing the exchequer €8.3 billion. Abolishing tax shelters on private hospitals and nursing homes could save €1.5 billion.

Increased pensions have lifted many older people out of relative and consistent poverty. Increasing social welfare rates for people with disabilities, lone parents and the unemployed would lift many more of these people out of poverty, and is one of the short-term more effective ways of impacting on health inequalities. The ESRI estimates that if every welfare payment was €230, it could halve the number of people at risk of poverty from 40 per cent to 20 per cent.[55]

In the mid-1980s, Ireland's gini coefficient (a standard measure of inequality) was 33.1, in the mid-1990s, it was 32.4 – the higher the number the more unequal the country. Therefore, there was a reduction in inequality between the mid-1980s and mid-1990s with a reduction in the gap between the richest and the poorest households. This trend continued until 2000 when Ireland's gini coefficient was 30.[56] By 2005, it had risen again to 32.

International comparative research shows that among developed countries it is not the richest societies that have better health, but those that have the smallest gap between the rich and the poor. Richard Wilkinson's work demonstrates that inequality and poverty increase death rates, that healthy, more equal societies are more socially cohesive. And that social cohesion is good for quality of life and health status. Wilkinson's research shows that more egalitarian, socially cohesive societies are good for everyone's health, not just the better off.[57]

So while Ireland has experienced a huge surge in its wealth at the turn of the twenty-first century, this has not translated into greater social cohesion. And the gini coefficient increased between 2000 and 2005 showing the opposite was happening, with greater wealth, there was also a greater gap between the richest and poorest.

Policies that can improve public health and reduce health inequalities

In Ireland, in 2009, the breadth of policies needed to improve public health and to achieve a reduction of health inequalities is just not on the policy or political landscape.

Ireland's health strategy had some of the rhetoric but little substantial commitment or targets to improve public health. 'Quality and Fairness' was a strategy primarily concerned with health services for the sick not the public's health. The Department of Health and the HSE are very much focused on the management of sickness services. The public health agenda has never got the political support required for it to be a policy driver. The public health infrastructure built up in the old health boards has been dismantled. When the HSE was founded public health had a national director and was one of the cross-cutting themes applicable to all the pillars and health and social care services. In the shake up of structures in the HSE that took place in 2008, public or population health, as it was called, was subsumed into the planning section. Apart from when there are crises in the public health arena, like the pollution of drinking water in Galway or outbreaks of legionnaires disease or MRSA, senior HSE public health officials are unheard of.

With a doctor in charge of the HSE who has worked all his life in hospitals, it is understandable, although unwise, for public health to be so far down the priorities of the health services. Effective public health policies are good for public health services because they keep people well and can reduce the ever-increasing demand on the public health system. Other public health issues are time bombs waiting to explode. Obesity, which is a growing public health concern with one-quarter of the population clinically obese in 2007, has the potential to overwhelm public health services. The causes of obesity lie mainly outside of the health system. Yet it is the health system that will have to deal with the impending epidemic. Likewise with smoking. And it is in this area that Ireland led the world by introducing a ban on workplace smoking.

The smoking ban

In March 2004, Ireland was the first country in the world to introduce a workplace smoking ban and it is for this measure more than any other that Micheál Martin is positively remembered during his tenure in the health ministry. It was a brave, public health measure that seemed impossible to implement in the run-up to its introduction. The hospitality sector, particularly pub owners, provided a fierce and vocal opposition to it. They said it was the end of the pub, the end of rural Ireland, the final nail in the coffin of personal freedom.

The smoking ban was decades in the making. Since the 1980s, there was growing evidence of the negative and detrimental impact of passive smoking on people's health, although this was ferociously denied by the tobacco industry. A diverse team of public health activists built up a body of knowledge based on the firm evidence showing the harmful impact of passive smoking on health. A range of Irish NGOs, public health doctors in the health boards and the Department of Health in co-operation with one senior civil servant in the Department of Health, and, subsequently, in the Office for Tobacco Control, Tom Power, led a successful policy and media campaign that resulted in the introduction of legislation to ban smoking in the workplace.

When Micheál Martin came into the Department of Health in 2000, he was open to persuasion that this was an issue to run with. It took longer to introduce than expected – and there were delays in its final implementation – but when it was finally introduced, despite all the fuss in the run-up to its introduction, it was very successful with 93 per cent compliance a year after implementation.

The smoke-free workplace is one of Ireland's major public health stories. It is estimated that about 160 bar workers lives are saved each year as a result of the ban,[58] not to mention the number of other bar drinkers' lives that are saved in the process. The measure changed behaviour overnight. Irish people now report standing outside bars and restaurants in countries where you are allowed to smoke. Many countries have followed suit. In fact, public health activists in Ireland have coined the phrase 'tobacco tourism' because of the number of international experts who come to Ireland to check out what was once considered an impossibility – a smoke-free Irish pub.

The elements that made it happen were: a strong scientific, evidence base; a long and informed, although contentious, media debate; a broad range of activists and spokespeople from a diverse range of sectors; strong political leadership and backup; and clear legislation.[59] It proved that vested interests, even the renowned tobacco lobby, could be won over. It showed that the public, even the Irish, could be persuaded to comply in the interest of public health. It demonstrated that clear leadership and legislation can have immense public health benefits. It has laid the way for other pioneering public health policy and legislation in Ireland.

Conclusion

Alas the smoking ban, albeit groundbreaking in its success, is a one-off for Ireland. The vast majority of policies that are implemented take no cognisance of their impact on health. Policies that promote good health and reduce health inequalities are consistently recommended by a range of organisations working in the public health and social justice field. These recommendations include the fairer redistribution of wealth and resources, better public service provision, the development of healthy, sustainable policies, which are good for the environment and good for people's health. However, such proposals are, in the main, largely ignored.

During a decade of booming economic and neo-liberal politics, of high spend and low tax, good health and a reduction of health inequalities was on the very edge of the policy and political scene. Perhaps in more turbulent economic times, post-2008, the public health agenda will be reawakened.

Chapter 8

Ignored yet essential: primary, community and continuing care services in Ireland

Although the vast majority of factors that improve people's health lie outside the health system, within the health system the vast majority of the population's healthcare needs can be met outside of the hospital system.

Good quality primary, community and continuing care services can prevent many people going to hospital in the first place and can ensure shorter stays for patients who need hospital care. As detailed in many parts of this book, many of the difficulties inside the hospital system are the result of shortages and inadequacies in the wider health system.

Primary care is usually the first point of contact for most people with the health services, and according to the WHO, 90–95 per cent of health needs can be met by primary care services.

Traditionally, primary care services in Ireland have been centred around GP services. As GPs operate as private providers and sole traders, their location and development has happened in an ad hoc manner, not always meeting the needs of local communities, particularly the most disadvantaged communities who may need them most. Healthcare budgets have always prioritised hospital care over community and continuing care budgets. In the past decade, there has been significant increased investment in staffing and the development of primary, community and continuing care most evident in increased budgets in services for older people, people with disabilities and children. But the increase was, and remains in 2008, insufficient to adequately ease the burden on the hospital system and to meet the demands of a rising and ageing population.

Primary care is the medical care a patient usually receives on first contact with the healthcare system, before referral elsewhere. It is an approach to care that includes a range of services designed to keep people well, from health promotion and screening of diseases to assessment, diagnosis, treatment and rehabilitation as well as personal social services. In Ireland, professionals in primary care, usually GPs, act as a gateway to many specialist and ancillary health and social care services.

Secondary care is a service provided by medical specialists who generally are hospital based. Community and continuing care services are those that are provided to keep people well or manage their health and well being in their own home and community. They include public health nursing, physiotherapy, social work services, family support, services delivered in local health clinics, the diagnosis and management of chronic diseases, ongoing care of older people and people with disabilities.

Although primary, community and continuing care provide the majority of health and social care services, there has been no effective policy dealing with and co-ordinating all of these services. While they are included in the health strategy, and a Primary Care Strategy was published immediately after its publication in 2001, services for the majority of community and continuing care are still delivered in a fragmented and disjointed manner. For example the diagnosis and management of chronic diseases are each dealt with by disease, while many other issues are dealt with by target group, e.g. children, older people, people with disabilities, despite the fact that there are obvious overlaps between conditions and groups.

The Primary Care Strategy

In 2001, within a week of the publication of the health strategy, the 'Primary Care: A New Direction' was published. This detailed a plan for extending primary care services across the country. An objective of the Primary Care Strategy was to ensure more direct links to specialist services and the seamless provision of health and social care services between the home, community and hospital.

The Primary Care Strategy outlined a blue print for comprehensive primary care services in Ireland. 'Primary Care: A New Direction' acknowledged that, up to 2001, Ireland's primary care infrastructure was poorly developed, services were fragmented, that there was limited teamwork and limited access to many health professionals.[1] It stated that there is a focus on treatment at the expense of a more balanced emphasis on prevention, health promotion and well being. The strategy detailed how communication between primary and secondary care can be poor or non-existent, how many services currently provided in acute hospitals could take place in the primary care setting and how accessing primary care services out-of-hours can be difficult and sometimes impossible.

The strategy proposed a new model of primary care that would involve the introduction of an inter-disciplinary team working in primary care provision. Members of the primary care team (PCTs) would include GPs, nurses/midwives, healthcare assistants, home helps, physiotherapists, occupational therapists, social workers and administrative personnel. The plan was also for a wider primary care network, which would be made up of other primary care professionals, such as speech and language therapists, community pharmacists, dieticians, community-welfare officers, dentists, chiropodists and psychologists. Each PCT would provide services to a population of approximately 7,000 to 15,000 people.[2] The strategy involved the recruitment of significant numbers of extra staff, but also the construction or alteration of buildings where these staff could work together to provide a new form of integrated, comprehensive primary care. The Prospectus and Hanly reports published in 2003 had also endorsed this shift from acute care to primary care.

Critically, though, the Primary Care Strategy did not commit to changing the accessibility of primary care, whereby everyone except medical card holders pay out of pocket to see their GP. On announcing the plan, Micheál Martin committed to extending medical card eligibility. However, this did not happen in 2003 or 2004 at which point the health budget, although continuing to grow, was curtailed.

Eight years after its publication, progress has been extremely slow in achieving the ambitious commitments for primary care heralded in 2001. The required budget to build up the infrastructure and staff the teams was not made available. Primary care teams have not materialised in most parts of the country and many central services, like public health nursing, and other ancillary services, like speech and language therapists, counselling and occupational therapists, have been over burdened, under-resourced and often remain disconnected from GP services.

In 2003, ten pilot Primary Care Teams were established but little else happened in the subsequent years to progress the realisation of the Primary Care Strategy. When the HSE was set up in January 2005, there were three central pillars to service provision, one of them was the Primary, Community and Continuing Care section. In 2006, under the leadership of newly appointed HSE CEO, Brendan Drumm, the 2007–2010 Transformation Programme was published, detailing six transformation priorities. One of the six priorities was 'to configure primary, community and continuing care services so that they deliver optimal and cost effective results'.[3]

Drumm brought a renewed effort to rolling out the primary care strategy, and shifting the public and political debate away from hospital care towards primary, community and continuing care. A range of detailed reports published in 2007 and 2008 show the numbers of patients who need not have entered hospitals in the first place and who were staying there unnecessarily because of the absence of services at primary, community and continuing care levels.[4] Drumm controversially challenges the supposition that there is a need for more hospital beds. He firmly articulates the view that if primary, community and continuing care services were comprehensive, fewer hospitals beds would be required.

The Primary Care Strategy promised 600 new primary care teams across the country. The 2006 social partnership agreement 'Towards 2016' renewed this commitment promising 'ongoing investment to ensure integrated, accessible services for people within their own community with a target of 300 primary care teams by 2008, 400 by 2009 and 500 by 2011. These targets will be reviewed in 2008 and out-of-hours GP services are to be developed as a priority'.[5]

This author has made frequent requests to the HSE in relation to the numbers of primary care teams up and running. Any responses obtained, and they are hard to get, contain different and inconsistent numbers, often contradictory to previous responses or public statements made by ministers and HSE management. There is no detail on the HSE website about how many teams are fully functioning or where they are. The most accurate information is often obtained from other sources outside of the HSE, such as Oireachtas Health Committee minutes, responses to Dáil Questions or the Comptroller and Auditor General's Annual Report.

According to the annual report of the Comptroller and Auditor General published in September 2008, 'by the end of December 2007, there were forty PCTs in development, including the original ten pilot teams. The target set for 2008 is to have 97 PCTs operational and to progress the development of a further 100 PCTs. The eventual aim is to have a total of 530 PCTs'.[6]

In May 2008, the HSE said 87 teams (not the 300 promised in 'Towards 2016') were fully operational. An RTÉ *Primetime Investigates* programme on the HSE aired in May 2008 found that just 16 per cent of these 87 teams were fully operational.[7] Communication with the author from the HSE press office on 3 October 2008 stated, 'the development of 87 [PCTs] were progressed in 2006–07 and an additional 113 teams are being developed in 2008. All of these teams are at varying stages of development with a total of 80 teams at fully functioning stage, i.e. holding clinical team meetings. As per the HSE Service Plan, the target set for 2008 is to have 97 teams at fully functioning stage by year end. As 80 teams are up currently at this stage, the HSE are confident that this target will be met'.[8]

In January 2009, HSE director responsible for primary care, Laverne McGuiness told the Oireachtas Dáil committee on health that by the end of December 2008, there were 93 teams in place. The target for the end of 2009 is to have 210 teams fully operating. The overall aim is to have a total of 530 primary care teams.

No matter which figures are believed, it is incontrovertible that, by the end of 2008, just a handful of primary care teams as envisaged in the Primary Care Strategy and in the Social Partnership Agreement were in place.

Currently, many of these professionals imagined as part of a team operate independently or under different line management. For example, GPs are independent contractors, whereas public health nurses, speech and language therapists and community welfare officers work out of completely separate service sections within the HSE. Co-ordination of these varied professions is a complicated management task, of which the details have never been worked out.

In reality, most people have access to a GP who may work with another GP and a practice nurse. So far only the pilot teams and a handful of other practices have such a comprehensive range of services attached to their practices. Also there are complications in relation to such new primary care teams as detailed in the strategy. While GPs are, in principle, available to all, those who have medical cards have free access, while those who don't, pay privately. However, other members of the primary care team are generally part of the HSE staff and are not automatically accessible to people without medical cards. Even if someone wants to buy such a service privately, e.g. occupational therapy, the services are not easily found in the private sector or if they are, they are independent of the primary care teams.

There are also variations across the country concerning whether or not allied professionals' services, working as part of primary care teams, are free. Some places charge for such services, others do not. The Department of Health has been reviewing eligibility for years. By February 2009, there was no outcome to the review. Speaking on RTÉ on 27 September 2008, Brendan Drumm said that uniformity would be introduced across the country based on the recommendations of the eligibility review.[9] No doubt, this will result in user charges for such ancillary care for everyone except those with medical cards.

According to the Primary Care Strategy, all individuals will be encouraged to sign up to a primary care team, and with a particular GP within the team. Enrolment will be voluntary. The Irish College of General Practitioners (ICGP) has called for compulsory registration with PCTs. Attending a proper primary care unit should involve an entire range of integrated services delivered by doctors, nurses, physiotherapists, etc. Another hugely important factor is location. As GPs are totally independent contractors, they can open a surgery wherever they want. Since the introduction of medical cards for all those over 70 in 2001, there has been an increased incentive for GPs to locate in areas where there is a high proportion of richer over 70-year-olds, as doctors are paid four times the rate to look after this group than for the people who already had a medical before the extension to all those over 70. Areas of south Dublin and Wicklow were known as the 'gold coast' because of the high numbers of richer older people living in those areas.

This combined with the absence of planning of the location of GPs for decades resulted in the absence of GPs in the areas most required. If, as planned in the Primary Care Strategy, the PCTs were operating out of buildings, developed by the HSE, then the planning and location of them is within the control of HSE planners. However, due to the lack of planning and resources, this largely has not happened. Instead, the private sector and GPs have been called upon to fill the gaps of public provision. As a result, there is no control over the numbers and location of so-called primary care centres.

Financing Primary Care

Central to more comprehensive primary care services and the implementation of the strategy is a sufficient budget. However, money allocated to primary care is still disproportionately low when compared to hospital care. Overall health spending in 2008 was €14.7 billion, the majority of which went directly towards HSE current spending. Of the €14.1 billion that comprises current HSE spend, €8.9 billion went under the heading of 'Primary, Community and Continuing Care (PCCC)', while €5.2 billion went to the National Hospitals Office.

A closer look at the PCCC spend shows that much of this is money that would normally be considered social spend, e.g.

care for older people (€1.8 billion), children and family services (€0.69 billion), or health and social care for specific groups, e.g. care for people with disabilities (€1.6 billion), and mental health services (€1.1 billion). There are two headings under the PCCC spend which include specific primary care services – Primary Care and Community Health (€1.9 billion) and Primary Care (Medical Card Services) Scheme (€1.7 billion). About €5 billion of the PCCC budget goes directly to primary care services as outlined in Primary Care Strategy, just one-third of HSE current spend.[10] Given that 90–95 per cent of health needs can be met through primary care, this proportional allocation to the primary care budget is very low.

The Primary Care Strategy costed its proposals at €1,270 million in capital investment and €615 million for annual costs of paying for teams' members and the operation of teams. This was based on 2001 pricing, estimating that each facility, i.e. newly built publicly funded, primary care centre would cost €2.5 million per facility.[11] This money never materialised. While a handful of publicly funded primary care centres have been built, the plan is for the majority of teams not to be housed in state-funded, purpose-built centres.

GP services in Ireland

GPs in Ireland are small, private, self-employed operators whose services are contracted by the HSE. In 2005, 35 per cent of GPs operated in single-handed practices, while the remainder worked in joint partnerships or as part of GP co-operatives. In 2008, many GPs are nearing retirement and there is a shortage of GPs alongside increasing numbers of women entering the profession. A survey of all graduates from GP training between 1997 and 2003 found that 70 per cent of them were female and that just 29 per cent of female GPs work full-time. It also found that twice as many males as females work at a senior partnership level in GP practices.[12] This survey revealed the changing face of Irish general practice with the majority of the GPs over 45 years of age being male and full-time workers, while the majority under 45 were female and worked part-time.

There has been a fall in the numbers of private-only practices but an increase in the numbers of GPs with private lists of over 2,000 patients. Although the numbers of GPs providing out-of-hours cover during the week and at weekends has dropped, 40 per cent of GPs participate in out-of-hours GP co-operatives.[13] Most GPs provide services for both private and medical card patients, with increasing provision of out-of-hours services.

Research carried out by the Irish College of General Practitioners in 2008 found that 27 per cent of GPs had closed their lists because they just could not cope with any additional medical card patients. There were significant variations in the geographical distribution of closed lists with parts of Dublin being particularly hard hit. More than half of the 1,300 GPs surveyed planned to retire before 2020.[14] There was a shortage of GPs in Ireland in 2008, with an annual intake of students at just 121 places. A report commissioned by the Department of Health previously recommended that the numbers of training places increase to 150 per annum by 2008.[15] The shortage of places combined with the high numbers of older and retiring GPs will pose significant problems in realising the primary care and transformation strategies as outlined by the HSE. In Ireland in 2007, there were 0.47 GPs per 1,000 compared to an EU average of 1 per 1,000 and 1.64 per 1,000 in Austria.[16] To successfully implement the Primary Care Strategy, adequate numbers of GPs are required.

Accessing GP care

GPs set the fees charged to private patients who pay per visit, while the HSE reimburses GPs per patient per annum for medical card holders, with rates based on age, distance from GP, etc. As discussed in Chapter 2, approximately one-third of the population has a medical card, while the rest pay out of pocket each time they see their GP. 'Free' access to GP services for those with medical cards ensures access to the central aspect of primary care for those on lowest incomes and in greatest medical need. Eligibility has been based on income levels determined by a means test, since the General Medical Scheme was introduced in 1970.

However, in December 2000, then Minister for Finance Charlie McCreevy made a radical change to eligibility by introducing free GP care to all people over 70 years of age. Such extension of the medical card scheme was not mentioned in the health and primary care strategies that had just been published. The Minister for Health, Micheál Martin was informed of the decision just the night before the budget. The move which was introduced in July 2001 was purely a political ploy to get older people's votes in the 2002 election and to distract from other measures introduced in the budget.

The introduction of universal healthcare for those over 70 was significant. Firstly, it demonstrates how political choices often take precedence over policy and evidence-based decisions. Secondly, it shows that financial restrictions were not the reason for not extending medical cards to other groups, e.g. it had been long campaigned to extend medical cards to people on low income who had not previously qualified, to all people with disabilities, to all children under a certain age. The medical card was extended to those over 70 who were not necessarily those who needed it most. Before the 2001 budget, anybody, including those over 70, who was on a low-income qualified on that basis. The move turned out to be a costly measure as the IMO did a deal with the Department of Health that ensured that GPs got an annual capitation grant for treating the over seventies group that was over three times the rate of other medical card holders. In 2008, GPs got paid €641 for wealthier 70-year-olds, whereas the rate for people on low income, under or over 70 years, was €141. The deal further incentivised the treatment of older, richer patients over poorer younger ones, thereby further motivating doctors to provide services in traditionally well-catered for middle and upper-class communities rather than poorer rural or urban communities. Organisations and advocates of older people speak positively about the introduction of the medical card for all those over 70 as it enabled them to access care at the earliest possible opportunity, without having to worry about the cost implications.

Research carried out by the ESRI showed the provision of medical cards is an effective pro-poor measure for those who qualify for them. It found that people with chronic illnesses, women and older people visit their GP more often and that charging for medical care has a direct impact on utilisation, i.e. those who have medical cards are more likely to visit their GP and visit more often.[17]

Research shows that people in Northern Ireland, where GP care is free to every citizen, visit their GPs more often than people in the south. In Northern Ireland, there are 3.8 GP visits per person per annum. In Ireland there are 3.3 visits per person per annum. Medical card holders in Ireland average 5.8 visits per annum whereas non-medical cardholders visit 2.2 times per annum.[18] The higher number of visits can be explained by poorer health status and medical card holders as public patients have slower access to hospitals services and, therefore, may rely on their GP for more care. People also have medical cards because of their low income or older age and, therefore, have a higher demand for GP services.

In addition, the rules are different for private and public patients of GPs, for example, a GP can write a prescription for a private patient for six months but only for three months for a public patient, so the public patient will have to return more frequently for prescription renewal. Austin O'Carroll, a GP based in Dublin's north inner city, whose group practice provides care for the disadvantaged neighbourhood in which it is situated and in a particular for homeless and drug-using patients, estimates that ten per cent of visits to his practice by medical card holders are primarily for form filling. This happens because of the administrative system in place which requires medical card holders to fill out many other forms for assistance, such as clothing grants and carers' allowance. The forms require a GP's signature. The medical card is important for people on low incomes not just because it gets the holder free GP care and medicines but because it acts as a gateway to other important safety nets.

O'Carroll also firmly believes that despite GPs', including his own, best intentions medical card and fee paying patients are treated differently. Because medical card holders have free access to hospital services and GPs get a capitation grant for them, he believes GPs give medical card holders shorter consultations, may discourage repeat consultations and are more likely to refer them to secondary care at an earlier stage.[19] This bias of how public and private patients are treated has been well identified in the literature on incentives for payment and analysis of health service provision. Dale Tussing, a visiting American economist who did a stint in the ESRI warned in the 1980s against the dual system of payment.[20] And again, in 2005, Tussing and Wren give great detail on the negative effects of the perverse incentives, i.e. if a doctor is paid one way for one type of payment and another way for other types, and if one is more profitable, they are more likely to treat the profitable patients preferably.[21]

Analysis of the Survey of Income and Living Conditions carried out by Central Statistics Offices shows there are also significant numbers of people in poverty and at risk of poverty who are without medical cards. Data from 2005 showed that 47,400 people in consistent poverty were without medical cards while 228,500 people at risk of poverty were without medical cards.[22] Comparative North–South research found that, in Ireland, 18.9 per cent of patients with medical problems had not consulted a doctor because of cost, compared to 1.8 per cent in Northern Ireland.[23] Those who do not have medical cards may put off seeking needed medical care due to the associated cost.

Access is also influenced by location of GP surgeries and accessibility as perceived by service user, e.g. people on medical cards have reported difficulty getting on a GP's list, people in rural areas and deprived urban areas may not have a GP in the locality, while some specific groups, such as Travellers and asylum seekers, also report difficulty in getting on a GP's list. Nationally, there is one GP for every 1,600 people, the European average is one GP per 1,200, while in Dublin's north inner city there is one GP per 2,500 people.[24] Fettercairn, a suburb in south County Dublin has a population of 6,000 people and has no GP.[25] Research shows that more deprived neighbourhoods and communities have fewer GPs yet a higher demand for them. People from disadvantaged communities are more likely to request home visits from their GPs, request more out-of-hour calls and have a higher use of hospitals' emergency departments.[26]

Research carried out in O'Carroll's group practice in Dublin's north inner city found that changes introduced in 2001 resulted in many medical card holders being removed from the medical card list without prior knowledge. Previously, medical card eligibility was reviewed every five years, but, in 2001, it was changed to an annual review. A review of people removed from the medical card list over a two and a half year period found that 87 per cent were removed from the GP practice list because of the non-return of review forms, while 60 per cent of these said they never received a review form. Their removal from the list resulted in ten per cent of patients not accessing GP care because they could not afford to and 80 per cent paying out of pocket to see a GP during the time that they were off the list. Ninety per cent of those removed were still eligible for medical cards.[27]

This study highlights the differences in the numbers of people who are eligible for medical cards and those who are actually in possession of them. Nine out of ten of those who had been dropped from the list were put back on it when they reapplied. In particular, it highlights how some of the people most at risk and in need of GP care, such as those on very low income, those with poor literacy, the homeless, and older people, are those most likely to loose their medical card through the review process. In 2008, the Department of Health was reviewing eligibility for medical cards and health services, a commitment ongoing since the 2001 health strategy, from which there was still no outcome in February 2009.

Why is there no free GP care for all?

Free GP care is the norm in the northern part of the island of Ireland. It is the standard across Europe. It makes total sense. If people can attend their GP or primary care service free at the point of entry, they are more likely to attend at an earlier point with a sickness or condition. The earlier the diagnosis and intervention, the better the outcome and the cheaper the treatment. So why has not Ireland even tried to introduce free care since Noël Browne's Trojan efforts over fifty years ago?

In the 1980s, Tussing advocated free GP care 'to encourage early, routine and preventative care'. In 2000, the Chief Medical Officer (CMO) of the Department of Health and Children's annual report, which focused on children advised considering free primary care to all children as a 'specific policy measure to redistribute resources' which 'will do most to create better child health'.[29] Internationally, there is evidence to show that free, accessible, high-quality, primary care services are a proactive way of reducing societal inequalities.

An early draft of the Department of Health's health strategy contained recommendations for a free primary care system where doctors could be health service employees, but these early, good intentions were won over by pragmatism and competing demands and did not make it to later, let alone, the final version.[30] In 2002, there was growing evidence that GPs might accept a state, salaried system of primary care if it provided access to all and improved quality of care.[31]

In the 2002 and 2007 general elections, Labour and Sinn Féin campaigned for free primary care for all, with differences in how that should be achieved. Labour saw its realisation through social health insurance, while Sinn Féin advocated a tax-based system like the British NHS, recommending its introduction to under-18s, before extending free medical care to all. In 2007, the Greens campaigned for the election on the basis of introducing free primary care for all under six year olds, a position also advocated by children's organisation such as Barnardo's and the End Child Poverty Coalition in the run up to the 2007 general election. Fine Gael recommended increasing eligibility so that 40 per cent of the population would be covered by medical cards.[32] While Fianna Fáil have not promised free primary care for over 50 years and the PDs have never made such empty undertakings. In fact, Michael McDowell in the run-up to the 2002 election declared free GP care as 'crazy, loony left' politics.[33] The Green Party reneged on their pre-election promise of free primary care for under sixes when they agreed a Programme for Government with the PDs and Fianna Fáil, which committed to increasing income thresholds for medical card eligibility, doubling the income limit eligibility for parents of children under six years of age and trebling them for parents of children with an intellectual disability under 18 years of age.[34] None of these commitments have materialised two years after the publication of the agreed Programme for Government.

Research carried out by Trinity College Dublin for the Adelaide Hospital Society has costed the extension of free primary care to all at €217 million.[35] This sum includes the additional GPs that would be required to staff such a service. Given the extent to which the benefits of free primary clearly outweigh the costs, it is hard to explain why it has never been introduced, particularly in the years where billions more were being spent on the Irish health service. It is particularly hard to explain given the timing of the Primary Care Strategy. However, it must be remembered, there is an inherent conservatism in Ireland and although Ireland has been liberalised socially and economically, economic liberalism was busy in the boom years of the Celtic Tiger benefiting those with money, not those without. Since the failed Mother and Child Scheme, it became the norm among the establishment to believe that people who had money should pay for basic services. Also the powers which stopped Browne's Mother and Child Scheme in the 1950s were still forces to be reckoned with in the early 2000s, particularly the medical profession. The negotiation of the deal for payment to GPs for people over 70 in 2002 and the consultants' contract agreed in 2008 demonstrated the power the medical profession still had over civil servants and the Department of Health.

In the years that followed the health strategy, choices were made at an explicit and implicit level as to where the money would go. Alas, neither common sense nor social solidarity prevailed. Equity and free primary care for all were not top of the priority list. It is ironic that one of the most common activities that public representatives do for their constituents is make the case for them to be eligible for a medical card, yet public representatives as a group, apart from Labour and Sinn Féin, have resisted advocating free primary care for all. Just another example of the anomalies in Irish health service and planning, where local parish pump politics override the national interest, policy content and the evidence base.

Increased privatisation and medicalisation of primary care services

Writing in 2005, Tussing and Wren came to the conclusion that the Primary Care Strategy, as outlined in 2001, was dead.[36] And, in 2005, they were correct. However, with the appointment of Brendan Drumm in August 2005, there has been a renewed interest in primary care but a slower, narrower, quite altered version of that originally planned. The primary care teams which are being 'rolled out' since 2006 are made up of fewer professionals than initially outlined with a greater emphasis on medical professionals. The money required for the 'state of the art' service, as wished for by all who welcomed the Primary Care Strategy in 2001, was never delivered.

As a result, its realisation has been much slower and has increasingly involved the participation of the private sector. Like nursing home and hospital care in Ireland the private sector has filled the gaps left open by the state's neglect. Instead of the ideal scenario envisaged in 2001, for-profit providers have rapidly entered the 'healthcare market'. Although the HSE appeared to prefer the public sector providing primary care facilities, in the absence of funding, pragmatism reigns and the 'roll-out' of the Primary Care Strategy is being driven by the 'public–private partnership model'. Interestingly, both the HSE's and Department of Health's special advisors on primary care in 2005 and 2006 have left their posts to take up positions in the private sector development of primary care services.

A good example of how the Primary Care Strategy was altered between 2001 and 2005 is Mulhuddart, County Dublin. Mulhuddart is an urban area of Blanchardstown, a community of 10,000 people with a rapidly growing population. It is an area with high socio-economic disadvantage, which up to 2005 had no GP, no pharmacist or health centre. In the late 1990s, Mulhuddart was rated amongst the highest deprivation ratings in the country. The community leaders in the area organised themselves into a Primary Health Group. They got funding from the Combat Poverty Agency as part of the Building Healthy Communities Programme to build the capacity of the community to participate in the development and implementation of the Primary Care Strategy in their area.

Initial research in 2003 found the development of local health services was the top priority of residents.[37] The government sponsored RAPID programme in the area prioritised the development of primary care facilities in its strategy for regeneration of the area. The Mulhuddart Primary Healthcare Group mobilised the community to press the case for action on primary care. They carried out a community consultation on their health needs and lobbied the local health board, the Department of Health and local politicians for primary care facilities for their local area. However, no money was forthcoming to develop a public primary care facility.

Harney, since taking up post as Minister for Health, emphasised the need for private investment to get the primary care centres up and running. And her views prevailed. In October 2005, Mary Harney opened the Mulhuddart 'primary care centre'.

The roll-out of primary care since 2005 is very different to Micheál Martin's 2001 plan, primary care centres are not located in HSE-owned primary care buildings with the multidisciplinary teams imagined. Instead, as is the case of Mulhuddart, it is run by private for-profit company. In

Mulhuddart, the primary care centre is owned and operated by Touchstone, a private company run by Fergus Hoban, a multimillionaire healthcare entrepreneur. Hoban who made his money through the pharmacy chain Unicare, which he sold to German pharmaceutical giant, Celescio for over €120 million, said at the opening of the Mulhuddart primary care centre, that he planned to open 60 centres around the country by 2011.[38] In the Mulhuddart centre, GPs who hire out rooms from Touchstone are located adjacent to a Touchstone pharmacist. Sean McGuire, who was appointed as Drumm's special advisor in 2005 on primary care, became a director of Touchstone, shortly after stepping down as the HSE's primary care advisor, just 18 months after taking up the post. Speaking on *Primetime Investigates* in May 2008, McGuire said that there was no conflict of interest in his role as advisor to Drumm and his subsequent directorship of a private, for-profit, primary care company.

Another person with an influential role in primary care policy who moved into the private sector was Mary Harney's primary care advisor, Tom Kelly. Kelly worked in the North Western Health Board and the interim HSE before being seconded to the Department of Health and Children to advise on primary care. In July 2007, he also stepped down from his advisory role, when he became a founding partner in Meret healthcare, another private, for-profit, primary healthcare company entering the Irish market.

The Mulhuddart model is being extended across the country, with GPs partnering with private for-profit companies and healthcare clinics to run primary care centres. In 2006, the HSE advertised for GPs interested in running primary care centres around the country. There were hundreds of GPs interested and, by 2008, some of the 87 primary care teams designated as up and running are these narrower, GP-run, for-profit, primary care centres. Mulhuddart is considered one of the 87 'fully functioning' PCTs according to the HSE.[39]

In 2008, the HSE advertised for further expressions of interests from 'individuals/companies who-are developing or are planning to develop health facilities at a range of locations which would facilitate the delivery of primary healthcare in conjunction with local General Practitioners'.[40] Under this scheme, the HSE is formally embarking on a form of public–private partnerships to implement the primary care strategy, although such a partnership was not articulated in the original strategy. The HSE rents accommodation for the public aspects of the primary care teams such as public health nurses, physiotherapists and other allied health professionals but the private providers such as GPs, dentists and pharmacists pay their own way. The GPs and developers build their own facilities and the HSE rent about 40 per cent of the floor space. In a 'Guidance Document for Primary Care Developments' available on the HSE website, it states that 'in the context of the multi-annual capital planning framework as part of the transformation process, the HSE will explore imaginative ways of providing primary care infrastructure in a timely and cost-effective manner including private provision and having regard to the fact that services are delivered through a mix of contracted providers and HSE employees'.

Speaking to the Oireachtas Health Committee in January 2009, HSE primary care director, Laverne McGuiness said, 'We will be leasing the public healthcare infrastructure elements with the GPs paying for their own accommodation in the Primary Care Centres. This approach has yielded significant discounts on the open market prices. The infrastructure programme aims to have all sites identified by the middle of this year, with the first group of 80 to open by the end of 2010 and the full complement to open in the course of 2011.'

The Irish Medical Organisation and medical professions

opposed to privatisation of health services have spoken out against the involvement of the private sector in funding and running of primary care centres, fearing they will be run in the interest of profit, not necessarily the needs of the local community. Even the HSE's own guidance document clearly stipulates the required clarity of relationship between pharmacies and the primary care centre, acknowledging the potential conflict of interest within the new primary care centres. In some areas, notably disadvantaged areas such as Irishtown, Tallaght and Inchicore in Dublin, Inisbofin, and Nenagh, the HSE is developing its own public primary care facilities. These publicly developed, funded and run facilities are much closer to those as originally envisaged in the Primary Care Strategy, whereby the facilities are built and run by the HSE. However, the predominant way of progressing the Primary Care Strategy in 2008 is through the private sector. Not surprisingly, by the end of 2008, private primary care practices were springing up all around the country in the absence of the government-backed initiative becoming a reality across the country.

Community and continuing care

While primary care services increasingly come under the remit of the private sector, there is also evidence of a shift in community and continuing care services moving in that direction. Community and continuing care services are all other health and personal social services, which are not primary care or hospital services. These include: public health; mental health; disability; child, youth and family services; community hospitals and local health clinics; continuing care services; and social inclusion services, such as those specifically for the homeless, Travellers, refugees, asylum seekers and drug users. Dealing with developments in a way that gives justice to the range, extent and deficit of services in any of these areas just mentioned could fill the pages of a book on its own. But, as mentioned in other chapters, they are a vital component of health and social care provision. Providing good quality community and continuing care services is essential for a fully functional health system.

Since 1997, there has been a growth in investment in community care services, but, like hospital investment, it was merely making up for the paltry investment of previous decades. A Department of Health commissioned report on 'Value for Money' published in 2001 found that between 1997 and 2001 there were 400 additional beds in community nursing units, over 1,000 new day places and ten new centres for older people with 880 extra staff added into the system. They also showed the increase in services for the disabled, an additional 1,650 residential places and 2,300 day places for people with intellectual disabilities, while the figures for physical disabilities were lower but still significant with 150 extra residential places and 400 more day places.[41] These improvements continued in the post-2002 period. However, what cannot be over-emphasised is the total absence of some services prior to this investment and the appalling quality of some of the services that did exist because of the vastly inadequate funding and the absence of standards, regulations and monitoring.

Good quality, accessible community and continuing care services are particularly necessary for people with long-lasting illness and disability, and people at risk. This group comprises older people, people with disabilities, children and families at risk, people with mental health difficulties and people with chronic illnesses. In order to give some insight into these issues, services for older people and mental health services are considered below.

Services for older people

Older people will be used as illustrative of service and policy developments, however, it is important to take into account that what has happened in older people services differs from those for people with disabilities or children and families at risk, where the majority of services still remain in the public or voluntary sector.

Irish life and society has changed fundamentally in the past 30 years. Families have become smaller, communities have become more fragmented and traditional caring roles have altered. According to the 2006 census, there are 161,000 carers in Ireland, about 40,000 of whom provide care for more than 43 hours a week. The Irish Carers Association estimate that family carers are providing 193.7 million hours of care a year, at a value to the economy of €2.5 billion.[42] Many of these carers are older people themselves. However, while many older people are still cared for by family members, fewer older people have that choice and are increasingly relying on public and private services to care for them. Also, as people are living longer because of better life expectancy and advances in modern medicine, there is a greater demand for state services, such as community supports, home helps, public health nurses and day care. Up to the 1980s, services for older people were under-developed, underfunded, and often provided on a charitable, voluntary or volunteer basis. State services for older people were also victim to the cutbacks of the 1980s and while the investment has increased significantly from 1997 onwards, it is still making up for decades of under-investment.

Residential care for older people

Older people's health and social care needs have hit the headlines at various times over the past decade, often in a negative manner. When trolley queues and poor conditions in emergency departments got public attention in the early years of the twenty-first century, one of the main explanations for the 'blockages' in A&E (as it was then known) was the problem of 'bed blockers'. This term was usually applied to older people who remained in hospital beds because of the shortages in long-stay nursing units and community supports, which prevented older people from leaving hospital in the first place. (This issue is dealt with in Chapter 4.)

This resulted in an increased investment in community and nursing home places but this investment did not meet demand. As a result, the health boards resorted to contracting beds in nursing homes from the private sector to meet the needs of older people. Simultaneously, the Finance Act was changed by then Minister for Finance Charlie McCreevy to incentivise the building and development of private nursing homes. A report published by Age Action in 2007 found that in 2006, there were approximately 9,500 long-term beds for older people in the public sector – which remained relatively static for the previous decade. But, in contrast, the private nursing home sector has grown rapidly due to tax incentives from 10,500 beds in 1995 to almost 18,000 in 2006. By December 2008, there were 10,543 public beds and 20,136 private long-term residential beds for older people.[43] In order to alleviate the pressures on acute hospitals and so free up beds for people in A&E who needed to be admitted, thousands of older people were moved into private nursing homes. And the increased dependency on the private sector happened without adequate standards in place or any independent monitoring of the quality of care.

As well as failing to provide sufficient numbers of nursing home beds, the health boards also haggled for the lowest possible price to buy care for older people in nursing homes. Research shows there is an immense gap between what the HSE pays for private contracted nursing home care and the actual cost of keeping someone in a nursing home. The location of a nursing home is also very important because it has a direct impact on the number of visits and the levels of support that person gets from friends and family. One of the downsides of the huge proliferation of private nursing homes is that it has happened at the whim of developers and investors, without any planning as to the location of the homes. As a result, many older people are ending up in homes, a long distance from their social network, which results in them being further isolated.

Of course, this dependency on the private sector happened silently, in an unplanned and unregulated way, as older people in need of long-term care did not have a loud voice in the booming Celtic Tiger years. It was a disaster just waiting to happen. It took an undercover team from *Primetime Investigate* to expose the abuse and neglect of older people that was taking place in one private nursing home in north County Dublin – Leas Cross. In the same way that bed blockers became common parlance in 2001, Leas Cross became synonymous with the state of care of older people in Ireland in 2005 and the years that followed. The nation was horrified by the images it saw on the programme, which was aired in May 2005 and exposed widespread abuse. Consultant geriatrician Des O'Neill, who carried out an independent inquiry into the case, described what was happening in Leas Cross as institutional abuse.[44] O'Neill concluded that there was no reason to believe that there were not more Leas Crosses across the country. The Leas Cross scandal exposed the state's neglect to inspect and monitor quality of care in private nursing homes which resulted in very poor quality care and in the early death of residents.

At the time, private nursing homes were inspected by HSE staff but with little effect as visits were notified and inspectors had little or no muscle to implement their recommendations or to punish non-compliers. Although, multiple promises were made in the aftermath of Leas Cross that all nursing homes would be independently inspected, four years on, both public and private nursing homes remain uninspected by an independent authority.

The HIQA was established in May 2007 and it has the responsibility to carry out such inspections. In August 2008,

HIQA published Draft National Quality Standards. These have been submitted to the Minister for Health and Children who has to carry out a regulatory impact assessment and develop new regulations for their implementation. Once the regulations are in place, the Social Services Inspectorate of HIQA will register and inspect all residential care settings, public, private and voluntary, against the National Quality Standards for Residential Care Settings for Older People in Ireland, and the regulations. It is likely that it will be at least summer 2009 before all nursing homes, public and private are inspected.

While it is reported that awareness has been raised and standards have improved, there are still older people living in substandard nursing home care in Ireland. In particular, public nursing homes, which are often housed in old buildings, sometimes disused hospitals or even workhouses, will be closed as they will be unable to meet the regulations required in the new national standards. At a public consultation held by HIQA when developing the draft standards, a manager from a public nursing home spoke about how they would have to close the next day if the regulations were introduced as they could never physically meet the guidelines. He detailed how the fire drill for their home was never carried out as the instructions for what to do for the older, infirm people on the upper floors in the event of a fire was to put them on top of a mattress and drag them down the stairs.

Up to 2005, people living in long-term residential care (such as publicly provided nursing home care for older people and long-term residential care for people with disabilities) were charged for this care, although legally it should have been provided for free. After a lengthy legal battle, in 2005, the Supreme Court ruled that those in need of such care were eligible for it, less 80 per cent of the non-contributory pension, and that residents had been charged illegally for their care. Some of residents illegally charged are now being reimbursed.

After the court ruling the government moved swiftly to legalise charging people for such care.

In response to this inconsistency in eligibility to state financial assistance for nursing home care by the HSE and other agencies (which led to many older people and their families unwittingly assuming the full charge of nursing home care, or else using the inadequate subvention system), a new system called the 'Fair Deal' was announced by the Minister for Health, Mary Harney in December 2006. The stated aim of the Fair Deal was to ensure fairness in relation to nursing home charges. However, groups working with older people, such as Age Action, say the so-called Fair Deal actively discriminates against older people because everyone in residential care will be charged for their care. Under the scheme, nursing home residents will pay up to 80 per cent of their disposable income towards the cost of their care during their lifetime, and up to 15 per cent of the value of their home after their death.

'Nobody would envisage that a young or middle-aged person who needed expensive heart surgery or cancer treatment would be asked to pay 80 per cent of their income and up to 15 per cent of the value of their home towards the cost. Yet we are proposing that older people who are paralysed by stroke or incapable of living in their own homes due to dementia would be charged in this way,' Eamon Timmins of Age Action said in response to the announcement of the Fair Deal. Also commenting on the Fair Deal, consultant geriatrician Des O'Neill, chair of the Irish Gerontological Society, said it is a 'cataclysmic shift in how essential health and social care services are provided for older people. It is a selective inheritance tax on people who suffer from strokes and dementia which reinforces Reagan's and Thatcher's myth of the burden of ageing. As the UK Royal Commission on Long Term Care stated, there is every reason to believe that it is totally possible to fully fund residential care for older people in Ireland through taxation and social insurance'.

The Fair Deal was meant to come into effect in January 2008 but was delayed because of legal and administrative issues. In July 2008, its implementation was deferred under the guise of government cuts until 2009. The legislation for it was published in October 2008 with a plan for implementation in 2009. Major concerns also remain over the capacity of older people to sign over such substantial assets for their care, and it is likely that there will be a limited amount of money dedicated to the scheme in any one year, insufficient to meet the needs of our aging population.

Community services

Only five per cent of older people will require long-term nursing home care at any one time, therefore, the majority of older people manage to live most of their last years at home and in their community. And it is here that home helps, public health nursing, as well as other vital allied professionals such as physiotherapists, occupational, and speech and language therapists, are essential in order to keep people at home and maintain their quality of life to the highest standard possible.

Speaking at an event for older people in north Clondalkin in July 2008, Minister Mary Harney spoke about 'the extra funding of over €400 million that was added to services for older people under Budgets 2006 and 2007 of which €190 million was for community-based services such as homecare packages, home helps, day care, respite and meals on wheels'.[45] And for anyone who has had a relative who receives care from home helps or public health nursing day-in, day-out, week-in, week-out, their care and contribution to quality of life is literally priceless. It is invaluable, because it would be very hard and very expensive to buy such quality of care. While it is possible to buy some of this care from private providers in urban centres, in many parts of the country such services are just not available.

Let's look at home helps as an example. Home helps are carers who come into people's homes and help them with the day-to-day aspects of life that they cannot do alone, such as dressing, washing, cleaning, cooking and preparing meals. The 2007 HSE Annual Report outlines the substantial increases in home-help hours and clients between 2006 and 2007 – increasing from over 11.4 million in 2006 to over 12.3 million hours in 2007, while the numbers of people receiving home helps increased from 49,578 to 54,736, nearly a ten per cent increase.[46] However, while this increase is a very positive development, it should be remembered that in September 2007, the HSE introduced cost-cutting measures that resulted in a freeze on home helps, i.e. it became increasingly difficult to get a home help if you did not have one in advance of the cutbacks. In the months following the introduction of the cost-cutting initiatives in autumn 2007, organisations working with older people, and nurses' and doctors' unions spoke out about the impact the cuts were having on people's quality of life and the knock-on impact on acute hospital services. Minister Mary Harney and the HSE management insisted, the 'cost containment measures' would not impact on frontline services. But they did. Some people had their home-help hours cut, others looking for the service were told the HSE were not issuing any further home-help hours. An examination of the HSE Service Plan for 2008 shows the true picture. Remembering that the home-help hours increased by nearly ten per cent between 2006 and 2007 and that cutbacks were introduced in 2007, that the population is ageing and there is a growing need for such services, the HSE 2008 Service Plan committed to deliver 11.7 million home-help hours in 2008. This was a cut in 600,000 home-help hours between what was actually provided in 2007 and what was planned for provision in 2008.[47]

All older people should enter their twilight years in the

knowledge, that they are entitled to good quality, accessible care whether it is in their home, in the community or in a residential setting. In Ireland at the beginning of 2009, such an aspiration is still a long way off.

Mental health policy

In 2006, an Expert Group on Mental Health established by the government, produced a new mental health policy for Ireland called 'A Vision for Change'.[48] It set out an ambitious ten-year programme of reform, with the aim of providing good quality, mental health services in the community, accessible to all. It was based on the principles of equity, inclusion, participation of users of mental health services and choice.

'A Vision for Change' focuses on strengthening individuals, strengthening communities and reducing structural barriers to mental health by reducing discrimination and promoting access to employment.

In Ireland, mental illness is considered a disability if the mental illness is classed as severe and enduring, however, there are no clear guidelines on how this is to be interpreted. Disability is one of the nine grounds covered by Equality Status acts of 2000 and 2004 and is included in the National Disability Strategy. The Equal Status acts requires the reasonable accommodation of people with disabilities (including mental health), in relation to goods and services, accommodation, health and welfare services. Equality employment legislation prohibits discrimination on disability grounds, including mental health.

Mental health status

The WHO defines mental health as 'a state of well being in which the individual realises his or her abilities, can cope with normal stresses of life, can work productively and fruitfully and is able to make a contribution to his or her community'.[49]

One in four Irish people experiences mental health problems at some stage in their lifetime. Yet, like good health, good mental health is a concern of everybody. One in ten people with a self-reported disability in Ireland describe themselves as having 'a mental, nervous or emotional problem'.[50] The WHO Regional Committee for Europe noted that 'poverty and mental ill health form a vicious circle: poverty is both a major cause of poor mental health and a potential consequence of it'.[51] People living in poverty are known to have lower self-esteem and higher stress. People from lower socio-economic groups have higher admission rates to psychiatric hospitals in Ireland and lower life expectancy than people from higher socio-economic groups.

Research carried out to inform 'A Vision for Change' with users of mental health services found that 68 per cent of respondents were dependent on social welfare, 47 per cent had the junior certificate as their highest qualification, 58 per cent were single, just 30 per cent in some form of employment, while 2 per cent were completely dependent on family with no source of direct income.[52]

The World Health Organisation, predict that, by 2020, depression will be the largest burden of disease globally. Women are twice as likely to experience depression, while men are more likely to commit suicide than women.

Research carried out in the Central Mental Hospital in Dublin found that more women than men had psychiatric illnesses.[53] However, there is evidence to show that men are less likely to seek help for their mental health.[54] It is estimated that nearly one in five under 16-year-olds will experience significant mental health problems at some period of their development.[55]

In 2004, depression accounted for 29 per cent of admissions to psychiatric hospitals in Ireland, while schizophrenia accounted for 20 per cent of admissions.[56] Some groups experience particularly acute mental health difficulties, such as children and young people at risk, homeless people, people with addictions, prisoners, minority ethnic groups, people living in isolation, people with disabilities, Travellers, lone parents, and isolated older people.

While there is some research in Ireland on people living in psychiatric institutions and a growing body of knowledge around suicide and para-suicide, there is an absence of research on the mental health status of the population and the needs of some of the most excluded groups. There is also a lack of knowledge around the causal pathways between poverty and poor mental health.

The cost of mental health

Mental health services in Ireland have always been underfunded.[57] While the actual amount spent on mental health services has increased, it has decreased as a proportion of the overall health budget. In 1984, 14 per cent of the overall health budget was spent on mental health services, in 2000 it was 8.1 per cent, in 2005 it was 7 per cent, in 2007 it was 6 per cent.[58]

In Great Britain and Northern Ireland on average, over 10 per cent of budget is allocated to mental health. Organisations working in the mental health arena have repeatedly called for 10–12 per cent of the health budget to be allocated to mental health, with a strong focus on prevention and inclusion of people with mental health difficulties.

The Mental Health Commission points out that the estimated cost to the economy of mental health problems in 2006 was over €3 billion, over two per cent of GNP.[59] And 60–80 per cent of all costs associated with mental health problems are outside of the health system.[60] A survey was carried out to inform the report on 'The Economics of Mental Healthcare in Ireland' which revealed that the public would be willing to pay more for community mental health services.[61]

Mental health services

Access to good quality mental health services is essential for people living with mental health difficulties and psychiatric conditions. 'A Vision for Change' outlined a comprehensive plan for how mental health services should be organised and funded. It recommends a shift away from acute psychiatric hospitals to comprehensive community services based on a recovery model.

It has 200 recommendations, proposing the establishment of fully staffed community mental health teams that will offer home-based services for people with mental health problems; closing down 15 remaining psychiatric hospitals, and using their funds to build new community mental health centres and residential units for those with chronic mental health conditions who need inpatient care; as well as involving mental health service users and their carers in their day-to-day care. When the plan was published in 2006, mental health service providers, users of mental health services, advocacy groups and NGOs all welcomed these developments.

However, three years later, the Irish Psychiatric Association, the Mental Health Coalition (a coalition of NGOs), the First and Second Annual Reports of the Independent Monitoring Group of 'A Vision for Change' and the Mental Health Commission have each criticised the slowness in implementation for the plan. The Irish Psychiatric Association are also critical of the government's failure to reinvest money gained from the sale of land from psychiatric hospitals into mental health services.[62]

Annually, the Report of the Inspector of Mental Health Services and now the Mental Health Commission have voiced concern over the poor standards in psychiatric hospitals and mental health services. Ireland has had very high rates of long-stay patients in psychiatric hospitals and while these are decreasing, the Report of the Inspector of Mental Health

Services in 2006 found 'the conditions of many remaining wards as entirely inadequate'.[63] It says that there are staff shortages in all community-based multidisciplinary teams, they are poorly managed and inadequately resourced.

Plans to enhance community mental health provision have been recommended since the 1960s and have not yet been realised. The Mental Health Commission has expressed concern that money intended for mental health services is being diverted into other health services. The Mental Health Commission has found that the promised National Mental Health Service Directorate in the HSE never materialised, new mental health catchment areas have not been formed, and there is no available information on how many mental health teams are actually up and running. The 2007 Annual Report is equally damning, stating that two years on from the publication of 'A Vision for Change' there 'was little substantial change in the provision and delivery of specialist and community mental health services'.[64]

A review carried out by the HSE in December 2007, found that more than 1,000 children are waiting for psychiatric assessment for more than a year. In total, there were 3,598 children waiting for psychiatric assessments, up 14 per cent from 2006 figures. Seventy per cent of all children were waiting up to a year for treatment. Delays in assessment and treatment for children with psychiatric conditions can accentuate their illness and cause additional problems long into their future.

The National Office for Suicide Prevention is receiving €3.5 million in funding in 2008, €2 million short of the government-endorsed 'Reach-Out' strategy, which outlined the resources required for developing prevention services.

Mental health organisations estimate the €150 million budget allocated to implement the new mental health strategy 'Vision for Change' over a seven-to-ten-year period is inadequate. An additional €25 million was allocated to fund new developments outlined in 'A Vision for Change' in 2005 and 2006, however, figures released to the Mental Health Coalition in 2007 showed that €23 million of this was not spent on new services, as it was used to 'shore up budgetary overspends'.[65] No additional money was allocated to fund new developments in 'A Vision for Change' in the HSE 2008 Service Plan. Mary Harney criticised the 2008 Service Plan saying it fell short of developments that could reasonably be expected in mental health.

The 2007 Report of the Inspector of Mental Health Services stated that in 2007, fewer than ten per cent of psychiatric catchment areas were able to offer a range of services to people with mental health problems. The inspector complained that there are no plans to improve services over the next five years and no additional funding for implementing 'A Vision for Change'.[67]

The Second Report on the Implementation of 'A Vision for Change' by the independent monitoring group is damning of the lack of progress made up to June 2008. In particular, it stated its concerns were the absence of clear identifiable leadership within the HSE to implement the strategy, the absence of a comprehensive implementation strategy for 'A Vision for Change' within the HSE who is responsible for 90 per cent of its implementation, that the Transformation Programme is taking precedence over 'A Vision for Change', that resourcing of community mental health teams is not prioritised, and the slow rate of progress on the development of child and adolescent mental health teams.[68]

Conclusion

The essence of the blueprints and the plans for what constitutes primary, community and continuing care that were published by the Department of Health between 2001 and 2006 and have been implemented since 2005 by the HSE were essentially good.

The Primary Care Strategy was a good plan. 'A Vision for Change' is an excellent blueprint for the future of mental health services in Ireland. The move to provide more and more older people with care in the community, be it in primary or community care, makes sense. Although, the Fair Deal is not a fair deal for older people.

Providing care for people in the community through primary and continuing care services makes sense for citizens on a social and personal level. It makes sense for government and for health service planners and deliverers for both economic and social reasons. People want to be cared for in their own home, if at all possible. And while primary care is generally a lower cost way of providing healthcare than secondary and specialist care, it is no less expensive in the long term as the expansion of primary care may end up meeting previously unmet needs, improving access and expanding utilisation. The general direction of Irish health policy has been made in the right direction. But, significantly, sufficient money has not followed the policies and plans – and, critically, some of it has been transferred in to the private sector without sufficient monitoring or regulation.

Central to fixing the problems faced by the health system in Ireland in 2009 is providing good quality, accessible primary, community and continuing care for every citizen. Of course, change takes time. But any close examination of developments and funding allocation since the establishment of the HSE show that the rhetoric of change and transformation is not backed up by action. For this to be achieved, there needs to be a greater proportion of funding allocated to these services, the plans already in place need to be implemented and there needs to be far greater integration of these services. There is no reason why Ireland should not plan to have a universal system of care for everyone, free at the point of delivery. Such a system seems a long way off early in 2009.

Chapter 9

The perfect storm ... universal healthcare for all

At the time of writing on 1 March 2009, over 17,000 people over 70 were having their medical cards withdrawn as they no longer qualified on the basis of age. The saga of the introduction of universal care for over 70s is a perfect example of the social and political fallout of the unintended consequences of an unplanned policy measure. It is also a great example of what happens when a nation is given a taste of a universal health system for some of its citizens, their reaction and the consequences of when it is taken away.

As already outlined, medical cards were introduced for all over 70 in 2001 as a purely political ploy to attract the grey vote in the run-up to the 2002 general election. Charlie McCreevy, the then Minister for Finance only told Micheál Martin, then Minister for Health, about the manoeuvre the night before the budget.

The extension of medical cards to everyone over 70 was not in line with health policy. It was not in the 2001 health strategy that was the blueprint of health policy in Ireland for the decade ahead. It was not costed. There was no evidence base informing this policy making sop. No deal had been done with the IMO to ensure these new over 70-year-olds who did not qualify on low-income criteria would be provided with 'free' primary care services on the same basis as those who qualified on the basis of their low income.

It was purely a device to get the Fianna Fáil–Progressive

Democratic government re-elected. The government went to the electorate in 2002 looking for time to implement their fantastic new health strategy. And it worked. It also worked for those over 70. Like the free public transport given the old-age pensioners by Charlie Haughey in the late 1960s, it was a very popular move. The country was in the middle of an economic boom. It could afford to provide 'free' healthcare for over those over 70. These were the people who had worked hard to create the environment for the Celtic Tiger. As people get older, they need more healthcare, surely this was a rational measure.

Charlie McCreevy, not known for his social leanings, introduced universal healthcare to a section of the Irish population, without any of the obstacles that his predecessors in Fianna Fáil encountered when they tried to do the same 50 years earlier. It was to be a social experiment Fianna Fáil would live to regret in a different economic landscape eight years on.

The scheme initially devised entirely by the Department of Finance, significantly not in Hawkins House, got the cost estimations wrong. They severely under-budgeted, reckoning it would cost €15 million a year. By the time of Budget 2009 when the Fianna Fáil–PD–Green government announced the withdrawal of universal healthcare for everyone over 70 in October 2008, the scheme was costing €243 million a year and was expected to grow by 14 per cent in the year ahead. Increasing numbers of older people, the high levy paid for richer over 70-year-olds and increasing drug costs were all contributing to the high cost of the scheme.

The deal agreed between the Department of Health and the IMO following the budget announcement in 2000 ensured that by 2008 GPs were paid €641 per patient per annum for these new richer, over 70-year-olds, while they were still paid the previously agreed €161 per low-income patient per annum who qualified for a medical card.

Organisations and advocates working with older people

praised it as a positive public health measure. Older people were more likely to go to their GP at an earlier stage of their illness because of it. Regular, unpaid for, attendances at their GP made the diagnosis and management of chronic diseases more manageable. Most medicines were covered by it. Some older people with private health insurance discontinued their schemes as they were entitled to free healthcare across the system, in the GP surgery and in hospitals. It kept older people out of hospital and took the burden of worry away from them; older people did not have to be troubled about paying for GP visits or for prescription drugs. They had access to a range of health and social care services which they were not automatically entitled to if they did not have the medical card.

From an equity perspective, it was argued that it was a regressive measure. The measure gave medical cards to older richer people, who did not quality for free medical care on the basis of their income, at the expense of young poorer people. It also fuelled the movement of GPs towards already well catered for middle and upper-class areas.

Between 1997 and 2007, there were significant decreases in the numbers of people with medical cards on the basis of income with 100,000 people losing their medical cards during the first two Fianna Fáil–PD coalition governments.[1] It happened silently and slowly as increases in the limits for medical eligibility did not keep in line with rising incomes. Up to 1997, at least one-third of the population had medical cards. By 2005, this was down to 25 per cent, when richer over 70-year-olds are excluded. In December 2008, 27 per cent of the population have medical cards on the basis of low income. A further three per cent have medical cards on the basis of their age. While the numbers with medical cards increased upwards post 2005 this was a reflection of increasing numbers on social welfare who qualified on the basis of their low income.

In the weeks before the early budget in autumn 2008, rumour abounded through leaks to the media that the government would abolish free medical cards to those over 70. It was put out there like many other fliers – such as the possibility of taxing or taking away child benefit from well-off parents – leaked to the media as a way of softening the actual content of the budget.

And then, on 14 October, Brian Lenihan in his first budget address as Minister for Finance dropped what was to become the most politically explosive announcements about healthcare in Irish politics in decades. The government was abolishing 'the automatic entitlement to a medical card for over 70s above the eligibility criteria' and planned to introduce 'an annual cash grant of €400 euro per person to over 70s without GP-only or full medical card from 1 January next year'. It was not clear from the budget speech if this was to apply to all over 70-year-olds or just to new over 70s, i.e. those who turned 70 after 1 January 2009. Everyone, including this author, assumed it was only the 'new' over 70 group. But we were wrong. Every person over 70 years of age who had qualified for their medical card on the basis of their age, not their income, would have to be means tested.

There was immediate political and media reaction. It was instantly recognisable that this was one of those moments when Fianna Fáil's common sense had not prevailed. Arrogance and thriftiness triumphed. Mary Hanafin, the first minister to be interviewed by the media after the budget speech, speaking on RTÉ Radio 1's *Drivetime* programme confirmed it would apply to everyone over 70.

Mary Harney held a press briefing on the detail of the estimates. Because the budget was published early, in response to the international and national economic crisis, the estimates were published on the same day. At the press briefing, Mary Harney said that there were 350,000 people over 70 with medical cards, that 140,000 of these had never been means tested. They would have to reapply for their medical card. For 210,000 people over 70 years of age, the status quo remained. Of the 140,000 others, she expected that 14,000 would still qualify on the basis of the means test, 35,000 more of them would get doctor-only medical cards, 70,000 would get the newly announced annual grant of €400 for the year. And 20,000 of those who were better off would get nothing. According to government, this new measure including the €400 annual grant would save the government €100 million. The world had never faced such dire economic conditions, stringent economic measures were required and this was one of them. Or so they said on 14 October 2008.

But a week is a long time in politics. Immediately, older people and the organisations representing them were up in arms. The opposition used it as the perfect opportunity to bash the budget – Fianna Fáil, the PDs and the Greens were hurting the old, the sick, the young and the poor. The budget speech had been full of rhetoric about protecting the most vulnerable. Yet the budget meant that over 100,000 people over 70 would loose their medical cards, that class sizes would get bigger, that people on low income were going to have to pay the newly introduced one per cent levy, no matter how low their income, and that 16- and 17-year-olds with severe disabilities would loose their income.

Fianna Fáil and Mary Harney, by this stage a minister without a party, came out strong. The abolition of a universal entitlement to medical cards for all over 70s was a necessary measure. It was in the interest of equity, according to Harney. In the Dáil, two days later, Mary Coughlan, as Tánaiste, came out fighting. Were the opposition really suggesting letting property tycoons and high court judges keep their medical cards when others were more in need of it? These were the words from a minister from the same party that introduced the measure eight years earlier. The opposition took a strong and unified stance against the measure. Interestingly, James Reilly, Fine Gael's spokesperson on health was the doctor who had negotiated the highly expensive deal for the IMO, as its president, in 2001. Jan O'Sullivan and Eamon Gilmore of Labour and Caoimhghín Ó Caoláin gave excellent, hard-hitting Dáil performances in opposition to the move.

Confusion abounded about who would keep the medical card and who would not. The medical card guidelines had always been complicated. But in the days that followed the budget announcement in October 2008, the HSE and Department of Health changed the guidelines and the limits on five different occasions. Prior to the Budget 2009 announcement, medical card thresholds were €201.50 for a single person and €298 for a couple. These were net income levels allowing for income after rent and other costs. So, if you were single with an annual income of €10,500 after costs you did not qualify for a medical card and if you were a couple with more than €15,600 per year after costs, you did not qualify. It was a very low bar, lower than the poverty line. The state pension was set above these levels, yet potentially over 70-year-olds on a state pension with minor additional payments, such as spouse's allowance, could have been excluded from receiving a medical card.

On Thursday, 16 October, two days after the budget announcement, the HSE issued a statement saying that the income threshold for a single person remained the same but for a couple it had been raised to €596 a week. The threshold for qualifying for a doctor-only card was also raised for couples (but bizarrely not for single people) to €895 a week. The single limit remained unchanged at €302. Within an hour of issuing this statement, the HSE press office recalled it. The Labour Party issued a press release showing the multiple change of rates that had appeared on the HSE and Department of Health's website and had then disappeared.

That Thursday afternoon, an urgent meeting between the Department of Health, the HSE and the minister was called. Early evening, the Department of Health issued a statement and Minister Harney went on the RTÉ *Six One News* to defend the position. New, higher guidelines were being put in place for those over 70. They were higher than those originally in place but lower than the HSE statement of earlier that day.

Another complicated scheme had been devised. Under the new guidelines, over seventies would qualify if their income, after other costs such as rent were taken into account, was less than €240.30 a week. Couples whose income was less than €480.60 after expenses would also qualify. Assets, except the family home would be taken into account, however, the first €36,000 of a single person's savings and €72,000 of a couple's savings would not to be included. Saving in excess of these amounts would be included in the assessment. Other allowances, such as for fuel and living alone, would not to be counted. For doctor-only medical cards, the income limit was raised to €360.45 for a single person and €720.90 for a couple, taking people's net income after other costs were taken into account and the same amount of savings were allowed. Others who would not qualify for either a medical card or a GP-only card, would get the €400 a year grant if their total weekly income is less than €650.

Speaking on RTÉ's news programme, Mary Harney insisted that this was not a climb down, that there would no longer be an automatic entitlement to medical cards for everyone over 70, that the thresholds were raised, that resources were being targeted to those that needed them most, and most importantly that €100 million would still be raised through this budgetary measure.

The government was under huge pressure, so much so they changed the parameters set by the measure within 48 hours of its announcement. But that was still not enough. The Taoiseach

Brain Cowen was due to travel to China to promote business links between China and Ireland. Tánaiste Mary Coughlan said it would be very unfaithful for members of Fianna Fáil not to tow the line in the absence of their leader. But, within 24 hours, Fianna Fáil backbenchers were going public against the move.

For Fianna Fáil backbench TDs and councillors with their eyes set on the local elections in June 2009, this was a drastic measure that needed further redress. One Fianna Fáil TD, Joe Behan, resigned from the party, while others spoke out against the measure. Joe Behan, a previously unheard of schoolteacher and TD from Bray, County Wicklow, went on the *Six One News* within 24 hours of Mary Harney's appearance and spoke of the move to take medical cards away from older people as 'an unwarranted attack on the elderly'. He said that 'to withdraw medical cards for this group is completely unforgivable and unacceptable and contrary to everything that Fianna Fáil stands for'. Consequently, he felt he 'had no alternative but to resign from the party'. He also spoke out against the increases in class sizes, how the young and elderly were the two sectors of society being asked to pay the price for current economic circumstances. He continued, 'Fianna Fáil have lost touch with the people, the Taoiseach and government have no option but to reverse this dreadful decision.' Most poignantly, he said, 'People like Eamon de Valera and Seán Lemass would be turning in their graves with the decisions made this week. This was not what Fianna Fáil stands for.'[2]

Fianna Fáil backbenchers, Tom Kitt, Mattie McGrath and Jim McDaid, said the decision needed to be reversed. Green Party TDs expressed their concerns about implications of removing the automatic right to a medical card. Independents Finian McGrath and Michael Lowry said they'd have to consider their support for the government. The government was in trouble.

Three hours later on that same Friday night, just three days after the budget announcement, Taoiseach Brian Cowen made an unprecedented move and went on the RTÉ *Nine O'Clock News* to allay the concerns of the public. He said that they would still 'have to get those savings [of €100 million]' but that they would engage in dialogue with doctors to 'change the structure of the scheme'. He reiterated how the government had to respect the budgetary parameters, that there would be no automatic entitlement, the current scheme was not sustainable and how he was hopeful with new arrangements in place more people will be able to keep their cards. They were 'setting up a process that will restructure the scheme and get a more acceptable outcome, that it was a pragmatic response to meet legitimate public concerns'. Brian Cowen's line was not a turn around but it was a significant backtrack to bring grass-roots Fianna Fáilers back on board.

The government was being put out in force to woo back the nation. Mary Harney, who had appeared as a double act with Brendan Drumm on the Marian Finucane Saturday morning radio show just a few weeks previously was back on to justify the scheme. In another gentle interview with Marian, Mary Harney admitted there was a major communications difficulty in the handling of the scheme but stood by her position saying someone like her should not be entitled to a free medical card. Brain Lenihan, the Minister for Finance who announced the controversial scheme went on the *Saturday Show* and the *Week in Politics* again defending the government line. The Sunday papers were full of the controversy. Cowen postponed his trip to China by two days to stay at home and manage it.

By Monday, the legitimacy of the whole scheme was being highlighted. The government under contract law could not negotiate a deal with the IMO. Also under law, the HSE would not be able to take medical cards from those over 70 for another three years. The momentum continued from opposition parties and groups working with older people.

Late Monday morning, Mary Harney spoke at an Amnesty International event on human rights and health, organised by her previous short-term PD colleague and friend Colm O'Gorman, by then Director of Amnesty Ireland. Speaking at the conference, she did not once mention human rights. After her brief conference appearance, she was door stepped by the media. Again she stood strong on it. She blew off rumours that she had threatened her resignation if the government did a turn around on the scheme, she reiterated her point that this was a government-wide decision. The principle would remain; everyone over 70 would have to be means tested for a medical card. She stated that the current situation was not fair nor financially sustainable, that she regretted any sense of confusion caused to older people.

By Tuesday morning, news broke that the Taoiseach Brian Cowen, the Minister for Health Mary Harney and leader of the Greens and Minister for the Environment, John Gormley, would hold an early morning press conference. Some sort of reversal was about to be announced.

Brian Cowen led the hastily scheduled press briefing, flanked by two distinctly uncomfortable looking ministers. The government had decided to set a new threshold at over three and half times the original limit. Only people whose income was more than €36,500 per annum for a single person and €73,000 per annum for a couple would not qualify for a full medical card (but now it was gross not net income being considered). Under the new scheme, according to the government, 95 per cent of those over 70 years of age would qualify.[3] Only the richest five per cent would be ruled out. This was responsive leadership according to Cowen. Colleagues, constituents and backbenchers had made it clear the government had made a mistake and this was their response. There was no apology except for the poor communications of the initial strategy, they did regret the anxiety caused.

But this was an about-turn by any standards – the €400 grant had disappeared, no older person would have a GP-only medical card, nearly all of them would be eligible for a full medical card. Those who had received them on the basis of age not low income or hardship would not have to undergo a means test but would be asked to notify their circumstances to the HSE. However, new applicants after the 1 January would be means tested.

Significantly, the principle of the universality was undone. The government was adamant the €100 million savings would still be made, they could stay 'within the board parameters of the budgetary arithmetic'.[4] Given that 95 per cent would keep their full medical cards, it seemed impossible that the same €100 million savings could be made.

It was an extraordinary volte face. Mary Harney looked dissatisfied but at least from her perspective, her policy and ideology of withdrawing universal care for over seventies remained. Whereas John Gormley was so uncomfortable, he was hardly able to speak about the issue. Instead, when it came to his turn, he just talked quietly about how much stress it had caused and how much work the Greens had done as a party over the weekend to rectify the situation. Gormely's party had gone to the electorate just 18 months previously with a promise of introducing universal healthcare to all children under six years of age. They had swallowed the bitter pill of co-located hospitals as part of the Programme for Government they signed up to, but undoing a universal right to healthcare must have galled them.

But confusion remained. Age Action had already arranged a public meeting for a city centre hotel. When they realised there were too many people to be accommodated there, the local church in Westland Row offered their space for the gathering.

Within an hour of the ending of the press conference announcing the fundamentally altered scheme, about 2,000 older people were in the church. There were songs and speeches. When John Maloney, Minister of State in the Department of Health, tried to speak, he was booed off the alter by a vociferous, angry crowd shouting 'don't you dare' and 'shame on you'.

News of the change in government policy was conveyed, but this was not enough. People were scared and angry, they wanted the principle of universality to remain, the government had targeted the old and the sick in society but they were not going to lie down and take it. The depth of anger and fear was palpable and hard to quell. Even those who would have kept their medical card all along now feared losing it. Plus, they saw it as the thin end of the wedge. If they took this away, next it would be the travel pass. The momentum remained.

Speaking on local radio after the announcement, Fianna Fáil senator from Cork, Dennis O'Donovan said, 'The sting was taken out if it, but the poison is not gone ... the government got a scalding on this one.'

The day after the press briefing, a rally on Dáil Éireann organised by Senior Citizens Parliament went ahead. A crowd of older people estimated at 15,000 gathered, in the words of one of the organisers Silvia Meehan, 'they came from Kerry and Donegal, from Connemara to Dún Laoghaire'. Marie Hoctor, Minister of State with responsibly for older people in the Department of Health, was booed off stage. So too was Ciaran Cuffe, backbencher for the Green Party. Banners in the crowd said, 'You might as well put a bullet through us', 'A budget to die for'. There were posters with Brian Cowen's image superimposed on to the posters for the film entitled 'No Country for Old Men [and Women]'. Commenting on the welcome sight of older people's activism on Kildare Street, one geriatrician watching found it fascinating that 'by going for 95 per cent cover, they [the government] have clarified that it is the doctrine of removing the entitlement rather than the money saving that is at issue – a formal erosion of inter-generational solidarity'.[5]

The government won a Fine Gael motion to reverse the decision by 84 votes to 71. Joe Behan and Finian McGrath voted against the government. The government expressed regret for anxiety caused and supported the new income thresholds proposed. The government allowed 95 per cent of 70-year-olds and over to keep their medical cards, but the people were still angry. Opposition politicians, councillors from all parties and members of the public stood by the principle of universality. Older people had been given this entitlement eight years previously and they were not prepared to lie down and have it taken away.

As the older people protested outside Dáil Éireann, government TDs huddled inside Leinster House, afraid to go out to the madding crowd, too distracted by the torment to sit at their desks.

A week and a day after the historic press conference, the Department of Health issued a press release saying the government accepted the new single fee to be paid to GPs for all people aged 70 and over of €290. By their own estimations, the government would save €16 million by paying GPs this rate and another €20 million by ending the entitlement to the medical card for the richest over seventies. They planned to save the rest from drug prescribing, which was already government and HSE policy and a mere red herring in the midst of the storm.

The government had instilled fear and panic into a large proportion of older people and withdrawn universal essential health and social care for just €16 million – hardly a prudent move.

Not since the march against the war in Iraq had Dublin city centre seen such a protest and not since the 1980s had Irish people mobilised on such a large scale on any domestic policy issue. And it was an exceptional crowd, made up for the main, by older people, some very able bodied, other less so, on crutches and in wheelchairs. And for those watching who had long advocated for universal healthcare, it was like the penny had finally dropped.

What had been introduced as a sinister ruse to get the votes of older people turned into one of Ireland's great public health experiments. The deal to pay GPs €641 for new 'richer' over 70-year-olds, while paying them €161 for their poorer counterparts was a bad one, it should never have been done in the first place, yet alone left for seven years before it was renegotiated.

The universal entitlement of medical card for all people aged 70 and over had made a difference to older people's lives. They knew they could go to their GP whenever they needed to, they did not have to worry about the costs of drugs or other health professionals. They were entitled to them for free.

Analysis of the census between 2002 and 2006 shows significant health gains for people aged 70 and over.[6] While it is not possible to directly correlate this relationship, it seems that older people's quality of life improved and their limiting illnesses and disabilities were reduced during this time.

Other research carried out for the National Council of Ageing and Older People which surveyed people in 2000 and in 2004 found improvements in health status between the surveys. Significantly, it found a doubling of uptake on the flu injection for over 70-year-olds between 2000 and 2004. All people in this age category are advised to get the flu jab. In 2000, 35 per cent in the eastern region got it, while 46 per cent in the western region, but by winter 2003–04 uptake had risen to over 70 per cent in both boards. In 2000, one in ten participants accessed a public health nurse, by 2004, this was up to one in five. GP use also increased during this period by at least one visit. Once again, while direct correlations cannot be made, the improved health, significantly improved access to a positive preventive measure like the flu jab and increased use of vital services like the public health nursing and GPs must be influenced by universal provision.[7] The knock-on impacts of keeping older people out of hospital is hard to quantify economically and socially, but international research shows there is a close relationship with free access to primary care services and better health outcomes.

No matter how stringent the economic situation in 2008, taking free primary care away from older people was a step backwards not forwards. Another change that the government had not reckoned for until it saw the crowds outside Leinster House was the realisation that a significant and outspoken section of the Irish population had learned what it was like to have universal healthcare.

Six months previously in March 2008, about 10,000 people took to the streets of Dublin demanding a better health service. Campaigners like Janette Byrne, Rebecca O'Malley and Susie Long had awakened a section of the Irish population to say enough is enough. The Dublin Council of Trade Unions, along with the Youth Branch of the Irish Congress of Trade Unions and Patients Together organised a march to campaign for a 'Decent Public Health Service'.

A quote from Susie Long led the rallying call: 'We need visionaries like Noël Browne who believed medicine should be only for the social good, not for profit. The long hospital waiting lists are indecent. The fear that drives thousands of people to purchase private health insurance so that they can access services that they are already entitled to is indecent.' They called for a good quality health service provided on the basis of need, not ability to pay. Those participating were a motley crew made up of dispirate grass roots movements which had spurted up all around the country opposing the closures of local hospitals, lobby patients and support groups. Irish people seemed to have had enough. Doctors, nurses, unions and left-of-centre opposition parties joined them in their demonstrations. Each was calling in some way or other for a universal health service, provided on the basis of need. The lone voices of senior hospital consultants like Orla Hardiman, Christine O'Malley, John Crown and Maurice Nelligan on the national airwaves and at public rallies. The growing momentum opposing government health policy was evident. But the groups were so disparate it was hard to maintain a unified force.

Another march was organised by the same groups in the first week in October 2008, just a fraction of those who had turned out at the rally in March were present. It seemed that momentum was lost.

And then the government announcement came on 14 October 2008 that mobilised older people and their families, that made many wake up and see the positive public health impact of McCreevy's ingenuity eight years previously. The government reversed the measures introduced in the 2009 Budget but they stood their ground on their firm rejection of universal healthcare – a suitable finale to the Celtic Tiger years.

Epilogue

Historians will look upon Ireland in the first nine years of the twenty-first century as an extraordinary time in the country's development. Unparalleled economic growth was followed by even more unexpected decline. The health services during this time were plagued by reform, yet incongruously, the Fianna Fáil/PD government in power since 1997, never even tried to get rid of the unequal system of care, which privileged private, wealthier patients over public patients. Even when they were joined by the Greens in coalition in 2007, who had campaigned on the basis of universal care for under six year olds, measures were introduced which exacerbated rather than reduced the two-tier nature of healthcare.

The health strategy published in 2001, under the stewardship of Minister Micheál Martin, remained largely unimplemented eight years after its publication. Many of the core components of it were not provided during the years in which Ireland had the most spending money ever witnessed in the history of the state. Up to the year the health strategy was published, the vast majority of health and social care in Ireland was provided by the not-for-profit sector – both publicly and privately – the private providers were generally voluntary, religious providers. Since 2001, there has been a vast encroachment of the private for-profit marketeers in to the healthcare arena, largely at the expense of the public health system.

This was driven by Charlie McCreevy while he was minister in the Department of Finance. His two unannounced, undebated changes to the Finance Acts in 2001 and 2002 led to the most mornentons realignment of the healthcare provision in the history of the state. His ability to permeate health policy making and implementation with a growing dependence on the market and neo-liberal economics can not be underestimated. This in turn was fortified when PD Mary Harney took over the health ministry in 2004 where she remained in early 2009. Their impact was and is everywhere to be seen.

By 2009, over two-thirds of all nursing home beds for older people are in the private sector; one-third of all inpatient hospital beds are in the private sector; government is relying on the private sector to build the hundreds of primary care centres committed to in 2001; public patients are still waiting for long promised additional 1,000 hospital beds to be built by private developers on the lands of public hospitals; €100 million euro was given away in 2008 to the private for-profit hospital sector in the form of the NTFP under the auspices of reducing waiting times for public patients, instead of investing the much needed money in the public health system. The great and the good of Irish business life have entered the healthcare market with gusto – with a common intent – to reap profits from the sickness of the Irish people and the failure of the government to provide an accessible, quality, public health service.

The expensive and concessionary new consultants' contract signed off by Mary Harney in late 2008 firmly institutionalised two-tier healthcare. As minister, she championed the eradication of the only aspect of universal provision within the health system by taking medical cards away from older, wealthier over 70-years-olds even though it had proved an effective health promoting, public health measure. The private sector was wooed and embraced first by the Minister for Finance and then by the health minister like never before.

There were some aspects of 'reform' and improvements during the Fianna Fail/PD reign. Expenditure on health quadrupled between 1997 and 2007, more and more services were being provided to more and more people. As the population grew and aged, there was increased activity across the health system. Some services were improved as a result of the increased investment, most evident in services for older people and people with disabilities. And while early in 2009, these were far from perfect or even comparable to many of our European neighbours, many of them were significantly better than they had been a decade before.

Within hospitals the seeds of change were beginning to be sown. Cancer care was transferred from 30 hospitals to just eight specialist centres in two years, quite an achievement in the hotbed of Irish health politics. While the benefits of improved quality care for cancer services are yet to be apparent in statistics, all the indicators are that Ireland must move up the European league tables in terms of cancer survival rates as a result of these changes. Professor Tom Keane's tenure as cancer tsar showed that change could be realised against the odds when leadership was provided and budgets ring-fenced.

The HSE, which got off to a disastrous start, was beginning to demonstrate that under a national management, without the interference of local politicians, uniform standards and services could be established and developed. While much more progress needs to be demonstrated by HSE senior management, some glimmers of hope were apparent in February 2009. A new director of communications was attempting to introduce a more transparent and accessible HSE. When they ran into extreme financial difficulty at the prospect of delivering the 2009 Service Plan in light of changing and constraining budgetary factors, Drumm spoke out publicly, putting the stark circumstances to its board and the minister, exhibiting a more nuanced and honest display of the politics of health in Ireland in 2009. However, much more leadership is required from senior HSE management, more accountability and democracy in how health services are provided.

The HSE Transformation Programme, the Primary Care Strategy and a 'Vision for Change' are good road maps for the delivery of primary care and mental health services – whether they are actually implemented to bring about the real improvements in health and access to services they detail as their intention is not evident early in 2009. The establishment of HIQA, albeit delayed in its foundation, is another ray of hope that standards will be in place and all healthcare institutions both public and private will be regulated and monitored. The work it has carried out to date, under the capable leadership of Tracey Cooper, is an indication that change for the better is possible in the Irish health service, even though it is is frustratingly slow to impact on the day-to-day experience of patients and the public.

It still amazes this author that the vast majority of Irish people do not realise the unique, complicated, unfair system of care that dominates the Irish health system. It disappoints and angers, that at the time this nation had most, that so much politically driven energy and resources went into developing and incentivising the public–private divide, instead of deconstructing the inherent inequality at the core of Irish health services.

Naomi Klein's *Shock Doctrine* outlines a very stark picture of what happens countries in times of shock and recession – how the private sector is facilitated to profitably fill the cracks of a crumbling society. What is unusual about Ireland is that when we had most, when we quadrupled our investment in healthcare, simultaneously and detrimentally, the private for-profit sector was championed into the healthcare market from the highest ministerial office in the land. At its most benign, this was irresponsible, at its most malevolent; it could be considered sabotage of the public health system.

At the time of writing in early March 2009, the HSE is rewriting its 2009 Service Plan. It is trying to find ways to cut one billion euro off its budget. If this materialises it will be the biggest ever cut back on a health budget experienced in the history of the state. Its impact will be felt hard and wide for years to come. Much of progress that has been made with recent investment will be undone. We will pay the costs for decades. We know that putting off seeking medical care in the short term is more expensive and costs lives in the long run.

About one-third of the health budget goes to hospitals, and hospitals are very important if you are sick and need care, particularly important is how you can access that care. Remedying the perverse incentives and blockages currently in place must be a priority. The remaining two-thirds of the health budget goes into primary and social care. This investment can make the difference between an old person being allowed to stay in their home instead of moving into residential care. It allows people with disabilities to get up in the morning. It provides protection and care for children at risk and the most vulnerable children and young people in our country. It provides shelter and care for people with mental illness and people who are homeless. It provides methadone maintenance for drug users, public health nursing for new mothers. It enables home helps to go into people's home and dress them in the morning or change their incontinence nappies. It allows the most basic aspects of human life to be fulfilled, the most basic human rights to be realised. These services cannot and should not be cut no matter what the economic circumstances. At a very minimum, current service must be maintained. At the optimum, this is the very time that investment should be made as people need the public health system more than ever in times of a recession. Investment in health and social care, especially much needed vital infrastructure and facilities, could be part of an economic stimulus package.

Perhaps, a positive outcome of the economic crisis facing Ireland and the world will be that it makes our choices starker.

These are social, economic and most fundamentally political choices facing our country. We can continue to go the way we have been going, fuelling the unequal, two-tiered healthcare system, aiding and abetting the for-profit sector to enter and dominate the Irish health market. Or, in these times of less, we can retrieve our humanity and realise that at last, at this critical juncture of our existence, it is time for solidarity. We can no longer stand on the sidelines and watch. The time is here to work towards, demand and provide the universal, good quality healthcare system to which we are all entitled. The choice is ours ...

Notes to Text

Chapter 1

1. 'Emergency department' is the term used for what are commonly known as A&E departments.
2. These were the charges at the time of writing in October 2008.
3. CSO, 'EU Survey on Income and Living Conditions' (EU-SILC) 2005, 16 November 2006. Available at: www.cso.ie/releasespublications/ documents/eu_silc/2005/eusilc_2005.pdf.
4. CSO, 'EU Survey on Income and Living Conditions' (EU-SILC) 2005, 16 November 2006. Available at: www.cso.ie/releasespublications/documents/ eu_silc/2005/ eusilc_2005.pdf.
5. Health Service Executive/PA Consulting, 'Acute Hospital Bed Capacity Review: A Preferred Health System in Ireland to 2020', detailed report, 2007. Available at: www.hse.ie/publications.
6. HSE. Final report on National Service Plan 2008 Deliverables. HSE. 2009. Available at: http://83.71.161.17/eng/Publications/corporate/Final_Report_on_NSP_2008_Deliverables.pdf.
7. Wren, Maev-Ann, *Unhealthy State: Anatomy of a Sick Society* (Dublin: New Island) 2003.
8. HSE. Final report on National Service Plan 2008 Deliverables. HSE. 2009. Available at: http://83.71.161.17/eng/Publications/corporate/ Final_Report_ on_NSP_2008_Deliverables.pdf
9. Ibid. HSE. 2009.
10. Combat Poverty, 'Health Policy Statement', 2007. Available at: www.combatpoverty.ie.
11. Daly, M. and Leonard, M., *Against all Odds. Family Life on Low Income in Ireland* (Dublin: IPA) 2002.
12. O'Reilly D., O'Dowd T., Thompson K.J., Murphy A.W., Kelly A., O'Neill C., Shyrane E., Steele K., Bury G. and Gilliland A., 'Consultation charges in Ireland deter a large proportion of patients from seeing the GP: results of a cross-sectional survey',

European Journal of General Practice 13(3):231–236, 2007.
13. Health Services Executive, 'Review of Adequacy of Child and Family Services 2005', 2008. Available at: www.hse.ie/eng/Publications/Children_and_Young_People/Review_of_Adequacy_of_Child_and_Family_Services_2005.html.

Chapter 2

1. Barrington, Ruth, *Health Medicine and Politics in Ireland 1900–1970*, (IPA) 1987, p. 274.
2. Wren, Maev-Ann, *Unhealthy State: Anatomy of a Sick Society* (Dublin: New Island) 2003
3. Tussing D.A,. Wren M.A., *How Ireland Cares*, (Dublin: New Island), 2005.
4. Barrington, R., *Health Medicine and Politics in Ireland 1900–1970*, (IPA) 1987, p. 274.
5. Wren, Maev-Ann, *Unhealthy State: Anatomy of a Sick Society* (Dublin: New Island) 2003, p. 49.
6. Barrington, R., *op. cit.*, p. 275.
7. Wren, Maev-Ann, *op. cit.*
8. Wren. *Ibid.*, p. 53.
9. Wren. *Ibid.*
10. Wren. *Ibid.* p. 60.
11. Wren. *Ibid.* p. 57.
12. Wren. *Ibid.* p. 64.
13. Wren. *Ibid.* p. 64.
14. Wren. *Ibid.* p. 76.
15. Wren. *Ibid.* p. 74.
16. Wren. *Ibid.* p. 78
17. Wren. *Ibid.* p. 78.
18. Wren. *Ibid.* p. 78.
19. Wren. *Ibid.* p. 78.
20. Wren. *Ibid.* p. 80.
21. Wren. *Ibid.* p. 80.
22. Wren. *Ibid.* pp. 81–82.
23. Wren. *Ibid.* p. 83.
24. Wren. *Ibid.* p. 83.

25. Wren. *Ibid*. p. 84.
26. Wren. *Ibid*. p. 87.
27. Wren. *Ibid*. p. 87.
28. Wren. *Ibid*. pp. 88–89.
29. Wren. *Ibid*. p. 94.
30. Department of Health, 'Shaping a Healthier Future', 1994.
31. Wren, Maev-Ann, *op. cit*., p. 98.
32. Wren. *Ibid*. p. 103.
33. Wren. *Ibid*. p. 100.
34. Wren. *Ibid*. p. 107.
35. Martin, Micheál, speech at the launch of 'Quality and Fairness – A Health System for You'. Mansion House. Dublin. 26 November 2001. Available at: www.dohc.ie/press/speeches/2001.
36. Department of Health. 'Quality and Fairness – A Health System for You'. Dublin. 2001.
37. Dáil Eireaan. Parliamentary Debates. Vol. 589. Wednesday, No. 1 29 September 2004. http://debates.oireachtsa.ie/ Xml/ 29/ DAL20040929.PDF.

Chapter 3

1. Department of Health, 'Quality and Fairness – A Health System for You'. Dublin. 2001. Available at: http://www.dohc.ie/publications/pdf/strategy.pdf
2. Department of Health, 'Audit of Structures and Functions in the Health System, 2003' (the 'Prospectus Report'). Stationary Office. Dublin. 2003. Available at: http://www.healthreform.ie/publications/prospectus.html.
3. Department of Health. 'Commission on Financial Management and Control Systems in the Health Service' (the Brennan Report), Dublin. 2003. Stationary Office. Dublin. 2003. Available at: http://www.healthreform.ie/pdf/brennan.pdf.
4. Department of Health, 'The Health Service Reform Programme', 2003. Available at: www.healthreform.ie/publications/reports.
5. 'The Health Service Reform Programme', 2003. Available at: www.healthreform.ie/structures/hse.
6. See: www.healthreform.ie/structures/hse.

7. Department of Health, 'Report of the National Task Force on Medical Staffing (Hanly Report)', 2003.
8. Martin, Micheál, speech at the launch of 'Quality and Fairness – A Health System for You'. Mansion House. Dublin. 26 November 2001. Available at: www.dohc.ie/press/speeches/2001.
9. Department of Health, 'The Health Service Reform Programme', 2003. Available at: www.healthreform.ie/publications/reports.
10. Statement from the Chairman of the Board of the HSE in relation to the 2006 performance-related award approved for the CEO, 14 September 2007. Available at: www.hse.ie/eng/newsmedia/.
11. Review Body on Higher Remuneration in the Public Sector – Report No 42. Available at: www.reviewbody.gov.ie/publications.
12. Callinan, Kevin, speech at the Impact Union conference, 15 May 2008.
13. Department of Health, 'Audit of Structures and Functions in the Health System, 2003' (the 'Prospectus Report'). Dublin. 2003.
14. Department of Health. 'Commission on Financial Management and Control Systems in the Health Service' (the Brennan Report), Dublin. 2003.
15. Browne, Maureen, *Irish Medical News* 'Opinion'. Available at: www.irishmedicalnews.ie/index.php/current-issue/view.
16. Confidential interviews with the author, December 2007 and March 2008.
17. Harney, Mary, Health Bill 2004: Second Stage, *Dáil Debates*, Volume 593, 23 November, 2004. Available at: http://historical-debates.oireachtas.ie/D/0593/D.0593.200411230024.html.
18. Tussing, D.A. and Wren, M.A., *How Ireland Cares: The Case for Healthcare Reform* (Dublin: New Island) 2005.
19. Staines, Anthony, inaugural lecture as Professor of Health Systems Research. Available at: www.dcu.ie/news/2008/may/s0508h.shtml.
20. Confidential interview with author, December 2007.
21. Review Body on Higher Remuneration in the Public Sector – Report No 42, *op. cit.*
22. Review Body on Higher Remuneration in the Public Sector *Ibid.* p. 90.

23. O'Meara, Aileen, 'Health workers swimming in treacle', *Sunday Business Post*, 23 March 2008.
24. Private Notice Questions in Dáil debate, 3 July 2008. Available at: www.oireachtas.ie.
25. Drumm, Brendan, 'HSE reforms aim to deliver first class integrated care to all', *The Irish Times*, 10 July 2008. Available at: www.irishtimes.com.
26. Private Notice Questions in Dáil debate, *op. cit.*
27. *Ibid.*
28. Interview on *Morning Ireland*, RTÉ, 4 July 2008. Available at: www.rte.ie/news.
29. O'Regan, Eilish, 'U-turn as HSE managers to be given local control', *Irish Independent*, 4 July 2008.
30. O'Meara, Aileen, 'Where the HSE has gone wrong', *Sunday Business Post*, 4 November 2007. Available at: www.archives.tcm.ie/businesspost/2007/11/04/story27974.asp.
31. *Ibid.*
32. Downes, John, 'HSE misses is own deadline for replying to Dáil questions', *Sunday Tribune*, 10 August 2008.
33. Fitzgerald, John, 'Management, Governance, and communications issues arising from the Review of Breast Cancer Services at Midland Regional Hospital', (HSE), February 2008. Available at: www.hse.ie.
34. Confidential interview by author with senior health official, December 2007.
35. *Ibid.*
36. Health Service Executive. National Service Plan 2009. Dublin. HSE. 2008. Available at: http://www.hse.ie/eng/Publications/corporate/National_Service_Plan_2009.pdf.
37. Donnellan, Eithne, 'Concern over lack of detail in HSE spending', *The Irish Times*, 26 March 2008.
38. Wall, Martin, 'One in six HSE posts is administrative, report finds', *The Irish Times*,15 May 2008.
39. Donnellan, Eithne, '20 per cent of HSE bonuses went to HR staff', *The Irish Times*, 14 July 2008.
40. Wall, Martin, 'HSE restructuring to shift staff into the community sector', *The Irish Times*, 13 May 2008.

41. McEnroe, Juno, 'Bad finance management cost HSE €20m a year', *Irish Examiner*, 5 July 2008.
42. Wall, Martin, 'HSE numbers down by 2,000', *The Irish Times* health supplement, 8 April 2008.
43. Health Service Executive. National Service Plan 2009. Dublin. HSE. 2008. p 3 & 8 http://www.hse.ie/eng/Publications/corporate/National_Service_Plan_2009.pdf.
44. Drumm, Brendan, quoted by Wall, M., 'Cowen criticism 'unreasonable'', *The Irish Times*, 15 July 2008.
45. See: www.ageaction.ie/news.
46. Spears, Madeline, conference speech at INO conference in Cavan, 9 May 2008.
47. Kelly, Michael, 'Steering a Policy Course' in McAuliffe, E. and McKenzie, K. (eds), *The Politics of Healthcare: Achieving Real Reform* (Dublin: Liffey Press) 2007, pp 29–30.
48. Confidential interview with the author, December 2007.

Chapter 4

1. OECD, 'Ireland: Towards an Integrated Public Service', p. 277. 2008. Available at: http://www.oecd.org/document/31/0,3343,en_2649_33735_40529119_1_1_1_1,00.html.
2. Wren, Maev-Ann, *Unhealthy State: Anatomy of a Sick Society* (Dublin: New Island), 2003 p. 104.
3. Kelly, Michael, 'Steering a Policy Course' in McAuliffe, E. and McKenzie, K. (eds), *The Politics of Healthcare. Achieving Real Reform*, (Dublin: Liffey Press) 2007, pp 29–30.
4. Wren, Maev-Ann, *op. cit.*, p 229.
5. Tussing, D.A. and Wren, Maev-Ann, *How Ireland Cares: The Case for Healthcare Reform* (Dublin: New Island) 2005.
6. Thomas, S., Normand, C. and Smith, S., 'Social Health Insurance: Options for Ireland' (Trinity College Dublin/Adelaide and Meath Hospital Society), 2006.
7. Department of Finance, '2008 Revised Estimates', 2008.
8. OECD Health Data 2008: Statistics and Indicators for 30 Countries. Available at: http://www.oecd.org/document/16/0,3343,en_2649_ 34631_2085200_1_1_1_1,00.html.

9. Wren, Maev-Ann, 'Universal health insurance – a realistic route to reforming Irish healthcare', a paper given to a public meeting organised by the Labour Party, January 2008. Available at: www.labour.ie.
10. Wren. *Ibid.*
11. Irish Congress of Trade Unions. 'Addressing the healthcare crisis'. Dublin. ICTU. 2007. Available at: www.ictu.ie.
12. OECD, 'Ireland, Towards an Integrated Public Service', 2008. *op. cit.*, p. 275.
13. OECD. *Ibid.* p. 277.
14. OECD. *Ibid.* p 277.
15. Thomas, S., Normand, C. and Smith S., 'Social Health Insurance: Further Options for Ireland', (Trinity College Dublin/Adelaide and Meath Hospital Society), 2008. Available at: www.adelaide.com. p. 21.
16. Thomas et al. *Ibid.* p. 22.
17. Thomas et al. *Ibid.* p. 22.
18. Wall, Martin, '1,200 hospital beds cannot be used, says report', *The Irish Times*, 6 October 2008.
19. Health Service Executive/PA Consulting, 'Acute Hospital Bed Capacity Review: A Preferred Health System in Ireland to 2020' detailed report, 2007. Available at: www.hse.ie/ publications/ 2007.
20. HSE. *Ibid.*
21. Thomas, S., Normand, C. and Smith, S., *op. cit.*, 2008, p. 24.
22. Thomas *et al. Ibid.*
23. Thomas, S., Normand, C. and Smith, S., *op. cit.*, 2006.
24. Morgenroth, E. and Fitzgerald, J. (eds), 'Ex-ante Evaluation of the Investment Priorities for the National Development Plan (2007–2013)', ESRI Policy Research Series 59 (Dublin: ESRI/DKM Economic Consultants), 2006.
25. Department of Health and Children, 'Quality and Fairness – A Health System for You', 2001. Available at: www.dohc.ie/ publications/2001.
26. Health Service Executive/PA Consulting, *op. cit.*
27. HSE. *Ibid.*

28. Department of Health and Children, 'Health in Ireland, Key Trends', 2007.
29. Health Service Executive, 'Annual Report and Financial Statement 07', 2008. Available at: http://www.hse.ie/eng/Publications/corporate/HSE_Annual_Report_and_Financial_Statements_2007.pdf.
30. OECD, 'Ireland: Towards an Integrated Public Service', *op. cit.*, 281.
31. OECD. *Ibid.* p. 279.
32. Wren, Maev-Ann, *Unhealthy State: Anatomy of a Sick Society* (Dublin: New Island), 2003.
33. OECD, 'Ireland: Towards an Integrated Public Service', *op. cit.*, p. 279.
34. Department of Health, 'Quality and Fairness. A Health System for You', *op. cit.*
35. Department of Health, 'Commission on Financial Management and Control Systems in the Health Service (the 'Brennan Report')', 2003.
36. Department of Health, 'Audit of Structures and Functions in the Health Systems (the 'Prospectus Report'),' 2003.
37. Health Service Executive, press release, 'New Consultants' Contract and Clinical Directorates are a Major Step Forward', 29 August 2008.
38. Tussing D.A. and Wren, Maev-Ann, *How Ireland Cares: The Case for Healthcare Reform* (Dublin: New Island) 2005, p. 20 T3.
39. ESRI. Annual Report Activity in Acute Public Hospitals in Ireland. Health Research and Information Division. December 2008. ESRI
40. Health Service Executive/PA Consulting, 'Acute Hospital Bed Capacity Review: A Preferred Health System in Ireland to 2020', *op. cit.*
41. Public Accounts Committee, published correspondence, Thirtieth Dáil. Correspondence received from Ray Mitchell, Head of Parliamentary Affairs, Health Service Executive (3), 7 February 2008. Available at: www.oireachtas.ie/viewdoc.asp?fn=/documents/Committees30thDail/PAC/Additional_Documents/ListofAdditionalDoc.htm.

42. Tussing, D.A. and Wren Maev-Ann, *Ibid.* op.cit.
43. Donnellan Eithne, 'Patients waiting up to 18 months for crucial cancer tests', *The Irish Times*, 1 March 2008.
44. Irish Cancer Society. Press Release: Wait times for crucial bowel cancer test show improvement/ However, 435 patients across the country are still waiting more than 6 months, 22 January 2009 www.ics.ie.
45. National Treatment Purchase Fund, Patient Treatment Register. Available at: www.ptr.ie/pages/forGPs.asp . Information accessed on 26 February 2009
46. Donnellan Eithne, 'Patients waiting up to eight years to see consultants', *The Irish Times*, 31 December 2007.
47. Donnellan. *Ibid.*
48. Donnellan. *Ibid.*
49. NTPF, The Patient Treatment Register, September 2005. Available at: www.ptr.ie/Pages/report/PTR_Report_200509.pdf
50. National Treatment Purchase Fund, 'The National Treatment Purchase Fund 2007 Annual Report', 2008. Available at: www.ntpf.ie/home.
51. Comptroller and Auditor General, 'Annual Report 2004', 2005. Available at: www.audgen.gov.ie/viewdoc. asp?fn=/documents/ annualreports/2004/ReportChap14.pdf.
52. National Treatment Purchase Fund, 'The National Treatment Purchase Fund 2007 Annual Report', 2008. Available at: www.ntpf.ie/home.
53. Comptroller and Auditor General, 'Annual Report 2004', 2005. Available at: www.audgen.gov.ie/viewdoc.asp?fn=/documents/ annualreports/2004/ReportChap14.pdf.
54. OECD, 'Ireland: Towards an Integrated Public Service', *op. cit.*, p. 279.
55. OECD. *Ibid.* p. 279.
56. Health Service Executive, 'Intercultural Health Strategy'. *op. cit.*
57. OECD, 'Ireland, 'Towards an Integrated Public Service', *op. cit.*, p. 279.
58. OECD. *Ibid.*
59. Health Service Executive, 'Intercultural Health Strategy'. *op. cit.*

60. Department of Health, 'Quality and Fairness, A Health System for You', *op. cit.*, p. 171.
61. See: www.patientstogether.com.
62. INO, press release. 'Overnight chaos in the emergency department of Galway University Hospital', Tuesday, 7 October 2008. Available at: www.ino.ie.
63. Health Service Executive, 'Emergency Department (ED) Task Force Report' 2007, p. 9.
64. Burke, Sara, 'Winners and losers in hospital targets', *Health Manager* magazine, October 2007, p. 12.
65. Harney, Mary, Minister for Health and Children, 'As for trolleys, some people spend all their time, perhaps 24 hours, being observed on a trolley. Recently, a close friend of mine who would be known to many members [of the Dáil] had such an experience in a Dublin hospital. He told me it was a very pleasant experience', Dail Éireann, 27th June 2007.
66. IAEM, press statement, 1 June 2008. Available at: www.iaem.ie.
67. Department of Health (UK), 'Emergency Care 10 years on: reforming emergency care' (NHS), 2007.
68. IAEM, press statement, *op. cit.*
69. McDonagh, Patricia, 'Family anguish as mother 39 dies alone in A&E toilet', *Irish Independent*, 26 January 2008.
70. Hardiman, O., 'The challenge of fixing our health service', 18 February 2008. Available at: www.irishhealth.com.
71. Health Service Executive, 'Emergency Department (ED) Task Force Report', *op. cit.*
72. Health Service Executive, 'Infection Control Action Plan', March 2007. Available at: www.hse.ie.
73. HPSC/Health Service Executive, 'Healthcare-Associated Infection and Antimicrobial Resistance-Related Data from Acute Public Hospitals in Ireland, 2006–2007', 2008.
74. HPCS. *Ibid.*
75. HIQA, 'National Hygiene Services Quality Review', 2007.
76. HIQA, National Hygiene Services Quality Review, 2008'. HIQA. Dublin. 2008. Available at: www.hiqa.ie.
77. See: www.hospicefriendlyhospitals.net/.
78. *Ibid.*

Chapter 5

1. See: www.hse.ie/eng/About_the_HSE/Map_of_Hospital_ Networks _and_HSE_Areas.pdf. Downloaded 12 September 2008.
2. Department of Health, 'Acute Hospital Summary Statistics, 1980-1997'. Available at: www.dohc.ie/statistics/key_trends/ hospital_care/table_3_1.html.
3. Department of Health and Children, 'Report of the National Task Force on Medical Staffing (Hanly Report)', 2003.
4. Department of Health. *Ibid.* p 15.
5. Department of Health. *Ibid.* p. 16.
6. Department of Health. *Ibid.* p. 18.
7. Martin, Micheál, TD, Minister for Health, speaking at the publication of the 'Report of the National Task Force on Medical Staffing', 15 October 2003. Available at: www.dohc.ie/ press/speeches/2003/20031015.html.
8. Mitchell, Olivia, press statement, 'Hanly Report Answers No Questions, Solves No Problems', 16 October 2003. Available at: www.finegael.ie/news/index.cfm/type/details/nkey/22682.
9. Hennessy M. *The Irish Times*. 'Opposition says report will only delay true reform'. 10 Oct 2003. www.irishtimes.com
10. Hanly Report: Statements (Resumed), *Dáil Debates*, Volume 575, 21 November 2003. Available at: http://historical-debates.oireachtas.ie/D/0575/D.0575.200311210004.html.
11. Kiely, Dr James, Chief Medical Officer, statement on 'Report of the National Task Force on Medical Staffing' (Hanly Report), 19 November 2003. Available at: www.dohc.ie/press/releases/ 2003/20031119c.html.
12. Deegan, G. and Donnellan, E., 'FF councillors reject Hanly plans', *The Irish Times*, 17 December 2003.
13. Donnellan, E., 'Debate on A&E cover in hospitals 'political'; Hanly'. *The Irish Times*, 16 April 2004.
14. Smith, Brendan, quoted in Hennessy, Mark, 'Divisions emerging between FF and PDs on election defeats', *The Irish Times*, 15 June 2004.

15. Harney, Mary, speaking at Joint Oireachtas Committee on Health and Children, *Dáil Debates*, Volume 39, 3 February 2005. Available at: http://debates.oireachtas.ie/.
16. Harney, Mary, speaking at Second Stage of Health Act, *Dáil Debates*, Vol. 593, No1. 23, November 2004. Available at: http://debates.oireachtas.ie/Xml/29/DAL20041123.PDF.
17. Kelly, Kevin, presentation at the Joint Oireachtas Committee on Health and Children, *Dáil Debates*, Vol. 45, 14 April 2005. Available at: http://debates.oireachtas.ie/DDebate.aspx?F=HEJ20050414.xml&Node=H3&Page=4.
18. McLoughlin, Pat, presentation at the Joint Oireachtas Committee on Health and Children, *ibid*.
19. Health Services Executive/Teamwork, 'Improving Safety and Achieving Better Standards: An Action Plan for Health Services in the North East', 2007. Available at: www.hse.ie/eng/Publications/Hospitals.
20. HSE. *Ibid*.
21. Department of Health, 'The Lourdes Hospital Inquiry: An Inquiry into peripartum hysterectomy at Our Lady of Lourdes Hospital, Drogheda', report of Judge Maureen Harding Clarke, 2006. Available at: www.dohc.ie/ publications/lourdes.html.
22. Department of Health. *Ibid*.
23. Health Service Executive, 'Transformation Programme 2007–2010', 2006. Available at: www.hse.ie/eng/Publications/Hospitals/HSE_Publications/Transformation_Programme_2007_-_2010.pdf.
24. Health Service Executive/PA Consulting, 'Acute Hospital Bed Capacity Review: A Preferred Health System in Ireland to 2020', detailed report, 2007.
25. Health Service Executive, 'Towards an Integrated Health Service or More of the Same?' background briefing, Health Forum Steering Group, 2008.
26. The Health Partnership/ARUP/York Health Economics Consortium, 'Recommended Location of a New Regional Acute Hospital in the North East', final report prepared for the HSE, 2008.

27. Ahern, Dermot, speaking on the RTÉ *Six-One News*, 4 April 2008. Available at: www.rte.ie/news2008/0404/navan.html.
28. OECD, 'Ireland: Towards an Integrated Public Service', 2008. Available at: www.bettergov.ie/attached_files/upload/IRELAND-Towards per cent20An per cent20Integrated per cent20Public per cent20Service.pdf.
29. HSE, Review of Acute Hospital Services in the Mid-West. HSE, Dublin, 2009. Available at: http://www.hse.ie/eng/Publications/Hospitals/ midwestreport.html
30. HIQA, 'Report of the investigation into the circumstances surrounding the provision of care to Rebecca O'Malley, in relation to her symptomatic breast disease, the Pathology Services at Cork University Hospital and Symptomatic Breast Disease Services at the Mid Western Regional Hospital, Limerick', 2008. Available at: www.hiqa.ie/ media/ pdfs/ HIQA_Rebecca_OMalley_Report.pdf.
31. Department of Health, 'Development of Services for Symptomatic Breast Disease', report of the sub-group to the National Cancer Forum, 2000. Available at: www.dohc.ie/ publications/pdf/symptomatic_breastdisease.pdf?direct=1.
32. O'Doherty, Dr Ann, 'Report of a clinical review of mammography service at Midland Regional Hospital Portlaoise for the Health Service Executive Mid Leinster' 2008. Available at: www.hse.ie/eng/Publications/ Hospitals/Clinical_Review_of_ Mammography_at_Portlaoise_Hospital.pdf.
33. Department of Health, 'Management, Governance and Communications issues arising from Review of Breast Radiology Services at Midland Regional Hospital Portlaoise', 2008. Available at: www.dohc.ie/publications/ fitzgerald_ report.html.
34. Campbell, Dr Henrietta, 'Report on the Independent Review of Symptomatic Breast Care Services at Barrington's Hospital, Limerick September 2003 to August 2007 (Department of Health and Children) 2008. Available at: http://www.dohc.ie/ publications/pdf/breast_care_services_barringtons.pdf? direct=1.
35. Department of Health, 'Building a Culture of Patient Safety', report of the Commission on Patient Safety and Quality

Assurance, 2008. Available at: www.dohc.ie/ publications/ building_culture_patient_safety.html.
36. Department of Health. *Ibid.*, p 209.
37. Harney, Mary, speaking at launch of the 'Report of the Commission on Patient Safety', 7 August 2008, attended by author.
38. Health Consumer Powerhouse, 'Euro Consumer Heart Index' (Sweden), 2008. Available at: www.healthpowerhouse.com/ files/euro-heart-index-2008.pdf.
39. HSE, Ireland: Take Heart. Audit of Progress on the Implementation of Building Healthier Hearts 1999-2005, HSE, Dublin, 2006.
40. Irish Heart Foundation/Department of Health. 'National Audit of Stroke Care', 2008. Available at: www.irishheart.ie/ iopen24/ pub/strokereports/stroke_report.pdf.

Chapter 6

1. Harney, Mary, speaking at Trinity debate 'That this house believes the Irish health system fails the disadvantaged', attended by author, 8 April 2008.
2. Department of Health, 'Quality and Fairness – A Health System for You', 2001, p. 43.
3. Wren, Maev-Ann, *Unhealthy State: Anatomy of a Sick Society* (Dublin: New Island), 2003.
4. Wren, Maev-Ann, 'Tax changes give a boost to private health clinics', *The Irish Times*, 2 May 2002.
5. Wren Maev-Ann, *Unhealthy State: Anatomy of a Sick Society*, *op. cit.*
6. Kelly, Michael, 'Steering the Policy Course' in McAuliffe, E. and McKenzie, K. (eds), *The Politics of Healthcare: Achieving Real Reform* (Dublin: Liffey Press), 2007.
7. Tussing, D.A. and Wren, M.A., *How Ireland Cares: The Case for Healthcare Reform* (Dublin: New Island), 2005.
8. Department of Health, press release, 'Tánaiste announces plan for 1,000 new public hospital beds over 5 years. Private beds in public hospitals will move to new private hospitals on public hospital campuses', 14 July 2005. Available at: www.dohc.ie.

9. See: www.hse.ie/eng/FactFile/HSE_Approach/National_ Hospitals_ Office/Hospital_Co_Location_Initiative.
10. Minutes of Cabinet Committee on Health and Children, 'Co-location of private hospitals on public hospital sites', March 2007. Obtained by author by FOI request on co-location, July 2008.
11. Drumm, Brendan, interviewed on *Morning Ireland*, RTÉ, 13 April 2007. Available at: ww.rte.ie/news/2007/0413/ morningireland. html.
12. Tussing, A.D. and Wren, Maev-Ann, *op. cit.*, pp. 361–362, Appendix 2.
13. Pollock. Allyson, 'Operating profits', *The Guardian*, 11 June 2008.
14. Tussing, A.D. and Wren, Maev-Ann, *op. cit.*, pp. 361–362, Appendix 2.
15. Cullen, Michael, 'Co-location hospitals are the key to a better healthcare system', *The Irish Times*, 24 July 2008.
16. Brian Cowen to Eamon Gilmore, 'Briefing note on the acute hospital co-location initiative', 14 May 2008, follow-up to Leaders Questions in the Dáil, 14 May 2008. Obtained through Labour Party press office by author.
17. Reilly, James, response to Dáil Questions on co-location, PQ 28060/08 to PQ 28066/08. Available at: www.hse.ie/ eng/Access_to_Information_PQs/Parliamentary_Questions/2008 _PQ_Responses/July_2008/Jul_9/James_Reilly_PQ_28061-08_Status_of_co-location_hospital_plans.pdf.
18. *Ibid.*
19. Minutes of Cabinet Committee on Health and Children, 'Co-location of private hospitals on public hospital sites', *op. cit.*
20. Donnellan, Eithne, 'State to earn €280 million from lease of lands from private hospitals', *The Irish Times*, 19 May 2008.
21. Dáil debate, 5 June 2008.
22. Health Services Executive board, press release, 'HSE Board Approves Co-Location Project's "Invitation to Tender" Documents', 19 April 2007.
23. Reilly, James, *op.cit.*
24. Reilly. *Ibid.*

25. Health Service Executive/PA Consulting, 'Acute Hospital Bed Capacity Review: A Preferred Health System in Ireland to 2020' detailed report, 2007.
26. HSE. *Ibid.*
27. Drumm, Brendan, quoted in O'Meara, Aileen, 'HSE expects a surplus of private hospital beds by 2020', *Sunday Business Post*, 21 January 2008.
28. O'Regan, Eilish, 'Consultants rush to snap up €1m private suites', *Irish Independent*, 21 March 2006.
29 http://www.eurocareinternational.ie/.
30. Mitchell, S., 'Quest defends itself over test claims', *Sunday Business Post*, 18 May 2008.
31. Donnellan, Eithne, 'US smear tests will miss 1,000 cancers', *The Irish Times*, 16 May 2008.
32. Wall, M. and Donnellan, E., 'HSE to implement reform of the hospital laboratory system', *The Irish Times*, 11 June 2008.
33. Pollock, A.M. and Godden, S., 'Independent sector treatment centres: the evidence so far', *British Medical Journal*, Vol. 336, 2008, pp. 421–424.
34. Pollock, Allyson, 'Farwell to the NHS', *The Guardian*, 1 July 2008.
35. Pollock, Allyson and Godden, S., *op. cit.*
36. Cuthbert, Jim and Cuthbert, Margaret, 'Lifting the Lid on PFI', *Scottish Left Review*, 3 December 2007. Available at: www.ukwatch.net/article/lifting_the_lid_on_pfi.
37. Pollock, Allyson, 'Operating profits', *The Guardian*, 11 June 2008.
38. Devereaux, P.J., Choi, P.T.L., Lacchetti, C., Weaver, B., Schunemann, H. J., Haines, T., Lavis, J. N., Grant, B.J.B., Haslam, D.R.S., Bhandari, M., Sullivan, T., Cook, D.J., Walter, S.D., Meade, M., Khan, H., Bhatnagar, N. and Guyatt, G. H., 'A systematic review and meta-analysis of studies comparing mortality rates of private for-profit and private not-for-profit hospitals', *Canadian Medical Association Journal*, 166, 2002, pp, 1399–1406.
39. Devereaux, P.J., Heels-Ansdell, Diane, Lacchetti, Christina, Haines, Ted, Burns, Karen E.A., Cook, Deborah J., Ravindran,

Nikila, Walter, S.D., McDonald, Heather, Stone, Samuel B., Patel, Rakesh, Bhandari, Mohit, Schünemann, Holger J., Choi, Peter T.-L., Bayoumi, Ahmed M., Lavis, John N., Sullivan, Terrence, Stoddart, Greg and Guyatt. Gordon H., 'Payments for care at private for-profit and private not-for-profit hospitals: a systematic review and meta-analysis', *Canadian Medical Association Journal* 70, 2004, pp, 1817–1824.

40. Horwitz, J.R. 'Making Profits And Providing Care: Comparing Nonprofit, For-Profit, and Government Hospitals', *Health Affairs* (Millwood) 24, 2005, pp. 790–801.
41. Port, F.K., Wolfe, R.A., Held, P.J., Bander, S.J., Lazarus, J.M., Lindenfeld, S.M., Nissenson, A.R., Owen, W.F. Jr, Qunibi, W.Y., Riley, D.J., Abboud, H.E., Ruma, J.J., Wick, G.S., Garg, P.P., Frick, K.D. and Powe, N.R, 'Ownership of Dialysis Facilities and Patients' Survival', *New England Journal of Medicine*, 342, 6 April 2000, p. 1053.
42. HIQA, 'The National Quality Standards for Residential Care Settings for Older People in Ireland', 2007. Available at: www.ihsab.ie/functions_shss_standards_residential_care.asp.
43. Mitchell, Susan, 'Private care in good health', *Sunday Business Post*, 25 November 2007.
44. Mitchell. *Ibid.*
45. Mitchell. *Ibid.*

Chapter 7

1. CSO, Irish Life Tables No. 15, CSO, January 2009. www.cso.ie
2. WHO, country profiles. Available at: www.who.int/countries, accessed 9 October 2008.
3. Department of Health, '2007, Health in Ireland, Key Trends', 2007.
4. Department of Health, *Ibid.*
5. CSO, 'EU Survey on Income and Living Conditions, 2005', 16 November 2006. Available at: www.cso.ie.
6. CSO, *ibid.*

7. Department of Health, 'SLÁN, Survey of Lifestyle, Attitudes and Nutrition in Ireland', main report, 2007. Available at: www.dohc.ie/publications/pdf/slan07_report.pdf?direct=1.
8. CSO, 'EU Survey on Income and Living Conditions, 2005', *op. cit.*
9. Department of Health, 'SLÁN, Survey of Lifestyle, Attitudes and Nutrition in Ireland', *op. cit.*
10. Balanda, K. and Wilde, J., 'A Report on All Ireland Mortality Data' (Dublin: Institute of Public Health in Ireland), 2001. Available at: www.publichealth.ie.
11. CSO, ' EU Survey on Income and Living Conditions (EU-SILC) 2006', 2007.
12. CSO, 'Measuring Irish Progress, 2007', 2008.
13. CORI, 'Socio-Economic Review, 2007', 2008.
14. CSO, 'EU Survey on Income and Living Conditions (EU-SILC) 2006', *op. cit.*
15. CSO. *Ibid.*
16. CSO. *Ibid.*
17. National Economic and Social Forum (NESF), 'Mental Health and Social Inclusion' (Dublin), 2007.
18. NESF, 'Mental Health and Social Inclusion' 2007. *ibid.*
19. Department of Health, 'A Vision for Change: Report of the expert group on mental health policy', 2006. Available at: www.dohc.ie/publications/vision_for_change.html.
20. NESF, 'Mental Health and Social Inclusion', *op. cit.*
21. Singleton, N. and Lewis, G., 'Better or worse: a longitudinal study of the mental health of adults living in private households in Great Britain, (ONS) 2000 and 2001.
22. Institute of Public Health in Ireland, 'Unequal at birth', (Dublin/Belfast: Institute of Public Health in Ireland). 2006. www.publichealth.ie.
23. See: www.cso.ie/newsevents/pr_censu2006vol5.htm.
24. Galway Travellers Support Group, 'Composite Submission to the National Intercultural Health Strategy from Travellers and Traveller Organisations Nationally', 2007.
25. Department of Health, 'National Travellers Health Strategy, 2002–2005', 2002.

26. Combat Poverty Agency, 'Health Policy Statement', 2007. Dublin, Combat Poverty. Available at: www.combatpoverty.ie
27. Health Services Executive, 'Intercultural Health Strategy', HSE, Dublin, 2008.
28. Health Services Executive, 'Intercultural Health Strategy', HSE, Dublin, 2008.
29. Cairde, 'Assessing the health and related needs of minority ethnic groups in Dublin's North Inner City. A Case Study of a Community Development Approach to Health Needs Assessment', (Dublin), 2006.
30. Galway Refugee Support Group, submission to the Health Services Executive, Intercultural Health Strategy Group, 'A framework for the healthcare and support needs of people from diverse ethnic backgrounds and cultures', 2007.
31. Kennedy, Harry, 'Mental illness in Irish prisoners' (National Forensic Mental Health Service), 2006.
32. Kennedy. *Ibid.*
33. Hannon, F., Friel, S. and Kelleher, C., 'The relative influence of socio-demographic, lifestyle, environmental factors and co-morbidity on self-related health in the Irish prisoner population', *Irish Medical Journal*, Health Research Board Unit for Health Status and Health Gain 1999–2007, Volume 100, Number 8, September 2007.
34. Department of Health and Children, 'Strategic Task Force on Alcohol, Second Report', 2004.
35. Department of Health and Children. *Ibid.*
36. National Advisory Committee on Drugs, 'Drug Use in Ireland and Northern Ireland 2006–2007', Bulletin 2, 2008.
37. Kelleher, Cecily, 'A Reflection on the evidence and future directions for policy and research', Irish *Medical Journal*, Health Research Board Unit for Health Status and Health Gain 1999–2007, Volume 100, Number 8, September 2007, p. 1.
38. Kelleher. *Ibid.*
39. Kelleher *Ibid.*
40. Segonds-Pichon, A., Hannon, F., Daly, S., Morrison, J.J., Bury, G., Murphy, A.W. and Kelleher, C., 'Socio-demographic, lifestyle and cross generation predictors of self-related health in mothers

during pregnancy', *Irish Medical Journal*, Health Research Board Unit for Health Status and Health Gain 1999–2007, Volume 100, Number 8, September 2007. p 11.

41. Fitzsimon, N., Fallon, U.B., O'Mahony, D., Loftus, B.G., Bury, G., Murphy, A.W. and Kelleher, C.C., 'Mothers' dietary patterns during pregnancy and the risk of asthma symptoms in children at 3 years', *Irish Medical Journal*, Health Research Board Unit for Health Status and Health Gain 1999–2007, Volume 100, Number 8, September 2007.
42. Fitzsimon et al. *Ibid.*
43. Delaney, L., Wall, P., O'hAodha, 'Social capital and self-rated health in the Republic of Ireland,. Evidence from the European Social Survey', *Irish Medical Journal*, Health Research Board Unit for Health Status.
44. Denny, K. and Doyle, O., 'Analysing the relationship between voter turnout and health in Ireland', *Irish Medical Journal*, Health Research Board Unit for Health Status and Health Gain 1999–2007, Volume 100, Number 8, September 2007.
45. Watson, D., Whelan, C.T., Williams, J. and Blackwell, S., 'Mapping Poverty: National regional and county patterns' (Combat Poverty Agency and IPA), 2005.
46. Department of Community Health and General Practice, 'People living in Tallaght and their health' (Trinity College Dublin), 2002.
47. Fettercairn Community Health Project. 'Taking the First Steps to a Healthier Future', Dublin. 2007.
48. Institute of Public Health in Ireland, 'Fuel Poverty', (Dublin/ Belfast: Institute of Public Health in Ireland). 2006. www.publichealth.ie.
49. Wilkinson, Richard, 'Ourselves and others – for better or worse: social vulnerability and inequality' in Wilkinson, R. and Marmot, M. (eds), *Social Determinants of Health* (Oxford University Press), 2006.
50. Nolan, B. and Whelan, C.T., *Loading the Dice: the study of cumulative disadvantage*, (Dublin: Oak Tree Press with Combat Poverty Agency), 1999. Whelan, C., Hannon, D. and Creighton, S. *Unemployment, poverty and psychological distress* (Economic and Social Research Institute), 1991.

51. Dáil Question, written response to Joan Burton, No 173 Ref: 11283/08.
52. Bank of Ireland Asset Management, 'Wealth of the Nation Report 2007', 2008.
53. DKM Economic Consultants, 'Irish wealth report of Investec', 2008.
54. Clarke, Vivienne, 'Cowen homecoming: Weekend long celebrations for Taoiseach in Offaly', *The Irish Times*, 12 May 2008.
55. Callan, T., Nolan, B., Walsh, J., Whelan, C. and Maitre, B., *Tackling low income and deprivation: developing effective policies*, 2008.
56. OECD, *Fact Book*, 2006.
57. Pickett, K and Wilkinson, R.G., The Spirit Level: Why More Equal Socieities Almost Always Do Better (Allen Lane), 2009.
58. Howell F. and Allwright, S., 'Smoke-free workplaces in Ireland: Cultural Shift Through Policy Change' in MAuliffe, E., McKenzie, K. (eds), *The Politics of Healthcare: Achieving Real Reform* (Dublin: New Island), 2007.
59. Howell et al. *Ibid.*

Chapter 8

1. Department of Health, 'Primary Care: A New Direction', 2001. Available at: www.dohc.ie/publications/ pdf/primcare.pdf.
2. Health Services Executive,'Service Plan for 2007' 2007. Available at: www.hse.ie/eng/Publications/corporate/HSE_National_Service_Plan_2007.pdf.
3. Health Services Executive, 'Transformation Programme 2007-2010', 2006. Available at: www.hse.ie/eng/Publications/Hospitals/HSE_Publications/Transformation_Programme_2007_-_2010.pdf.
4. Health Service Executive/PA Consulting, 'Acute Hospital Bed Capacity Review: A Preferred Health System in Ireland to 2020', detailed report, 2007. HSE/Teamwork, 'Improving Safety and Achieving Better Standards. An Action Plan for Health Services in the North East', 2007. Available at: www.hse.ie/ eng/

Publications/Hospitals/. Health Service Executive, 'Towards an Integrated Health Service or More of the Same? background briefing', Health Forum Steering Group, 2008.

5. Government of Ireland, 'Towards 2016, A Ten Year Framework Social Partnership Agreement 2006–2016', 2006.
6. Comptroller and Auditor General. 'Annual Report of the Comptroller and Auditor General 2007' (Stationary Office), 2008. Available at: http://audgen.gov.ie/ documents/ annualreports/ 2007/AnnualReport2007b.pdf.
7. *Prime Time Investigates: Through the looking glass*, 26 May 2008. Available at: www.rte.ie/news/2008/0526/ primetimeinvestigates.html.
8. Health Services Executive, response to press query by author, 3 October 2008.
9. Drumm, Brendan, speaking on *Marian Finucane Show*, 28 September 2008. Available at: www.rte.ie/radio1/ marianfinucane/1084847.html.
10. Department of Finance, 'Revised Estimates of Public Services', 2008. Available at: www.finance.gov.ie/documents/REV2008/ REV2008English.pdf.
11. Department of Health, 'Primary Care: A New Direction', *op. cit.*
12. O'Kelly, F., O'Kelly, M., Ni Shuilleabhain, A., O'Dowd, T., 'National Census of Irish General Practice Training Programmes'.
13. O'Dowd, T., 'Structure of General Practice in Ireland 1982–2005 (Department of Public Health and Primary Care, Trinity College Dublin), May 2006. Available at: www.medicine.tcd.ie/ public_health_primary_care/research/reports/GP_Structure.pdf.
14. Irish College of General Practitioners, 'Survey of GPs', 2008. Available at: www.icgp.ie.
15. Buttimer, J., 'The Report of the Postgraduate Medical Education and Training Group' (Department of Health and Children), 2006. Available at: www.dohc.ie/publications/buttimer.html.
16. Irish College of General Practitioners, press statement, January 2008. Available at: www.icgp.ie/go/about/press_releases/ 551D621E-19B9-E185-832727A1824E9F44.html.

17. Layte, R., Nolan, A., Nolan, B., 'The Health Divide: Income, Health and Healthcare' (Combat Poverty Agency), 2007.
18. McGregor, P., Nolan, A., Nolan, B. and O'Neill, C., 'A Comparison of GP visiting in Northern Ireland and the Republic of Ireland' (ESRI), 2006.
19. O'Carroll, Austin, presentation on Access to Primary Care, to ISPA annual conference, 'Who pays? Access and Equity in the Irish Healthcare System', 25 September 2008.
20. Tussing, cited in Wren, Maev-Ann, *Unhealthy State: Anatomy of a Sick Society*, (Dublin: New Island), 2003.
21. Tussing D.A. and Wren, Maev-Ann, *How Ireland Cares: The Case for Healthcare Reform* (Dublin: New Island) 2005.
22. Combat Poverty Agency, 'Health Policy Statement', 2007. Available at: www.combatpoverty.ie/publications/ policystatements/ 2007_Policy_HealthPolicyStatement.pdf.
23. O'Reilly, D., O'Dowd, T., Galway, K.J., Murphy, A.W., O'Neill, C., Shryane, E., Steele, K., Bury, G., Gilliland, A. and Kelly, A., 'Consultation charges in Ireland deter a large proportion of patients from seeing the GP: results of a cross-sectional survey', *European Journal of General Practice*, 2007, 13(3), pp. 231-236.
24. O'Carroll, Austin, presentation on access to primary care, to ISPA annual conference, 'Who pays? Access and Equity in the Irish Healthcare System', 25 September 2008.
25. Fettercairn Community Health Project (FCHP), 'Taking the First Steps to a Healthier Fettercairn', FCHP Participatory Rapid Appraisal Report, (Dublin) 2007.
26. Crowley, Phillip, *Health Inequalities and Irish General Practice in Areas of Deprivation* (Irish College of General Practitioners), 2005
27. O'Carroll, A. and O'Reilly, F., 'There's a Hole in the Bucket: An Analysis of the Impact of the Medical Card Review Process on Patient Entitlement to Free Healthcare', *Irish Medical Journal*, Volume 101 Number 1, January 2008. Available at: www.imj.ie//Issue_detail.aspx?issueid=+&pid=2732&type=Papers.
28. Tussing, cited in Wren, M.A., *Unhealthy State, Anatomy of a Sick Society*, *op. cit.*

29. Department of Health, 'Annual Report of the Chief Medical Officer for the year 2000', 2001, p. 7. Available at: www.dohc.ie/publications/cmo_2000.html.
30. Wren, Maev-Ann, *Unhealthy State: Anatomy of a Sick Society*, *op. cit.*
31. Wren. *Ibid.*
32. Burke, Sara, 'Voters have healthy choices of plans', *Irish Examiner*, 11 May 2007.
33. McDowell, cited in Wren, Maev-Ann, *Unhealthy State: Anatomy of a Sick Society*, *op. cit.*
34. Department of An Taoiseach, 'An Agreed Programme for Government. A Blueprint for Ireland's Future 2007-2012', 2007. Available at: www.taoiseach.gov.ie/attached_files/Pdf percent20files/Eng percent20Prog percent20for percent20Gov.pdf.
35. Thomas, S., Normand, S., Smith, S., '*Social Health Insurance: Future Options for Ireland* (Trinity Collage Dublin Health Policy and Management and the Adelaide Hospital Society), 2008.
36. Tussing, D.A. and Wren, M.A., *op. cit.*
37. Cosgrove, Sharon, 'Mulhuddart Primary Health Research Report for the Primary Healthcare Group Mulhuddart' (Dublin), 2004.
38. Touchstone Healthcare Group, 'Building Communities of Care'. Available at: www.touchstone.ie/downloads/THG_ Commuities.pdf.
39. Kibred, Bernie, from PCCC, HSE, speaking at a Combat Poverty Primary Care conference, June 2007.
40. Health Service Executive, 'Guidance Document for Primary Care Developments', 2008. Available at: www.hse.ie/eng/ Publications/Primary_Care/Guidance_Document_for_Primary_Care_Developments.html.
41. Department of Health/Deloitte and Touche, 'Value for Money Audit of the Irish Health System', 2001.
42. The Carers Association, 'Pre-Budget Submission 2008. Delivering on Social Partnership priority actions for 2008', 2008. Available at: www.carersireland.com/documents/ PreBudget2008_000.pdf.

43. HSE, Final Report on National Service Plan Deliverables for 2009. Available at: http://83.71.161.17/eng/ Publications/ corporate/ Final_Report_on_NSP_2008_Deliverables.pdf.
44. O'Neill, Des, 'Leas Cross Report' (HSE), 2006. Available at: www.hse.ie/eng/Publications/Older_People_and_Nursing_Home s/Leas_Cross_Report_.pdf.
45. Harney, Mary, speaking at launch of the 'Report on the Needs of Older People in North Clondalkin and Palmerstown', 8 July 2008. Available at: www.dohc.ie/press/speeches/2008/ 20080708. html?lang=en.
46. Health Service Executive, 'Annual Report and Financial Statements 07', 2008.
47. Dáil Éireann, 'Nursing Home Support Scheme Bill 2008', 9 October 2008.
48. Department of Health, 'A Vision for Change: Report of the expert group on mental health policy', 2006. Available at: www.dohc.ie/publications/vision_for_change.html.
49. World Health Organisation, 'Mental Health'. Available at: www.who.int/mental_health/en/.
50. Department of Health, 'A Vision for Change: Report of the expert group on mental health policy', *op. cit.*
51. World Health Organisation, *Resource book on mental health, human rights and legislation,* (Geneva). Downloaded on the 6 June 2006 from: www.who.int/mental_health/policy/ who_rb_ mnh_hr_leg_FINAL_11_07_05.pdf.
52. Department of Health, 'A Vision for Change: Report of the expert group on mental health policy', *op. cit.*
53. Kennedy, *et al.*, *Mental illness in Irish prisoners: Psychiatric morbidity in sentenced, remanded and newly committed prisoners* (Dublin: National Forensic Mental Health Service), 2005.
54. McKeown, K., Clarke, M., *Male mental health in Ireland*, (Dublin: One Foundation), 2004.
55. Department of Health and Children, 'Annual report of the chief medical officer', 2001.
56. Daly, A., Walsh, D., Comish, J., Kartolova O'Doherty, Y., Moran, R. and O'Reilly, A., 'Activities of Irish psychiatric units and hospitals 2004' (Dublin: Health Research Board), 2005.

57. Department of Health, 'A Vision for Change: Report of the expert group on mental health policy' *op. cit.*
58. O'Shea, E. and Kennelly, K., *The Economics of Mental Healthcare in Ireland* (Mental Health Commission, The Irish Centre for Social Gerontology and Department of Economics, NUI Galway), 2008. Available at: www.mhcirl.ie/docs/The_Economics_of_Mental_Health_Care_in_Ireland.pdf.
59. O'Shea et al. *Ibid.*
60. McDaid, 'Mental health and social exclusion: An overview', in Thompson Coyle, K. (ed.), *Public policy, poverty and mental illness: Opportunities for improving the future*, occasional paper No. 1, (Dublin: Schizophrenia Ireland), 2004.
61. O'Shea E. and Kennelly K., 'The Economics of Mental Healthcare in Ireland', *op. cit.*
62. Irish Psychiatric Association, 'The lie of the land: Psychiatric Service Land Disposal and Failures and Delays in Capital Development of Community Based Mental Health Services' (Dublin), 2008.
63. Mental Health Commission, 'Annual Report 2006, including the Report of the Inspector of Mental Health Services' (Dublin), 2007.
64. Mental Health Commission, 'Annual Report 2007, including the Report of the Inspector of Mental Health Services'. Available at: www.mhcirl.ie/annualreports.htm.
65. Irish Mental Health Coalition, *The Emperors New Clothes* (Dublin), 2008.
66. Mental Health Commission. Annual Report 2007, *op. cit.*
67. Mental Health Commission. *Ibid.*
68. Independent Monitoring Group of 'A Vision for Change. The Second Report of the Expert Group on Mental Health Policy', 2008. Available at: www.dohc.ie/publications/ vision_for_change_2nd_report.html.

Chapter 9

1. Wren, Maev-Ann, 'Time for Ireland's healthcare to be rated universal', *Sunday Tribune*, 26 October 2008.

2. Beehan, Joe, TD, interview on RTÉ *Six-One News*, 17 October 2008. Available at: www.rte.ie/news/2008/1017/6news.html.
3. Government statement regarding medical card for people aged seventy and over, issued at press conference at Government Buildings, 22 October 2008.
4. Cowen, Brian, speaking at press conference at Government Buildings, 22 October 2008.
5. Email to author, 22 October 2008.
6. Wren, Maev-Ann, 'Medical card experiment was in rude health, why shelve it now?' *Sunday Tribune*, 19 October 2008.
7. O'Hanlon, A., McGee, H., Barker, M., Garavan, R., Hickey, A., Conroy, R. and O'Neill, D., 'Health and Social Services for Older People II: Changing Profiles from 2000 to 2004' ('HESSOP II'), (National Council of Aging and Older People), 2005.

Epilogue

1. Klein, Naomi, Shock Doctrine. The Rise of Disaster Capitalism. Penguin. 2007.

Index